INTO THE SHADOWS

America's Unsolved
Mysteries and Tales
of the Unexplained

TROY TAYLOR

FALL RIVER PRESS

New York

FALL RIVER PRESS

New York

An Imprint of Sterling Publishing
387 Park Avenue South
New York, NY 10016

© 2002 by Troy Taylor
Text designed by Maureen Slattery

This 2007 edition published by Fall River Press by arrangement with the Author.

ISBN: 978-0-7607-9078-6

Manufactured in the United States of America

2 4 6 8 10 9 7 5 3

NOTE FROM THE PUBLISHER: Although the Author and all affiliated with this book have
carefully researched all sources to ensure the accuracy of the information contained in this
book, we assume no responsibility for errors, inaccuracies, or omissions.

TABLE OF CONTENTS

Introduction

EVERYONE LOVES A MYSTERY

It is human nature for us to love a mystery. We all love to be intrigued by the mysterious and tantalized by the idea of something that cannot be solved. For this reason, murder mysteries, courtroom dramas and books about ghosts and the paranormal have been immensely popular for decades. We love to question, to wonder and be baffled by those things that we believe to be unexplained. Of course, most fictional mysteries are usually solved by the intrepid detective in the closing pages of the book or the last reel of the film, but what of mysteries that cannot be solved? What of real-life mysteries for which no explanation exists?

Our history is filled with such enigmas and puzzles. In unsuspecting places we find tales of crimes and of disappearances for which all clues have vanished over the passage of time. It is unlikely that we will ever find know the true identity of Jack the Ripper or whatever became of the infamous skyjacker D.B. Cooper, yet we remain fascinated with each and every unsolved case. I have long been obsessed with such mysterious stories and obviously, you are as well, or you would not be holding this book in your hands.

My own interest in the unexplained came about in childhood. In addition to stories of ghosts and hauntings, I was also fascinated with anything that reeked of the unknown and the unsolved. I pored through every book that I could find on mysterious happenings, unexplained disappearances, unsolved crimes and more. It's likely that such reading material was far from appropriate for the age when I first began delving into it and some would point this out as a warning to parents who don't want their children to turn out like me! Regardless of what age I started exploring the unknown, I was certainly hooked by junior high and began exhausting my local library, bookstores and mail order catalogs for any books that I could find on the subject.

Many of the books contained remarkably similar tales and I soon realized that others shared my obsession. Many of the stories, like that of the Lindbergh Kidnapping, were sad and tragic, and others, like the tales of treasure on Oak Island, sparked visions of adventure that I hoped to live as an adult. Some of the tales were simply haunting and have stuck with me after all of these years. And one of them, I have never forgotten.

One of the mysteries from my childhood reading has been considered by some to be one of the greatest mysteries of all time. It began in an old burial vault that was located on a high, windswept hill on the Caribbean island of Barbados.

During the days of the slave trade, in the early 1800s, rum and sugar created huge fortunes in the West Indies. Wealthy plantation owners, who believed that their displays of power should extend beyond their homes and offices to their final resting places, constructed homes and government buildings here on a grand scale.

Such was the vault near Christ Church on Barbados. It was hewn from stone and constructed from coral and concrete. The large stone blocks were firmly cemented together, creating walls that were nearly two feet thick. The floor space inside measured twelve feet by six feet and was reached by several descending steps. A huge slab of blue marble, effectively sealing the vault until it was required to admit another coffin, closed off the entrance.

It should be carefully noted that there was no way to enter into this tomb, save for the removal of the slab. Regardless, between the years of 1812 and 1820, someone, or something, managed to enter the tomb and wreak havoc on the contents, without leaving a single clue behind. The events were completely inexplicable to the Chase family, who owned the tomb and abandoned it in 1820, and they remain inexplicable today.

The tomb was built in 1724 and even the first burial here remains somewhat of a mystery. A man named James Elliot constructed it and on May 14 of that same year, the remains of his wife, Elizabeth, were allegedly placed inside. This is according to records, which also state that the tomb was not re-opened until 1807, when it was found to be empty. Whatever became of the body of Elizabeth Elliot is unknown.

In 1807, the Walrond family purchased the vault and the body of Mrs. Thomasina Goddard was placed inside.

The Chase family purchased the vault a year after this interment. They were wealthy plantation owners on the island. On February 22, 1808, the vault was opened for the first time by the family to admit the body of Mary Ann Maria Chase, the infant daughter of Thomas Chase. At that time, the Goddard coffin was found to be undisturbed. A few months later, in July, another of the Chase daughters, Dorcas, also died. There was nothing out of the ordinary reported about the vault until August 8, 1812, when it was opened again for the burial of Thomas Chase himself.

On that date, a startling sight greeted the mourners and a workman, who was actually the first to enter the tomb. He cried out when he saw the coffins of the two Chase daughters standing on end against the northeast wall. There was no sign that anyone had entered the vault, or that the door had been disturbed. The children's coffins were placed beside that of Thomasina Goddard, which lay undisturbed. The heavy, lead-enclosed casket belonging to Thomas Chase was then carried inside by eight men and deposited on the floor. The mourners then left and the stone masons cemented the marble slab back into place.

Four years passed and on September 22, 1816, the vault was opened again to admit the small coffin of a boy named Samuel Ames. The stone slab was removed and a vivid memory of four years before immediately sprang to mind. The interior of the vault was in wild disarray. The coffins were scattered about and tipped over, including the immense coffin of Thomas Chase, which was found standing against one wall.

Once again, the vault was sealed, only to be opened again just eight weeks later to admit the body of Samuel Brewster, who had been killed in a slave uprising. The slab was pulled aside and mourners lined the area around the doorway, hoping for a glimpse inside the now infamous tomb. They discovered another gruesome sight. The coffins were scattered about and stacked on top of one another. Only the original Goddard coffin was undisturbed but in the confusion around it, the old wood had broken apart, scattering her bones onto the floor. They were carefully collected and wrapped and then placed near the wall as the rest of the vault was again organized into some semblance of order.

The unexplained desecration of the tomb caused "great astonishment" on the island, wrote an early chronicler of the events, Sir Robert H. Schombaugh. He wrote that "no signs were observed that the vault had been opened without knowledge of the family." The Chase family naturally launched an inquiry into the events, but nothing could be found. The vault appeared to have been sealed the entire time.

Many of the plantation owners blamed the desecrations on the slaves. It was thought that many of them were restless, as proven by the recent disturbance that had taken the life of Samuel

Brewster, and now were vandalizing the graves of their masters. This still did not explain why the door slab showed no signs of being opened.

Others suggested flooding, although there was no indication of this outside of the tomb. In addition, the vault had purposely been constructed on high ground. It was also suggested that earthquakes might have inflicted the damage, but there was no sign of this in any of the other tombs on the island.

Three years later, the vault was opened again. On July 17, 1819, the body of Thomassina Clarke, another member of the family, was scheduled to be interred there. By now, the weird story of the vault was known all over the island and even attracted the attention of the Governor, Lord Combermere, who went out of his way to make sure he was present for the service. Predictably, the vault was once again disturbed. All of the leaden coffins were tipped over and scattered about. Only the Goddard remains were undisturbed. Thomas Chase's coffin stood against one wall while the others were thrown about the chamber.

Lord Combermere was so fascinated with the mystery that he personally led a search of the tomb. They investigated every inch, looking carefully for secret passages, underground doors or any signs of digging. They finally gave up, still finding nothing to explain the phenomenon.

Finally, Miss Clarke's coffin was brought in and all of the coffins were rearranged with those of the adults on the floor and the children's stacked atop them. Then, at Lord Combermere's direction, fine sand was spread on the floor so that if anyone entered the vault, his or her footprints would be seen. The slab was then sealed back into place and the Governor's personal seal was affixed to it in front of witnesses.

In April 1820, Lord Combermere ordered that the vault be opened again. There was no one to be buried at that time, but as he was traveling in the area, he asked the local rector, Reverend T. Orderson, to have it opened for his inspection. According to

Nathan Lucas, a witness who was present at the time and who drew "before and after" sketches of the chamber, the coffins were again scattered about.

The cement was broken from the door and then they attempted to remove the slab. Unfortunately, it refused to budge. It eventually took ten slaves to get the door open and when entry was forced, they discovered what was causing the difficulty. Thomas Chase's huge casket was turned upside-down and was jammed against the marble slab. The other coffins were also strewn about the room but to the amazement of the men who entered the tomb, not a single footprint marred the sand on the floor!

Shortly after, the Chase family removed their relatives from the vault and it has been abandoned ever since.

What explanation could there be for the moving coffins? Earthquakes? Retreating waters? The restless spirits of those interred within? Obviously, natural explanations have been attempted to explain the bizarre disturbances. However, these explanations were all eliminated decades ago. All that we seem to have left to us is the supernatural.

Author Sir Arthur Conan Doyle, who embraced the unexplainable, suggested that the disturbances were created by "forces" that reacted to the lead in the Chase family coffins. While it is true that the wooden Goddard coffin was always undisturbed, it has never been quite clear what these forces may have been. Doyle suggested that perhaps they were the spirits of the Chase family, unable to pass on to the other side because of the lead chambers.

Sir Arthur also considered the idea that perhaps energy expelled by the workers who moved the heavy coffins into the vault may have been trapped inside when the door was sealed. If this was the case, perhaps this electrical-type energy was able to move the coffins around inside the vault.

So, what are the answers behind this strange mystery? It is certain that we will never really know for sure and the vault today is not providing any answers. It remains there on Barbados, its black, open mouth swallowing the daylight that attempts to pierce the shadows below. The stone interior is still cool and dry to the touch but nothing rests inside save for the dust of the centuries and the eerie memories of yesterday's strange events.

Tales such as this one had a remarkable effect on me as a child and, without a doubt, led me to pursue the profession in which I am presently embroiled. For as I read these books, I always vowed that someday, I would collect my own such stories, and this book is the result of that vow.

Unlike most of the other books that I have written, this book is not entirely filled with ghosts. While stories of the mysterious and the unexplained have managed to creep into some of my other works, you will find a greater abundance of such tales within these pages. The majority of the stories here will be tinged with the supernatural, although some will not, however in every case, I found the account just too chilling, too strange or too mysterious to not include it. The stories that you are about to read are simply my favorite tales of the unexplained and hopefully, as you read this book, you'll share my enthusiasm for them.

Everyone loves a mystery.

Troy Taylor

Chapter One

HISTORY'S MYSTERIES

History, Haunts & Unsolved Enigmas from America's Past

The history of America is mired in unsolved mysteries. So many questions exist and remain unanswered that to this day, we have no clear cut answers as to who the first people on this continent actually were, where they came from, where some of them vanished to or even who actually discovered America first.

Not long after Columbus landed in the New World, the people of Europe began speculating as to the origins of the people who already lived here. Columbus, who thought he had landed in India, assumed that they were Indians. When he realized his mistake, theories began to be tossed around as to who the natives were and where they had come from.

One theory had it that they were survivors of the lost continent of Atlantis, Plato's mythical continent that was supposed to have been lost to disaster and floods centuries ago. Others believed that the Native Americans were the descendants of the lost tribes of Israel, who had been exiled to Assyria in the Old Testament but had not been heard from since.

The first to move beyond the myths and legends were the Spanish friars who came to the Southwest in the 1500s. Jesuit missionary Jose de Acosta suggested that the Indians had reached America by way of an overland route from Asia. Today, most scholars would agree that his ideas were correct. More credit was given to his research in the later 1800s after Charles Darwin theorized that human beings first evolved in Africa and then spread throughout the world. Fossil evidence seems to suggest that American inhabitants came about much later and most believe that an overland bridge once existed between Siberia and Alaska, where the waters of the Bering Strait now flow.

But even with this widely accepted idea, they are still those who disagree as to when the first Americans arrived, citing archaeological evidence that argues dates both before and after the end of the last major Ice Age. But no matter when these ancient people arrived, they managed to leave their own mysteries behind.

WHO WALKED AMERICA BEFORE COLUMBUS?

The Secrets of the Mound Builders

The first European explorers who dared to wander away from the shores of the New World and began to brave the interior regions of the country discovered Native Americans who roamed the land. Most of them had no written language and little in the way of organized communities. However, scattered in places like present-day Ohio, Wisconsin and Illinois, they discovered strange mounds, altars, burial sites and what appeared to be ruins where towns and villages once stood. It seemed that a civilization, far advanced of the current natives, had once prospered in these places. The greatest of these lost civilizations had been in the Mississippi River Valley. Who were the mysterious dwellers who lived here? It remains a mystery. They have been called the "Mound Builders," thanks to the monuments of earth they left behind, but the people have so utterly disappeared that their true identity will never be known. They left only silent graves and magnificent mounds in their wake, located in places like Cahokia.

At Cahokia, near present-day Collinsville, are the remains of Illinois' most ancient city. The site boasts a number of mounds but one main centerpiece. It is sometimes called "Monk's Mound" after Trappist monks who farmed the terraces of the structure in the early 1800s. It is a stepped pyramid that covers about 16 acres and was apparently rebuilt several times in the distant past. At the summit of the mound are the buried remains of some sort of temple, further adding to the mystery of the site. The mounds intrigued the settlers who later came to this area and they believed them to be evidence of some long vanished and forgotten culture. As they dug into the mounds, they found extraordinary artifacts like pottery, carved pipes and stone trinkets, effigies of birds and serpents made from copper and mica, and vast numbers of human bones.

During the time of the Middle Ages, Cahokia was a larger city than London and yet today, it is an abandoned place about which we know almost nothing. It is generally believed that about 20,000 people once occupied Cahokia, living inside a wooden stockade that surrounded various pyramids. The site is named after a tribe of Illiniwek Indians, the Cahokia, who lived in the area when the French arrived in the late 1600s. What the actual name of the city may have been in ancient times is unknown. The site is believed to have existed from 700 A.D. until its decline in 1300. By 1500, it is thought to have been completely abandoned.

So, what happened to the Mound Builders of Cahokia? Some archaeologists believe the last survivors of the Mound Builders were the Natchez Indians of the Lower Mississippi Valley. These Indians were known for being devout worshippers of the sun, which may explain the uses of the mounds at Cahokia and the so-called "Woodhenge" of the site. These 48 wooden posts make up a 410-foot diameter circle and by lining up the central observation posts with specific perimeter posts at sunrise, the exact date of all four equinoxes can be determined.

It has been suggested that the Mound Builders abandoned the area because of overcrowding or contamination of the local water supply, while others have theorized that it was a breakdown of the civilization itself. Around 1500, the Mississippi Valley was seized by a religious movement that has been dubbed the "Death Cult." A new type of grotesque artwork became prevalent, portraying winged beasts, skulls and weird faces. The rituals practiced during this period of decline are unknown, but scholars have imagined them to be quite dark. Some have even hinted at human sacrifice and cannibalism. Regardless, this proved to be the death knell for the civilization.

According to legend, a bearded and robed god had originally visited the Mound Builders and inspired them to love one another, live in harmony with the land and build the great earthen works. But later, they degenerated to human sacrifice and warfare during the Death Cult period. The possible survivors of the Mound Builders, the Natchez, were described by the French as being the "most civilized of the native tribes," but their tribal traditions sometimes had dark elements to them. It was reported that in 1725, the death of a chieftain touched off a sacrificial orgy when several aides and two of the chief's wives agreed to be strangled so they could escort him into the next world.

Could the degeneration of the Mound Builder's society have brought the civilization to ruin? Perhaps, although many people still consider the Cahokia site to be a sacred place. In August 1987, the Monk's Mound was the meeting place of more than 1,000 people who took part in a worldwide "harmonic convergence" that was designed to bring peace to the planet. Many Native Americans and metaphysical groups believe Cahokia is a source of powerful psychic energy even today.

The Disappearance of the Anasazi

In late 1840s and early 1850s, Americans were moving ever further west and explorations were funded by the United States government to map out areas of the southwest, which had been previously been controlled by Mexico. In 1849, the first of these explorations entered Chaco Canyon, located in northwestern New Mexico. U.S. Army Lieutenant James Simpson led the expedition and what he discovered in the canyon convinced him that the Aztec Empire of Mexico must have extended much further north than was previously thought. Only an advanced civilization could have constructed the magnificent buildings that now stood in ruins before him. Nestled against the walls of the canyon were stone structures unlike anything he had seen before. The largest of the buildings, Pueblo Bonito, stood five stories tall and had hundreds of rooms inside of it.

Simpson was, of course, wrong in his thinking, for archaeologists were later able to date the ruins to centuries before the rise of the Aztecs. The city had been built by a mysterious tribe that the local Indians called the "Anasazi." These vanished people had created an outpost so advanced of the Hopi and Zuni in the region that many would come to believe that it was actually a Roman city that had been built in the American southwest.

Perhaps this thinking came about because of the roads. Like the Roman roads of the Old World, many broad avenues connected Pueblo Bonito to nine great houses and some 75 other settlements around Chaco Canyon. It is believed that the Anasazi used the roads to carry building supplies and timbers while constructing their dwellings and to transport the tremendous amount of turquoise that was mined in distant canyons and brought back to the city. The Anasazi were remarkably wealthy and remains of exotic gems and pottery have been found. Their society was also supported by a sophisticated irrigation system that used dams, terraces and reservoirs to sustain life in the barren desert.

They remained in Chaco Canyon for nearly 100 years and then abandoned the city and moved north into southwestern Colorado. Here, they created architecture that was even more stunning, building their homes right inside the caves that are found throughout the steep cliffs of the canyon. Most of these dwellings here at Mesa Verde are still largely intact today.

And it is here where the ghosts of the past are sometimes seen roaming the empty and abandoned dwellings. These apparitions are most often encountered near the pit houses, or *kivas*, located on the floor of the canyon. These smaller buildings had holes in the floor that likely served as spiritual gateways to the other side. Archaeologists, park guides and tourists who have come face to face with the inhabitants of the past find their lingering presence to be just another of the mysteries of the place.

Perhaps the greatest of the puzzles is why the Anasazi would have abandoned the city at all? And just where did they go when the left? There have been many theories suggested, including one by archaeologist Harold Gladwin in 1957 that theorized the Anasazi had been under attack. He believed that this was why they had left their more scattered homes in Chaco Canyon and had moved to the cliff dwellings at Mesa Verde. Protected by the canyons and cliffs here, they had managed to hold out for more than 100 years before being wiped out. But wiped out by whom? Gladwin and others believe that the attackers must have been the people who later became known as the Navaho and the Apache. Moving south from Canada, they were the last people to reach the southwest before the Spanish came north from Mexico. Navaho tradition suggests that this may be correct for the word "Anasazi" comes from a Navaho word that means "ancient enemies."

The only problem with this theory is that no evidence exists to say that war or fighting ever occurred at Mesa Verde. The dwellings here were obviously just abandoned, not burned out or sacked, and look as though the inhabitants simply packed up and walked away one day. So, why would they leave?

Some experts have suggested a great drought that forced the Anasazi to abandon even their irrigated city. Others claim that an epidemic might have wiped out most of the inhabitants, forcing the others to flee. This could be the case, however no mass burial sites have ever been discovered. Other theories have included a disruption in the turquoise trade, a break down of the civilization that turned the tribe against itself or perhaps a religious upheaval that drew the Anasazi south and into the emerging Kachina religion.

Needless to say, the mystery remains unsolved. Unlike other tribes, such as the Hopi or the Navaho, there are no Anasazi to ask today of their traditions of the past or mythology. The tribe completely vanished into the sands of the distant past.

Who Discovered America?

While the upheaval and mass exoduses of the Native Americans were taking place within the confines of the New World, the Europeans were landing on the eastern shores of the country. But who actually arrived here first? Tradition, of course, tells us that "In 1492, Columbus sailed the Ocean Blue," and he managed to land somewhere pretty close to America. However, there have long been theories that Columbus was far from the first explorer to discover the New World. There may have been many who came before him (aside from the Native Americans) and some have even stated that Columbus just happened to be the "first white European, financed by a government," who landed in the New World, and thus, got credit for its discovery.

Regardless of what school of thought the reader might belong to, they would have a hard time ignoring the barrage of theories that range from the Chinese, the Phoenicians and even ancient African explorers. All of these camps (and others) claim to have evidence through often questionable sites and relics to legends passed on by Native Americans to prove that the nationality of their choice was the first to arrive.

The Sagas of the Vikings, the Irish and the Welsh in Early America

One of the most convincing stories of pre-Columbus explorations of the New World was the saga of the Vikings. According to ancient Icelandic traditions, the first European to discover America was Biarni Heriulfson. Biarni was a trader who often crossed the ocean between Norway and his home in Iceland. In the summer of 985, he decided to return home from Norway and spend the winter with his father. He arrived to find that his father had departed for Greenland, a land that had been recently discovered by Eric the Red. Biarni followed, but managed to miss Greenland and end up at some new land instead. This new land would later be called America but he was not impressed with the place and he soon set sail for Greenland to join his family.

Others were stirred by Biarni's journey however. The new land sounded appealing, especially when compared to Greenland, a cold and frigid place that was anything but green. The son of Eric the Red, Leif Ericsson, spoke at length to the trader and then purchased his boat from him. He assembled a crew and then set sail for Biarni's new world. He called the place "Vinland" and he lived there for a year before returning home.

Other Norse expeditions followed, including one led by Leif's brother, Thorvald. The Viking sagas say that Thorvald was later killed in Vinland by the "Skrellings," the fierce local inhabitants. The surviving members of the party returned to Greenland and another expedition followed. This one was led by Leif's brother Thorstein and his sister Freydis. They attempted to colonize the region but were again driven off by the natives. This time, the Norsemen did not return and for the next 500 years or so, and the Native Americans had the land to themselves.

Or so the stories go. To most people, the sagas were mere tall tales of the Vikings and not a true history. Many scholars disagreed and set out to find proof that the Norsemen had come here first. For years, most of the evidence that was developed, from rune stones to ruined towers, turned out to be false information or poor hoaxes. But a Norwegian archaeologist named Helge Ingstad refused to give up. He traveled thousands of miles up and down the American coast, searching for traces of the Vikings. His journeys led him to believe that Vinland ought to be in northern Newfoundland, as the landscape seemed to match the descriptions in the Viking sagas. He searched for years, but found nothing.

Then in 1960, Ingstad made a remarkable discovery near a small village called L'Anse aux Meadows in Newfoundland. He noted a number of indistinct overgrown elevations in the ground that appeared to be the ruins of old buildings. Their shapes were similar to ancient Norse buildings that had been uncovered in Iceland and Greenland, and it certainly seemed that they could be old enough to have been Viking settlements. Ingstad began to excavate, and in 1964 he and his men discovered what they believed to be proof of a Norse settlement. It was a spindle-whorl that was exactly like those used in Norse countries and unlike anything that would have been used by the inhabitants of Newfoundland at the time.

Ingstad was delighted but as with any other controversial find, the critics still found something to be bothered about. They disagreed with Ingstad's findings on the basis of the name of the place, Vinland or "Wineland," as it was sometimes translated. According to the sagas, Leif had named the new land after the wild grapes found there. Botanists stated that the northern limit for wild grapes on the East Coast was Massachusetts. They would never grow as far north as Newfoundland, or would they?

Historians came to Ingstad's rescue. They suggested that just because grapes don't grow in Newfoundland now, they might have between 1000 and 1200. It is a fact that the vineyards of Western Europe at that time extended farther north than they do today. It's also thought that perhaps the explorers may have mistaken wild berries for grapes or even that Leif exaggerated about the fertility of the place with a fanciful name. After all, his father certainly had no qualms about giving Greenland a misleading name to attract settlers.

But no matter whether Newfoundland was the Vinland of legend or not, the discovery of the ancient Norse settlement did prove that the Vikings were in America long before Columbus was and that they were the first Europeans to land in the New World. Or were they? If we accept the fact that the Norse sagas may be based on fact, then we have to admit that some of the other ancient tales may have some truth to them as well. As we have already noted, there is evidence to say that the Vikings reached the New World long before Columbus, but what if someone else arrived long before the Vikings? And what if that someone else may have been the source of the tales that led to the Norsemen's journeys?

During the early years of Christianity in Britain, a desire to spread the word led many Irish monks to travel widely. After the fall of the Roman Empire, they began to journey to Western Europe to spread the gospel. One such monk was St. Brendan, who was born in 484 in County Kerry. In Ireland, May 16 celebrates the feast of St. Brendan the Navigator as he was responsible for establishing numerous churches and monasteries along the west coast of Ireland. Brendan also traveled to Scotland and Wales but the most famous of his travels is recorded in the *Navigatio Brandoni* or the "Voyage of Brendan."

This Irish epic, which is believed to have been recorded first in the Eighth Century and then later translated into Latin, tells of the monk's search for the "Promised Land of the Saints" or Paradise. According to the story, Brendan and a number of fellow monks started on their journey in a *curragh*, a wooden fishing boat that was covered with ox-hide leather. They encountered many mythical obstacles along the way, from demons to giant fireballs in the sky, but eventually they reached a land that was rich in fruit and green with vegetation.

For centuries after, explorers searched in vain for "Brendan's Island" but eventually gave up. Although it was a well-known story in medieval times, most came to believe the land had never really existed at all. Much later though, scholars began to look at the story a little closer and noted some striking similarities in the descriptions and locations of actual spots in the Atlantic that Brendan was supposed to have passed during his voyage. They began to feel that Brendan's new land had not been an island at all, but rather the shores of America.

And while it's no proof that the actual voyage of St. Brendan was anything more than a legend, a writer named Tim Severin duplicated it in 1976. Intrigued by the possibilities of the Irish landing in the New World before the Vikings, Severin built a boat called the *Brendan* and made it an exact replica of a *curragh* from the Sixth Century. He set sail, and following the path laid out in the account of the wandering monks, he eventually landed in Canada.

But if Irish monks and Viking explorers are not intriguing enough for you, what about a Welsh prince? The stories of Prince Madoc ab Owain Gwynedd have had probably more of an impact on the accounts of European settlement in America before Columbus than any other. He has been credited with not only exploring the New World but in leaving his mark behind by way of building sites, descendants and language. How much truth there is to the story of Madoc's explorations is unknown, but Madoc himself was a real person who lived in Wales around the Twelfth Century. He was a renowned sailor and, according to the stories, left Wales in 1170 and sailed westward, where he found a new land. He returned to Wales with tales of the new places that he had found and hundreds of his countrymen left Wales to follow him across the sea.

The wondrous land that Madoc described to his friends and followers in Wales was believed to be what is now Mobile Bay in Alabama. Scholars feel that ocean currents would have carried him into the Gulf of Mexico and the attractive bay would have made a natural landfall for the expedition. In addition, they cite a number of pre-Columbian forts that have been discovered up the Alabama River. Local Cherokee Indian traditions state the forts were built by the "White People." The three forts, said to be unlike anything constructed by the Indians of the immediate region, were built along a route that settlers might have taken from Mobile Bay and up the Alabama and Coosa Rivers to the Chattanooga, Tennessee area. Some have even suggested that the ruins of the forts bear a remarkable resemblance to similar structures in Wales. One fort, which was discovered on top of Tennessee's Lookout Mountain, is said to be nearly identical to Dolwyddelan Castle in Gwynedd, the presumed birthplace of Madoc.

Accounts have been created to suggest that the settlers slowly moved northward, creating forts along the way, before constructing the more elaborate fortress at Lookout Mountain. This site took months or years to complete, but the hostility of the local Indian tribes forced the settlers to move further up the Coosa River to build another stronghold at Fort Mountain, Georgia. However, this structure was probably more hastily constructed and only shielded Madoc's Welshmen for a time. Eventually retreating from Fort Mountain, the settlers built a series of minor forts in the Chattanooga area, before moving north to the forks of the Duck River, near what is now Manchester, Tennessee. Here, they built their final fortress, called Old Stone Fort. The fortress was enclosed by high bluff and high stone walls and boasted a 1200-foot long moat that surrounded the fort's 50 acres. A number of archaeologists have stated that the engineering that went into Old Stone Fort surpassed the skills of the Native Americans at that time.

What happened to the Welshmen becomes more speculative after they abandoned Old Stone Fort. Cherokee legends tell of wars that existed between the tribe and the white men who built the stone forts. Eventually, a treaty was reached and the settlers agreed to leave the area and not return. According to the legends, they followed the Tennessee River down to the Ohio and then to the Missouri for great distance,"but they are no more white people, now they all become Indians."

Based on these stories, many have come to believe that the Welshmen were eventually assimilated by the Indians and explorers would later tell stories of having encountered "bearded Indians" and Native Americans with pale skin tones and blue eyes. And while most of them never claimed an ancestry of Welsh (by the 1700s, little trace of their Welsh forebears would have remained), many of the strange Indians would speak a language remarkably similar to that spoken in Wales.

While a number of tribes have been considered as possible descendants of Madoc and the Welsh settlers, the most likely is the Mandan tribe. The Mandans had been repeatedly driven north and west by their enemies; when a Mandan village was visited by a French explorer, Sieur de la Verendrye, in 1738, he described them as "white men with forts, towns and permanent villages laid out in streets and squares." He stated that their customs and lifestyles were unlike any of the other tribes that he had encountered and noted that many of the men sported beards. The Mandan were repeatedly driven out of their villages and decimated by the Sioux. By the 1830s, less than one-third of the tribe remained and most of them were wiped out by a smallpox epidemic in 1837. The tribe is considered to be extinct today but they do lay claim to being the only Indian tribe never to have been at war with the United States.

And while the Mandan were certainly an unusual tribe, were they the descendants of Twelfth Century Welsh explorers? No one really knows for sure, although mainstream scientists consider the stories of Madoc to be nothing more than folklore and accept no connections between the Welshmen and the stone forts of Tennessee. They negate the accounts and theories to the realm of pseudo-archaeology and wishful thinking, but obviously not everyone feels this way, including the Virginia Cavalier Chapter of the Daughters of the American Revolution. In November 1953, they erected a monument at Fort Morgan at Mobile Bay, Alabama that reads in part: "In memory of Prince Madoc, a Welsh Explorer, who landed on the shoes of Mobile Bay in 1170 and left behind, with the Indians, the Welsh language!"

AMERICA'S MYSTERY SITES

Haunted Tunnels, Relics & Altars

America is filled with mysterious places—there is no question about that. The unsolved mysteries come about when we try to determine just who built some of these sites, when and why? We have already discussed some of the strange stone forts of Tennessee and Georgia, which some believe to be relics from Prince Madoc's journeys through pre-Columbian America, but there are many others.

Some of the most famous stone forts in America are those of southern Illinois. Many of these structures have disappeared over the years, but several remain to puzzle curiosity-seekers today. They have been studied many times over the years, but so far, no one can comprehend their purpose. According to Loren Coleman's book, *Curious Encounters*, there are at least 10 pre-Columbian forts in southern Illinois and others may exist in the remote areas of the Shawnee Forest, a vast and mysterious wilderness that engulfs a large portion of state. These walled structures are located on high bluffs, facing outward in rough alignment between the Ohio and Mississippi Rivers. The walls face steep cliffs on both sides, but may be approached from behind. While only one of them, near Stonefort in Saline County, has a water source inside of it, all of them have stone-lined pits where water could be stored.

The question remains as to what these forts were used for? Who built them and why? The puzzle may never be solved, but one has to wonder: if the forts truly are scattered in a rough line between the two rivers, what enemy were the inhabitants trying to keep out? Or stranger yet, were they trying to keep something else within?

Many of America's most mysterious sites have not been constructed but are undoubtedly man-made. Strangely, many of them have been dated back to periods when the regions were supposedly uninhabited, or show engineering and design that was thought to have been impossible for people of the day.

Such is the case with the thousands of worked copper mines that are located in northern Michigan and on Isle Royale in Lake Superior. The mines were discovered by French missionaries in the 1500s but they reported that the local Indians knew nothing of their origin. This seemed odd to researchers until more recent times, when carbon dating of debris in the excavations revealed that the mines had been dug more than 4,000 years before.

Other tunnels and shafts of similar vintage have been discovered elsewhere in America. Along a trail that skirts a mountain ridge in northern New Jersey and southern New York State is a series of exploratory tunnels that may have been dug by someone seeking ore. No one knows who cut the tunnels, but they are believed to have been carved in prehistoric times.

Perhaps stranger still are the sites where standing rocks, monoliths and chambers have been found. Many feel that these sites were left behind by Old World cultures that came to America long before the land was officially explored. Some feel that the chambers and standing stones are remnants of an ancient Celtic community, which flourished in New England in the centuries before Columbus, but the riddle remains unsolved.

However, some of these formations can be traced back over 12,000 years to the end of the last Ice Age when large melting glaciers left assorted debris behind. Rocks tumbled out of the receding ice and as years of wind and water weathered away the soil, precariously balanced tumbles of boulders remained. This explains how many of the sacred sites that were so revered by the Indians came to be, but not all of them.

When it comes to the chambers and carefully constructed stone sites, we know that they were definitely constructed by man. Such locations have gone by many different names and have been attributed to many different groups. They have also been thought to have had a variety of purposes, ranging from solar temples to Colonial root cellars. Debunkers of the theory that the chambers and sites were built by an ancient people state that they are nothing more than storage cellars that were constructed during the Colonial period. This is despite the fact that many of them seem to be much older and that there are no real references to the chambers in first-hand accounts from the period. In addition, where would the colonists have gotten the idea for them? Stone-chambered root cellars simply do not exist in England, so if the colonists did devise these root cellars, the idea for them did not come from their homeland.

So, if the colonists did not build the dirt-covered root cellars, but merely used existing ones, why again did they never mention them in their writings, save for a few vague references to "man-works"? These scant notations seem to point to the idea that the chambers preceded the arrival of the colonists. If this is the case, then who built them and why? Many of them are located deep in the woods and away from the nearest farms. Almost all that have been discovered have no trace of mortar or insulating material and are merely cold, bare stone. The empty interiors of these stone crypts hold many secrets and riddles for which no answers have been found.

Mystery Hill

Of all of America's mysterious stone sites, Mystery Hill in New Hampshire is unquestionably the most famous. This rugged hill, strewn with ancient ruins, is located in North Salem and has been the source of controversy and debate for years. There are no real answers as to what the site was used for, who built it, or why. Possible builders include Irish monks, Phoenician traders and Celtic mystics, but most experts disagree that any of these groups constructed the site. They believe that the markings on the stones show that none of the structures were worked on with stone tools. All of the mentioned groups would have had access to steel by the time Mystery Hill was built, so why would modern tools have not been used?

Some experts who have worked on the site believe that it was a Native American culture that disappeared long before the coming of the British colonists to New England because the only identifiable artifacts are either Native American or Colonial. However this conservative theory does not explain the stones bearing unusual markings and writings that cannot be identified. These markings, along with local legends, say that the site may have been built, or at least used by, occultists and mystics of early New England. They were thought to be attracted to the place because of its unusual nature and may have performed all manner of rituals here.

These theories aside, it seems that the structure was here long before the colonial-era mystics. The ruins on Mystery Hill appear to have been part of an astronomical calendar with an outer ring of stones surrounding the many buildings. The sun, moon and stars rise over certain stones and specific or important dates seem to be marked by others. Could the site have been constructed by some long vanished culture that understood the solar and lunar cycles?

Perhaps, but what has caused Mystery Hill to gain a reputation as a strange and blighted place? Anyone who visits here can tell you that the area has an unusual feel to it and it affects everyone differently. For instance, author H.P. Lovecraft visited the site in 1937 and was so unnerved by it that he was inspired to write his book *The Dunwich Horror*, a classic New England tale of terror. These strange feelings and reports of an odd presence may be explained by the fact that most of the major building have been constructed over strong magnetic fields. But how did the original builders, colonial farmers or ancient dwellers know this?

Covered by a complex of stone walls, chambers, underground passages, monoliths and weird inscriptions, Mystery Hill was discovered in 1826. The first person to be associated with it was Jonathan Pattee, who built a house among the ruins here that same year. He and his family lived here for almost 30 years, and stories circulated about the Pattees' odd behavior and strange manner. They were avoided by many local residents and were the likely inspiration for the Whateley family in Lovecraft's 1930s story. In the 1850s, the Pattee house burned to the ground and the family moved away. The charred remains of the old foundation were eventually covered by years of undergrowth.

For years after, local residents referred to the nearby stone structures as "Pattee's Caves." They assumed that the old farmer had constructed the chambers for some unknown reason. The family was considered eccentric anyway, and the structures seemed to be further proof. While it seems unlikely that Pattee built the structures, he and his family did use them, and more recent excavations have discovered rusted nails, kitchen utensils and broken china within the buildings and passageways.

The first person to challenge the local folklore was an insurance executive from Connecticut named William B. Goodwin. He purchased Pattee's Caves in the 1930s and set out to show the world that not only did Pattee not construct the site, but Irish monks had actually built it in the Twelfth Century. While he had little evidence of this, he did bring attention to the site and many began to wonder just who might have constructed it.

In 1945, Dr. Junius Bird of the New York Museum of Natural History conducted the first investigation of Mystery Hill and released a report of contradictory findings, stating that while evidence did exist from the colonial era, he believed the stone slabs had been constructed at an earlier date. In the 1950s, another investigation, conducted by a Yale archaeology graduate student, concluded (with thin evidence) that the site was originally constructed by American colonists and then was reconstructed by Jonathan Pattee in the 1820s. Unfortunately, this believable but likely inaccurate report has caused many to dismiss the site as nothing more than a colonial rock pile with an undeserved reputation.

A few years later, the property was purchased by Robert Stone, an electrical engineer who lived nearby. Stone changed the name of the place from Pattee's Caves to "Mystery Hill—America's Stonehenge" and also established the first ongoing research project at the site. It has been through his dedication that the ruins here have been saved from bulldozers and developers.

Throughout the 1960s and 1970s, the mystery behind the site grew deeper and every new investigator applied his own interpretation to the stone structures. After astronomer Gerald Hawkins shocked archaeologists with his analysis of Stonehenge, Mystery Hill was then seen as a megalithic astronomical site. In 1975, when author Barry Fell pointed out that the stones at the site appeared to have markings that resembled Iberian Punic script, Mystery Hill was seen as an outpost for the Celts. During the 1980s, it was seen as a Phoenician trading post, a Viking fort and an ancient Druidic site (among other things) and the explanations continue to change with cultural fashions and whatever is popular among academics and new age thinkers.

All of this supposition just makes the place even more mysterious, as no explanation will likely ever be found. Either Jonathan Pattee, or someone who came before him, went to a lot of effort to fashion this site. Of course, who that may have been is just one of Mystery Hill's unsolved questions.

The Mystery of Burrow's Cave

In 1982, a man named Russell Burrows, from the small southern Illinois town of Olney, was out looking for Civil War relics with his metal detector when he discovered a mysterious cave. Situated along a branch of the Little Wabash River, the cave would seemingly rival all others that had come before. The cave's startling contents would set a long-held standard of American archaeology on its ear by seemingly providing evidence that visitors from the Old World may have reached the center of the North American continent long before it was generally believed. That was the claim anyway, but were the contents of the cave merely an elaborate hoax? Did the weird figures and strange carvings really just prove that trickery was alive and well in southern Illinois?

The discovery of enigmatic archaeological finds is nothing new in America. For many years, scientists and ordinary people have happened upon everything from the skeletal remains of nonexistent visitors to implausibly located ancient coins to bizarre writings and carvings to mystery stones in ancient languages. So what makes Burrows Cave so different? Perhaps it is the sheer number of oddities: ancient corpses, relics, strange inscriptions and thousands of black stones that have been carved with symbols and languages seemingly unknown in the Illinois country of earlier times. Almost immediately, mainstream scientists dismissed the discovery as a hoax. More charitable critics suggested that the carvings may have been placed in the cave and forgotten by an innocent hobbyist years earlier. They believed this unknown person would have never dreamed the stones would be accepted as genuine.

Other researchers were not so quick to dismiss the site and continue to study the artifacts today. They believe that it might be possible that the stones are real and that ancient travellers journeyed up the Mississippi to southern Illinois. With the death of party members, the unknown clan created the hidden tomb and filled it with the carved stones to pass the time in this harsh and uncivilized land. Is this possible?

One thing is sure, whether authentic or not, the cave was certainly well hidden. Russell Burrows was walking along a wooded path and literally stumbled onto the opening. As he fell, he dislodged a massive stone that, if it had not jammed, would have flipped over and deposited him into a stone chamber that was 12 feet deep. The stone had then been designed to turn over and seal the intruder into the chamber—permanently. Instead, the trap door stayed open allowing Burrows to notice the strange carvings and writings on the bottom of the stone. Peering deeper into the cavern, Burrows saw a wall with a huge face that had its eyes fixed on the deadly trap door. This nearly fatal discovery would begin a mystery that remains unsolved today.

For those who have seen the carvings and artifacts from the cave, most confess to being mystified and understandably skeptical.

The stones have a disturbingly amateurish look to them that does not conform to the types of ancient drawings we are used to seeing. Some would say that this is because of the conditions the ancient travellers were forced to work under, while others would say this provided proof of the hoax. Many of the other theories about the artifacts have puzzling questions and theories concerning them.

One thing that is always pointed out is that the writings on the stones (in tongues like Egyptian, Punic, Libyan, Greek and Arabic) make no sense in the languages of their scripts. Skeptics say the writings were obviously done by someone illiterate in these languages who simply copied the text from somewhere else. However, those who continue to study the stones offer alternate explanations. They point to the fact that the writings show a curious consistency and may actually be made up of an older language that provided a basis for the others. It's also possible that this is an unidentified script that is similar to other recognizable languages. The early American settlers noted that the Algonquin language of the American Indians sounded like Hebrew. This is often pointed out by groups (such as the Mormons) who believe the Native Americans were actually part of the Lost Tribes of Israel.

Another criticism is that the engravings do not fit with historical precedents as we know them, but could they represent something previously unknown to archaeologists? At the time of this writing, the cave has received very little attention from mainstream archaeology and most readers have never heard of it. No archaeological digs have been conducted, and supporters of the cave's authenticity have complained that the lack of attention is a conspiracy to suppress evidence that doesn't fit into the standard way of thinking by scientists. These complaints don't really seem valid because it is Burrows and his associates that have prevented any close investigations of the site and its artifacts. In fact, most people have no idea where the cave is even located. According to Burrows, the location of the cave has not been divulged due to fears that it will be looted and destroyed by relic hunters. However, there are claims that Burrows and others have already removed thousands of artifacts from the cave and sold them to private dealers. One man claimed that he purchased hundreds of pieces from Burrows, only to find that they were fake and worthless. Accounts like this that have resulted in few scholars supporting the authenticity of the cave.

Most scholars who have looked into the cave feel that it is strange that one site would hold such a large number of rock carvings as no similar artifacts have been found at other locations in America. Supporters of the authenticity of the cave argue this by saying that the cave was a central repository of ancient artifacts. Scholars also point out that if ancient European or Middle Eastern cultures had made contact with tribes in North America, there would likely be folktales or stories about "mysterious people from the East." Instead, there are none, aside from a few tales to say that some contact was made with "white people" but none to say that the contact lasted long enough to result in the intricate carvings and artifacts in the cave. Supporters of the cave have argued this too, falling back on the idea that academics are suppressing the evidence of ancient contact.

Not surprisingly, most archaeologists have labeled Burrow's Cave as a hoax, infuriating not only the cave's supporters but also those middle of the road researchers who feel that the artifacts should not be dismissed prematurely and without sufficient study. The problem is that no one can actually study the site because they don't know where it is and aren't allowed to see it by those in control of the cave. It deserves to be studied, despite the amateurish look of the artifacts and the unsettling, recent news that some of the site's supporters may have questionable intentions. If the cave turned out to be legitimate, it would represent a find with staggering repercussions. However, if it was revealed as a hoax, it would hopefully mean embarrassment and exposure to those who have managed to mislead people looking for validation of their beliefs in ancient American cultures.

So, is the cave real or a hoax? No one really knows for sure, although sadly, the evidence seems to point to the idea that it may be a fraud. To this date, Burrows, and possibly some of his close associates, are the only ones who have apparently been inside the cave. No one else knows its location and even the owner of the land remains anonymous. Some people have been taken to a wooded area and have been told the cave is nearby and at least one was shown a rock ledge and was told that it was the entrance, but none of them were taken inside of it. The only evidence that it even exists is Russell Burrow's testimony. He claims that he doesn't take anyone into the cave because it has been taken over by the state of Illinois and they won't allow him into it. This is in contradiction to a letter from the Illinois State Archaeologist's Office, which stated that no one has ever registered the site.

Recently, even more disturbing news has come to light about the honesty of some of the participants in the site. In 1999, an announcement was made that the cave location had been revealed and was going to be excavated. At that time, representatives from *Ancient American* magazine and Discovery Resources (a California-based research organization) joined forces to open and investigate the cave site. Early in their joint venture, nearly two decades after the cave was discovered, they were surprised to learn that the landowner of the site had no previous contact with Russell Burrows. They were forced to enter into an agreement with the owner before they could gain access to the site.

After 42 months of fund raising and arranging for professional assistance from geologists, archaeologists, experts in excavation, metal detection and ground penetrating radar, they finally began opening the cave. However, almost as soon as they began, they were stunned to learn that someone had purposely attempted to collapse and seal off the cave. Formerly open spaces had been filled with rubble, and there were indications that the doorway to the cave had been intentionally destroyed.

The organization was again surprised when Russell Burrows then completely reversed his story about the site's location, saying that the cave they were excavating was not the same underground site that he had displayed artifacts from. He now insisted that Burrow's Cave was more than 40 miles away and that the organization was working on a site known to local Choctaw Indians as a treasure trove. According to Burrows, the real cave was now being excavated by an anonymous archaeology team from an unidentified major university. He claimed that work was taking place at the real site with artifacts being removed and examined. The unnamed professor in charge was allegedly turning all of the artifacts over to Burrows when he was finished with them because the landowner had deeded them to him.

Befuddled and irritated, the organization re-named the site from Burrow's Cave to the Embarras Tomb, named for a local tributary of the Wabash River. The archeologists continued to believe this was the original cave that had been discovered and looted by Burrows in 1982, thanks to ground-penetrating radar. The radar showed the cave's interiors to be a close match to those indicated on the map provided by Burrows years before. Continued surveys have verified other underground tunnels and cavities that were also identical to those represented on the Burrow's Cave map.

Their surveys also discovered underground locations that were filled with precious and semi-precious metals and objects made from copper and gold. As far as the organization was concerned, this seemed to be the original site that Burrows reported two decades before. So, why did he change his story and attempt to lead them to a new site? Burrows' behavior seems to be as mysterious as the relics that have allegedly come from the tomb. Are they real or fake? Even those with a limited knowledge of ancient artifacts would admit that the publicly displayed pieces look like fakes, created by someone who looked through some old books and copied the designs onto stone. Most of the carved pieces depict the same human male and seem to have been created by the same person. Several of the pieces have even been recognized as copies of known artifacts that have been depicted in books over the years.

But once again, we can't be too quick to rule out anything. Burrows Cave, or the Embarras Tomb as it is now called, may be a legitimate find, or it may be an elaborate hoax, but until it can be thoroughly studied, it will remain a mystery. Is the cave a real archaeological site? And if not, then why was it created? Who would stand to gain from such an expensive, elaborate and time-consuming hoax? Is it all a mistake? Could the stones be the work of some strange hobbyist who never expected his creation to be found? At this point, Burrows Cave is as much a mystery as it was in 1982.

The Lost & Ancient City of the Grand Canyon

Not only is Burrows Cave far from the only American site where evidence of an ancient culture is said to exist on this continent, but it is also not the only location where supporters believe that the evidence left behind is being suppressed by mainstream science. For years, the Grand Canyon in Arizona has been considered a place of great beauty and mystery but for many researchers and amateur archaeologists, it is also a place that is shrouded in secrecy. Many believe that within the depths of the canyon, there exists a place that would turn American archaeology upside down and would be one of the most amazing discoveries in history. What is this discovery, you might ask? It is nothing less than an underground city of Egyptian origin that is hidden away inside of one of the Grand Canyon's many walls.

The magnificent Grand Canyon has been a place of wonder since the Spanish explorers first looked down from the rim at the Colorado River far below. Conquered first by explorer John Wesley Powell in the 1860s, the canyon has been the scene of both tragedy and mystery ever since.

Emory and Ellsworth Kolb were the foremost photographers of the Grand Canyon in their time. Between 1901 and 1941, they captured the magnificence of the canyon in a way that no one has done, before or since. The Kolbs literally moved onto the rim of the canyon to photograph and film the area, constructing a combination home-studio into the side of the cliff. They posted a sign outside and that read "Bright Angel Toll Road. Riding Animals, Pack Animals, Loose Animals, $1.00 each."

By 1928, a steady stream of tourists were handing dollar bills to the Kolbs for the privilege of straddling a burro from a nearby stable and heading down into the canyon. They were surprised one day in November 1928 by a young couple named Glen and Bessie Hyde who came knocking at the studio door, having hiked up the canyon from down below. The introduced themselves to the Kolbs and explained that they were honeymooners who had spent the past 26 days rafting on the treacherous Colorado River. They asked the Kolbs to take their photograph standing on the rim of the canyon. They would come back to get the photo after their trip.

After doing so, Emory Kolb asked them about their boat and they explained that they had built it themselves in Idaho and they planned to navigate the canyon with it. Despite the rapids, they did not have life preservers. Kolb was shocked and warned against such foolhardiness. Glen Hyde laughed off the warnings but Kolb could see that Bessie was nervous about the journey ahead. He told himself that the girl did not want to go back on the river. As the couple prepared to depart, Kolb's daughter Emily came out of the studio to greet the young couple. Emily was very neatly dressed and Bessie Hyde took one look at her own weary clothing and then spoke aloud. "I wonder if I shall ever wear pretty shoes again," she said. Then, she turned and followed her husband down Bright Angel Trail.

The night was November 16 and none of the Kolbs slept well that night, worried about the haunted young woman named Bessie Hyde. Both Emory and Emily kept thinking about the girl's parting words. By early December, there was still no sign of the Hydes. Finally, Kolb initiated a search of the area, which included a small plane that flew down through the inner gorge of the canyon. This was the first time that such a flight had been attempted. The pilot spotted Hyde's boat snagged in the rocks of the river.

Emory Kolb joined the rescue party and hiked down from the rim. When they reached the boat, they found everything packed and secure. The food, clothing and even the couple's books were neatly put into place. All that was missing were the Hydes. The search party combed the area, but they were nowhere to be found. If they had made it down the river, Bessie would have been the first woman to successfully navigate the canyon. As it was, she had disappeared—vanished without a trace. Even after all of these years, no trace of the Hydes has ever been found and this haunting mystery has remained unsolved for more than seven decades. Sadly, Bessie would never have the chance to wear pretty shoes again.

In 1893, the Grand Canyon was declared a national forest preserve and in 1908, a National Monument. It finally became a National Park in 1919 and today is visited by more than 3 million visitors each year. Very few of these visitors are aware of the mysteries that continue to plague the Grand Canyon, including what may be one of the greatest archaeological mysteries in American history.

In 1909, a lengthy article appeared on the front page of the *Phoenix Gazette* newspaper. According to the story, an explorer and hunter named G.E. Kinkaid, who had spent "thirty years in the service of the Smithsonian Institution," had reported an amazing discovery within the depths of the Grand Canyon. Kinkaid claimed to have found, about 2,000 feet above the Colorado River, a vast underground city that had been carved from solid rock. His employer, Professor S.A. Jordan, wanted the find to be further investigated as it was deemed to be of major importance, and in 1909 was allegedly doing just that.

The newspaper went on to say that "the archaeologists of the Smithsonian Institution, which is financing the expeditions, have made discoveries which almost conclusively prove that the race which inhabited this mysterious cavern, hewn in solid rock by human hands, was of oriental origin, possibly from Egypt, tracing back to Ramses."

According to the report, the city was found to be nearly a mile underground and accessible by way of a long main passage. This led to a massive chamber from which other passages radiated outward like the spokes of a wheel. Kinkaid claimed that the team from the Smithsonian had explored several hundred rooms and had discovered weapons, copper instruments, carved idols, urns of copper and gold and carved inscriptions that appeared to be hieroglyphics of Egyptian origin. In one chamber, they found a large crypt that was said to contain many well-preserved mummies. Each of them had been entombed with weapons, leading the explorers to believe that the chamber was a burial site for soldiers.

The explorers theorized that upwards of 50,000 people could have lived in the immense underground city and that possibly the ancestors of the Indians who resided in the area in 1909 may have been slaves or servants of those who lived in the cave. The civilization, they believed, existed thousands of years before it was generally thought such a culture could have lived in America. "Professor Jordan," Kinkaid was quoted as saying in the newspaper article, "is much enthused over the discoveries and believes that the find will prove of incalculable value in archeological work."

A story like this must have been stunning in 1909. The Grand Canyon city could be regarded as the oldest and most unusual archeological discovery in American history and yet today, it is largely forgotten. The Grand Canyon is filled with places and geological formations that have been given Egyptian names. So why is this city never mentioned in textbooks, especially with a formidable authority like the Smithsonian Institution involved in its discovery?

Largely because the Smithsonian now claims that neither the discovery, nor its discoverers, ever existed. Many ask how such a thing could be possible, especially after the extensive newspaper coverage the site was given? *The Phoenix Gazette* claims that the story must have been a hoax, and the Smithsonian discourages any inquiries on the subject. In fact, they claim to have no records that G.E. Kinkaid or Professor S.A. Jordan ever worked for them at all.

Could the story have been a complete fabrication—or could it be that the discovery was so monumentally important that it was covered up?

Author David Hatcher Childress, who has written scores of wonderful books including *Lost Cities of North and Central America*, became intrigued by the story of the Grand Canyon's Egyptian City several years ago and decided to look into it. The first thing that he did was to call the Smithsonian Institution and explain that he was researching the 1909 newspaper story about the rock-cut vaults and the Egyptian artifacts. He wondered if anyone could provide him with further information. A staff archaeologist informed him very quickly that not only had no Egyptian artifacts ever been found in North or Central America, but that the Smithsonian had never been involved in any such excavations. Neither she nor anyone else that Childress spoke with could find any record of the discovery or of explorers Jordan and Kinkaid.

Of course, it can't be ruled out that the entire story was an elaborate newspaper hoax, but the fact that it was on the front page of the paper and continued on for several pages, named the prestigious Smithsonian and gave a highly detailed account, does lend a great deal to its credibility. It does seem hard to believe that such a story would come out of thin air. Many then ask the question as to whether or not the Smithsonian is covering up this remarkable revelation. If the story were true, it would radically change the ideas of pre-Columbian settlement in America. Is the idea that ancient Egyptians came to America thousands of years ago so preposterous that it has to be erased from all records? Could the Smithsonian be more interested in maintaining the recognized standard than in releasing information that could change all of the ideas that currently exist?

You might believe that only conspiracy nuts would think the Smithsonian Institution was trying to engineer a cover-up of the Grand Canyon's Egyptian city. You might believe that, but don't be too quick to judge. A look at a hiker's map of the Grand Canyon does reveal that much of the area on the north side of the canyon has Egyptian names. The region around Ninety-four Mile Creek and Trinity Creek has points and formations with names like "Tower of Set," "Tower of Ra," "Horus Temple," "Osiris Temple" and "Isis Temple." And while this is not so strange if you consider that perhaps the early explorers of the area were inspired by the discoveries that were taking place in Egypt at that time, it's not the most unnerving part of the puzzle. What is strange is that this part of the Grand Canyon is totally off-limits to hikers and visitors "because of dangerous caves." It's interesting that the exact same area that was described in the 1909 articles by Kinkaid is now a forbidden zone, where no one is allowed inside.

Is something being hidden away within the shadowy confines of the Grand Canyon? Or are the tales of an underground city and Egyptian relics merely part of an elaborate hoax from the last century? Perhaps only time will provide the answers to another historical, unsolved mystery.

RELICS THAT SHOULDN'T EXIST

The Wyoming Mummy & Friends

Lost cities, strange relics, unexplained artifacts, mysterious forts— all these are a part of America's hidden history, but wait, because things are going to get even stranger.

Several human skulls with horns were found inside a burial mound at Sayre, in Bradford County, Pennsylvania in the 1880s. Reports say that except for the horns, which protruded from the skulls about two inches above the eyebrows, the skeletons were perfectly normal human males, and except for the fact that they were about seven feet tall. They were estimated to have been buried around 1200 A.D. And while some have suspected this to have been some sort of religious hoax (devils in America, that sort of thing) the find was reportedly made by reputable people, including a

Pennsylvania state historian, Dr. G.P Donehoo, and two professors from the American Investigating Museum and the Phillips Academy in Andover, Massachusetts: A.B. Skinner and W.K. Morehead. The bones were sent to the American Investigating Museum in Philadelphia, where they later disappeared.

In 1879, a skeleton that measured nine feet, eight inches tall was found in a stone burial mound in Brewersville, Indiana. A mica necklace was found around its neck and a human image that was formed of burnt clay was nestled at its feet. The mound was excavated by Indiana archaeologists, scientists from New York and Ohio, a local physician named Dr. Charles Green, the owner of the farm where it was found, and a man named Robison. The bones were then stored in the Robison grain mill until 1937, when a flood washed the mill away.

In 1888, seven skeletons were found in a burial mound near Clearwater, Minnesota. Each of them has double rows of teeth in the upper and lower jaws and all had been buried in a sitting position, facing the nearby lake. The skulls were described as having unusually low and sloping foreheads and prominent brows.

Another strange discovery took place in 1911 near Lovelock, Nevada. Two miners began working the rich bat guano deposits in Lovelock Cave and had removed several carloads of guano before coming upon a collection of Indian relics. Soon afterward, they also discovered a mummy, a six and a half foot-tall person with "distinctly red hair." According to the legends of the local Paiute Indians, a tribe of red-haired giants (called the Si-te-cahs) had once lived in the area and had been the mortal enemies of the other tribes. The tribes had finally all banded together to drive the red-haired ones away. A mining engineer from Lovelock, John T. Reid, became convinced that the discovery of the mummy substantiated the Paiute legend and spent years collecting evidence that the mysterious tribe had existed.

A year later, the discovery of the mummy, along with the other relics, caught the interest of the University of California at Berkeley and the Nevada State Historical Society and they sent an archaeologist named L.L. Loud to investigate the cave. He managed to salvage a number of other artifacts from the mining operation. His excavations were followed in 1924 by M.R. Harrington, from the Museum of the American Indian in New York. He too collected artifacts, but found no other bones. He also asked that the original mummy be reburied so that the Indian workers on the site would stop complaining about the disrespectful treatment of the remains.

His requests were ignored and over the next few years, more red-haired remains were found in the Lovelock area. After measuring the bones and fragments of bodies, Reid and others were able to determine that the bodies belonged to people who had stood from six to nine or even ten feet-tall.

Today, a few of the remains, including a skull, some bones and a few artifacts, are still located at the Humboldt Museum in Winnemucca, Nevada. There are also artifacts from Lovelock at the Nevada State Historical Society in Reno, but no bones. There is no mention there of giant people, but the fact that the red-haired Indians did exist is no longer disputed.

In 1891, the skeleton of a massive man that was wrapped in copper armor was found inside a large burial mound in Ohio. The skull was fitted with a copper helmet and side pieces, also of copper, encased the jaws. The arms and torso were also covered in armor and, on either side of the head were wooden deer antlers, also wrapped in copper. The mouth of the skeleton was filled with large but decayed pearls and a necklace of bear teeth and pearls circled the neck. The body of a woman was also discovered next to the giant.

In October 1932, two prospectors were seeking gold in a ravine at the base of the San Pedro Mountains, southwest of Casper, Wyoming. Cecil Main and Frank Carr were working along the edge of the rocks and thought they spotted some indications of gold in the stone walls of the ravine. They inserted dynamite into some cracks in the gulch and started blasting away the rock. As the resulting dust cloud began to disperse, they discovered that a small cavern had been hidden behind the wall and they wandered inside. It appeared to be a natural cave, although the entrance had apparently been covered over years before. They looked around, never imagining what they were about to find. Sitting on a small ledge inside of the cave was a mummified man with his legs crossed. His hands were folded onto his lap and his skin was brown and wrinkled. The face was oddly proportioned with a flat nose, a low forehead and a wide mouth with thin lips. In spite of his strange features, he appeared to be an ordinary person, except for the fact that he was just 14 inches tall.

As the prospectors peered closer, they couldn't believe their eyes. The tiny mummy did not appear to be that of a child, but rather a smirking old man. Bewildered, they carefully removed the figure from the ledge and took it back with them to Casper, where it attracted a lot of interest. It was displayed in sideshows for several years and then was purchased by Ivan Goodman, a Casper automobile dealer, who took the mummy to New York. He wanted to show it to scientists, who, after hearing of the discovery, were naturally skeptical. Most suspected that the mummy was a hoax but anthropologist Dr. Harry Shapiro from the American Museum of Natural History agreed to take a look at it. He was intrigued enough by his initial examination to organize an x-ray examination of it. He was still nearly positive that he would find the mummy was either a clever fabrication, or the body of a deformed child.

Instead, he found that "Pedro" (as the mummy was dubbed on the carnival circuit) possessed an undeniably man-like skeleton, in spite of his size. The figure had a complete set of ribs, fully formed arms and legs, a backbone that had once suffered an injury and even a fractured left collarbone. This broken bone could have been part of the injuries that Shapiro deduced had killed the little man. It seemed that the flat appearance of the mummy's head came about when Pedro was hit with a violent blow to the skull while still alive. A dark substance on the head was found to be exposed brain tissue and congealed blood.

Shapiro then began trying to discover Pedro's age at the time of death. He noted that his skull had been closed (before the injury), which means that the mummy could not have been an infant, as a baby's skull does not close for some time. He also found that Pedro had a full set of teeth, along with large and pointed canines. Shapiro estimated that Pedro had been about 65 years old when he died and that his death had not been in recent times, but far back in history. He had apparently been given a ceremonial burial at the time of his death.

These findings sparked more interest and debate and many spoke of the legends of the Shoshone and Crow Indians of Wyoming, who told tales of the "little people" that had once lived among them. Could Pedro have been one of these little people? Some believed so (and many still do), but other scientists would later refute Shapiro's findings.

In 1950, after the death of Ivan Goodman, the mummy became the property of Leonard Wadler. What became of it next remains a mystery for the mummy was never seen again. And while it may have vanished from public eye, interest in it refused to die.

In 1979, Pedro's photos and x-rays were given to Wyoming University anthropologist George Gill, who completely disagreed with Shapiro's theories about the mummy. He announced that the remains were not of a small adult, but rather of an infant suffering from anencephaly, a condition in which most of the brain and cranium do not develop. While this could account for the state of Pedro's head, it does not explain his adult features and full set of teeth. But a French zoologist named Dr. Francois de Sarre came up with an explanation for Pedro's features in 1993. He stated that the mummy was that of a deformed infant to which the skin of an adult male had been molded, as headhunters do when creating shrunken heads.

Could he have been right? Even Dr. Gill surmised that Pedro might have been a member of an unknown prehistoric race of small people. The race might provide the basis for the Native American legends of the little people, descriptions of which are very close to

Pedro. According to these traditions, the small people even killed their own when they became ill—by smashing their skulls in with a rock!

CROATOAN!

What Became of the Lost Colony at Roanoke?

There were 90 men, 17 women and nine children who were left in the American wilderness in July 1587. These hardy souls came to what is now the coast of North Carolina in pursuit of the unknown. Among them was a woman named Eleanor Dare, the daughter of the colony's first governor, John White. She was about to give birth to a girl named Virginia, who would be the first European child born in the New World. White stayed in America for the birth of his granddaughter and then he set sail for England to arrange for supplies for the colony. This journey took him more than three years to complete. When he returned, he found that Eleanor and Virginia, along with the rest of the colonists, had vanished without a trace, leaving behind nothing but a mysterious message and what has become four centuries of unanswered questions. The only clues were the letters "CROATOAN," carved on a post and "CRO" on a nearby tree.

White and his man could only assume that the missing colonists had carved the letters before abandoning the colony, but what did they mean? White had left specific instructions that they should carve a cross on the post if they were in trouble. Did this mean that they had left the colony willingly? If so, where had they gone? Could they have joined the friendly Indians on Croatoan Island? If they had, then they had again ignored White's orders. He had told the colonists to head north towards Chesapeake Bay if they were in trouble, but Croatoan was south of Roanoke Island.

Several search parties were sent out but bad weather forced White to return to England. The colonists were abandoned to their mysterious fate, but were not forgotten. Years later, John Smith would launch several expeditions from the Jamestown Colony to try and determine the fate of those who went missing at Roanoke. He never learned what happened to them and neither have the scores of historians, archaeologists and curiosity-seekers who have followed in his footsteps.

The Sixteenth Century is often called the Age of Exploration. European governments were anxious to stake their claims in the New World and England was no exception. Queen Elizabeth granted a number of charters to men who were willing to finance expeditions and to start colonies in America. By using private funds to launch English colonies, the money would not be taken from the official coffers and yet England would be able to lay claim to land before France or Spain could do so. The investors would then receive enormous land holdings and hopefully, wealth and great status. Rich men jumped at the chance to start their own colonies, never dreaming of the great risks involved.

In 1584, Queen Elizabeth granted a charter to a favorite of the royal court, the privateer Sir Walter Raleigh. He quickly organized a voyage to the New World and appointed Philip Amadas and Arthur Barlowe as captains of two of his vessels. They departed from England in April 1584 and a few weeks later, landed on one of the islands that now make up the outer banks of North Carolina. They stayed for a few months, exploring the area and meeting with a tribe of Indians who lived on Roanoke Island, located between the outer banks and the mainland. Amadas and Barlowe returned to England with two of the Indians and with reports of timber, wild fruit, and forests and water teeming with game and fish. The Queen was impressed with their reports, and the new land was dubbed "Virginia."

The next spring, Raleigh sent seven ships carrying 108 men back to Roanoke Island. Their mission was to establish an outpost and to set up a base for attacking Spanish ships. England and Spain were at war at the time and Raleigh made his fortunes seizing ships as a privateer (an inflated word for pirate). The leader of the expedition, Sir Richard Grenville, left the fledgling colonists at Roanoke and immediately set sail back to England to get more supplies. He left a man named Ralph Lane in charge of things at the settlement.

Lane and his men built a fort at the north end of the island and, while they waited for supplies, they refused to hunt or fish and began taking food from the local Indians. At first, the natives were as generous as they had been with Amadas and Barlowe, but eventually, they began running out of food they could share. When they turned the colonists away, the settlers became enraged and raided the Indian village, burning their houses and slaughtering a number of the Indians, including the chief who had befriended them. The Indians did not retaliate openly, but for the next several months, quietly raided the settler's fish traps. The friendly relationship between the Native Americans and the colonists had come to an end.

Meanwhile, Grenville's return to America with the supplies was delayed and he did not leave England until the spring of 1586. In June of that year, while Grenville was still making his way across the Atlantic, Sir Francis Drake happened to anchor off the outer banks and some of his ships sailed in to Roanoke. There, the sailors found the colonists in a sorry state. A number of the men had died from disease, their supplies gone and the fort in ruins. Hungry, miserable and desperate, they managed to convince Drake that they were in danger of eminent attack by the Indians. Drake, unaware of the incident that had occurred with the Indian village, offered to take the colonists back to England.

Two weeks later, when Grenville arrived, he found the fort deserted. But unwilling to abandon England's claim in the New World, he left fifteen men at the outpost with two years' worth of supplies and again returned home.

Even after Raleigh received word about how poorly the Grenville-Lane colony had fared, he refused to give up. He had already lined up a number of volunteers for another colony, this one to be started near Chesapeake Bay. He promised each of them land grants of 500 acres or more. Raleigh appointed John White the governor of the colony. White already had experience in America, having been a part of Lane's original colony. He was convinced that the new settlement would succeed.

On May 8, 1587, White and the colonists set sail from England on three ships. The group included White's daughter Eleanor, her husband Ananias Dare, and the two Indians who had been brought to England with Amadas and Barlowe. White's pilot was Simon Fernandez, a Portuguese navigator who had also been part of the 1584 voyage. The journey from England to America, with a stop in Puerto Rico, took about two and a half months.

Although they had actually planned to sail straight on to Chesapeake Bay, White decided to stop at Roanoke Island on July 22 to check on the status of the fifteen men who had been left by Grenville. This simple plan would seal the fate of the colonists for their journey would take them no further. There had been tensions between White and Fernandez throughout the trip. They had begun when White prohibited him from raiding Spanish ships during the journey; by July, Fernandez was anxious to return to England. When the group reached Roanoke, he refused to take them on to Chesapeake Bay. With that, the settlers were stranded on Roanoke Island.

Dark signs marked their arrival. The fort that had been built by Lane's colonists had been destroyed. Of the fifteen men that Grenville had left behind, there were no traces of them, save for the skeleton of a man found in the ruins of the fort. The colonists nervously took up residence and began to try to salvage what they could of the outpost. A few days later, Indians killed one member of the colony, George Howe, while he was fishing for crabs. The settlers retaliated by attacking the village they believed belonged to the hostile Indians, but they killed a member of a friendly tribe, a Croatoan, instead. Fortunately, one of the Indians who had returned with them from England was a Croatoan, and he interceded to prevent more bloodshed.

Over the course of the next month, the settlers unloaded all of their supplies from the ships and started rebuilding the fort. They also constructed a small village of houses. On August 18, Eleanor Dare gave birth to her daughter, Virginia. The birth of this little girl was a joyous time in the colony, but dark days were still ahead.

During the month that was spent revitalizing the remains of the first colony, the fall hurricane season began to get closer and closer. Simon Fernandez was anxious to set sail for England. It was too late in the year to plant crops and the colonists had only a few months' worth of supplies so it was decided that someone would have to return to England with Fernandez and bring back food and provisions. The leaders asked that John White take the responsibility and he reluctantly agreed. A short time later, he left with Fernandez, leaving his family behind. He had arranged with the colonists that, if they moved their settlement from the fort, they should carve their destination in a visible location. If they had to leave because of an attack, they were told to add a Maltese cross to the carving.

Ocean storms prevented White from reaching England until November. Once there, he hurriedly gathered food, supplies and weapons and within four months had a fleet of ships together to sail back to Roanoke. Before he could leave, it was learned that Spain was organizing an armada of ships with which to attack England. The English Navy needed the ships that White planned to take to America, and White was left with only the two smallest ships in his fleet. He reorganized, and then finally set sail. Unfortunately, during the journey, the captains of the two ships tried to seize a French vessel and were badly damaged by the larger ship. They were forced to return to England.

White spent the next year and a half trying to get ships and supplies for the Roanoke colony. Desperate, he was finally able to buy a passage to Roanoke with a fleet of privateers in 1590. On August 15, they anchored off the outer banks. From their position, they saw a column of smoke rising from Roanoke and White was hopeful that his family and the rest of the colonists were still alive.

The next day, he and a party of men set out for the island in two boats. The signal fire turned out to be nothing more than burning brush. And things got worse from there.

As the boats approached Roanoke, one capsized and six men drowned. They reached the island and made camp. Their accounts tell of seeing an eerie light in the woods. It was believed to have been another brush fire. Finally, on August 18 (three years to the day of Virginia Dare's birth), White returned to the Roanoke settlement. He discovered that all of the houses had been torn down, and the area around the village was surrounded by a barricade made from fallen tree trunks. The settlement was overgrown and silent, but there were no skeletons and no signs of slaughter or death. It was as if everyone had just picked up and walked away. On a post, someone had carved out "CROATOAN" and on one of the fallen timbers, the letters "CRO" had also been etched. There was no Maltese cross added to the words, which must have eased White's anxiety somewhat. It was bad enough to find that his friends and family had vanished, but it would have been worse to know they had been in mortal danger as they fled.

White led his men to nearby Town Creek, located south of the settlement, where the settlers had left their boats and where they had fortified the outpost with several small cannons. Both the boats and the cannons had also vanished. The search party was left with no clues, and a vast stretch of wilderness to search. White was saddened but not distraught. He truly believed that, with no sign of the Maltese cross, the colonists had left Roanoke voluntarily. So, he boarded the ships and returned to England. He was unable to raise the money to come back and search for them again; he died in 1606, never knowing the fate of his family in the New World.

The colony was simply considered lost and no one searched for them until after 1607 (except for a half-hearted effort in 1602), when the Jamestown colony was founded. Sir Walter Raleigh had been in no position to look for his lost colonists. He had secretly married while all of this was occurring in America, and when

Queen Elizabeth found out, she did not take it well. She imprisoned her former lover and his new bride in the Tower of London; when he was released, he was exiled from the court. In 1595, Raleigh set sail for South America, the problems of the lost Roanoke colony all but forgotten. As long as he could claim that the colonists were probably alive somewhere, and their bodies were not found, Raleigh could maintain his patent on the colony. He did send a party to make a quick search for the settlers in 1602, but they found no trace of them.

In 1607, the first successful American colony, Jamestown, was founded in Virginia. The settlers here made several attempts to find the lost colonists from Roanoke but could find no evidence of where they had gone. In 1608, John Smith was told a chilling story by Powhatan, an Algonquin chief and the father of Pocahontas. According to Powhatan, the Roanoke settlers had lived with the Chesapeake Indians for a number of years but had been massacred by a confederacy of Indians led by Powhatan himself. He even showed Smith a few metal items that he claimed had belonged to the murdered colonists. The Jamestown settlers decided this explanation was accurate to explain the missing group, but not everyone believed it.

For that reason, the true fate of the Roanoke colonists has never been discovered. No physical evidence has been found to show what route they took when they left the fort and no one, living or dead, was ever discovered who could prove they had once been part of the settlement. Over the years, the lost colony entered the realm of legend, and stories were sometimes told of blue-eyed Indians with English names living in the backwoods of North Carolina.

Another legend involves the ghost of Virginia Dare herself. An old Indian story had it that the Chesapeake Indians adopted a blue-eyed white girl, and as she grew into a beautiful young woman, she aroused jealousy among the men of the tribe. A medicine man was said to have turned Virginia into a young doe to prevent her from marrying any of the men but one heartsick brave tracked the doe for years, believing that she would eventually return to her human form. It is said that the ghostly form of a white deer is still some-times seen in North Carolina, just north of Fort Niagara and along the Thomas Hariot Trail.

Still another legend tells of a ghost ship that was spawned by the desperation of John White as he looked for the lost colony. First reported in the 1600s, a spectral, three-masted sailing ship has been sighted for more than three centuries off the shores of Roanoke Island. The ship vanishes just as quickly and mysteriously as it appears, often slipping into a bank of fog and fading away.

All legends aside, it seems that the fate of the colony is just as haunting as any ghost story can be. What became of the settlement at Roanoke? Historians have posed a number of theories (of course); one is that John Smith was correct and that Powhatan's confederacy did kill the settlers. Such a massacre would obviously explain why no trace of them has ever been found.

Another theory is the colonists went to live with the friendly Croatoan tribe, which fits with John White's finding of the word "CROATOAN" carved into the post. This theory has been ques-tioned, based on White's own writings. In 1587, he noted that the Croatoans feared that the English settlers would wipe out their already limited supply of corn. This suggests that they had too little food to support their own tribe, not to mention 100 additional peo-ple. Some believe that perhaps the Croatoan assisted the settlers in leaving the outer banks and that the colonists then joined up with a tribe on the mainland. Eventually, they were assimilated into the tribe and this might explain the stories of the pale-skinned Indians.

It has also been suggested that perhaps the Croatoans actually killed the colonists. This seems unlikely given that one of the num-ber who came from England was a returning member of the tribe, and also because the Croatoans had always been supportive of the settlement. But could there have been tensions that White didn't know about, just as there had been with the original settlement? Perhaps, but we have to remember that there were no signs of vio-lence at the fort, and nothing to indicate that any of the colonists had been killed. This theory, along with the idea that a group of Spanish explorers attacked the colony is further questioned because of the lack of a Maltese cross at the site. This was the agreed upon sign of attack or danger, and yet it was nowhere to be found.

Historians and archaeologists are still searching for the lost colony and hope that someday, the missing pieces of the puzzle will miraculously appear. Until then, we are left with many unanswered questions and one of the enduring mysteries of American history.

The Eerie Mystery of the Mary Celeste

The Famous Lost Ship and Her Vanished Crew

History is filled with many mysteries of ships and the sea. There have been accounts of crews, passengers and even entire ships that have vanished without a trace. For instance, in 1849, a schooner called the *Hermania* was discovered off the English coast. Her masts had been blown away, her crew was missing, but the lifeboats were still in place. The ship appeared to have weathered a storm, and yet there was no indication as to where the captain and crew had gone. They had simply disappeared.

In 1855, a ship called the *James B. Chester* was found adrift in the mid-Atlantic. The ship was in perfect condition, but the compass and all of the ship's papers were gone. It also appeared that the crew's possessions and gear had been hastily packed up and carried away. Strangely, all of the lifeboats were still in place, but the crew had vanished.

Some mysteries of ships don't even involve the sea. The Mississippi and Ohio Rivers had their share of unexplained disappearances during the height of the steamboat era. Perhaps the most famous lost riverboat was the *Iron Mountain*, a large paddlewheel steamer that was famous on both of the rivers. The steamer was greater than 180 feet in length and, in addition to carrying passengers, towed freight barges as well.

In June 1874, the *Iron Mountain* set off for New Orleans, carrying 57 passengers and towing a string of barges behind her. As she reached midstream and approached a bend in the river, her pilot gave a long blast on the steam whistle. The *Iron Mountain* rounded the bend, and was never seen again. Her barges were later found, adrift on the river, with their tow ropes cut clean through. No trace of wreckage from the steamer, nor bodies of passengers and crew, were ever found. Hundreds of miles of river bottom were dragged, but without success.

Other riverboats should have seen the *Iron Mountain*, but none had. Except for a few deep holes that were thoroughly dragged, there was no water deep enough to have completely covered the huge riverboat. If she had been wrecked or burned, there would have been bodies and debris. Instead, there seemed to be no earthly explanation for the disappearance of the ship. In more recent times, some researchers have come to believe that the vessel fell victim to river pirates, which were common along the Mississippi in those days. This explanation came about thanks to the stories of strange sounds that have been heard on the river at night. Many fishermen and river workers have claimed to hear screams and cries that seem to come from nowhere. These eerie noises usually include the voice of a woman, who cries out for help in French. When the witness searches for a source for these sounds, one is never found. Those with a taste for the supernatural believe the cries come from a ghostly passenger who vanished with the *Iron Mountain* many years ago. The passenger manifest of the ship recorded several French-speaking passengers on board. The other voices are those of the fellow passengers, it is thought, also calling out for help.

It is believed that pirates plundered, burned and pillaged the boat, robbing and raping the passengers. Their bodies were then buried in the forests along the river. The *Iron Mountain* herself was scrapped and dismantled, with its various sections being hidden where they would never be found. Could the ghostly voices be seeking justice, or even merely rescue, from the other side?

But of all of the ships in history, none has a more haunting reputation that the infamous *Mary Celeste*, a vessel from which the entire crew inexplicably vanished and was never seen again!

The afternoon sun was glistening off the waters of the North Atlantic where a sailing ship called the *Dei Gratia* was on course from New York to Gibraltar on December 5, 1872. Suddenly, across the bow, a two-masted square-rigger appeared over the horizon. The ship's course was unsteady and as the wind veered, the vessel shifted aimlessly. The captain of the *Dei Gratia*, David Reed Morehouse, could see no one at the helm. He ran up a signal, but there was no reply.

A boat was lowered and the captain, the second mate and two crewmen cast off toward the silent ghost-like ship. As they rowed closer, they saw her name painted across the stern, *Mary Celeste*. Morehouse was stunned. He knew the captain of this ship, Benjamin Spooner Briggs, and in fact had a passing friendship with him. The two men had dined together less than a month before when their ships had been loading cargo at neighboring piers in New York. The *Mary Celeste* had set sail for Genoa on November 5, ten days before the *Dei Gratia* had left port.

The dinghy was tied up to the larger ship and Morehouse and the mate climbed aboard. What they found on the ship has remained a mystery for well over a century. The deck was empty. No crew member came forward to meet them. They searched the ship from stem to stern, but there was no one on board. The vessel was absolutely deserted, but if the crew had abandoned her, they had left everything behind.

The hull, masts and sails of the *Mary Celeste* were all sound. The cargo, which consisted of barrels of crude alcohol, was all intact. There was plenty of food and water. Sea chests and clothing lay dry and undisturbed. In the galley, a meal was being prepared and still hung over a dead fire. The table in the captain's quarters had been set for breakfast and then had been abandoned halfway through.

There was porridge on one of the plates and the remains of eggs on another. Next to one plate was an open bottle of cough medicine with its cork lying beside it.

The ship itself was seaworthy and most things were in their proper place. It looked as though the entire crew had suddenly winked out of existence. Whatever had occurred, Morehouse realized, had taken place a short time before. None of the food had rotted and nothing metal had rusted in the sea air. Everything on the ship, including money and valuables, was intact. The only thing that seemed to be missing was the ship's chronometer. However, not everything had come through unscathed. There was water found below deck and a number of the sails were tattered. Rope and canvas was scattered about on the deck. More searching revealed that while the chronometer was missing, the ship's compass had been smashed into pieces.

Captain Morehouse suspected mutiny, but if this had occurred, how had the crew escaped? All of the ships' lifeboats but one were still on board. There was no way that everyone on board the *Mary Celeste* could have squeezed into one lifeboat. There had been a crew of seven on the ship, along with Captain Briggs, his wife Sarah, and their two-year-old daughter Sarah Matilda.

The men searched and did find a few clues to support the mutiny theory, although few of them made sense. In one cabin, they found a cutlass that was smeared with what could have been blood. They found similar stains on the starboard deck rail, near a cut that looked as though it had been made with an ax. On each side of the bow were strips of wood that had been cut from the deck. The strips were six feet long, but why they had been cut was anyone's guess.

Morehouse checked the ship's log and found the last entry was dated for November 24, ten days before. At that point, the *Mary Celeste* was passing north of St. Mary's Island in the Azores, which was more than 700 miles away. If she had been abandoned after the entry, then the ship had sailed itself, unmanned and unsteered, for more than a week and a half. Such a feat seemed impossible.

Morehouse believed that someone had to have been working on the ship for at least several days after the final log entry. But who?

And where had everyone gone? Disease? Madness? Or something far more sinister? Morehouse decided to abandon the ship in the Atlantic. Faced with his own superstitions, and those of the sea, he was too frightened to sail the *Mary Celeste* to Gibraltar. Only the wisdom of his first mate, and the promise of salvage money for the vessel, convinced him to tow the ship the rest of the way to shore. Both of the ships arrived in the Gibraltar harbor one week later. Instead of salvage money, Morehouse was met with an official order from the British Admiralty's office to seize the *Mary Celeste* for an immediate investigation. What they discovered was more questions than answers!

The *Mary Celeste* had always been known as an unlucky ship. Originally called the *Amazon*, the first captain of the ship died just 48 hours after his appointment. On her maiden voyage, she collided with a fishing boat off the coast of Maine and damaged her hull. During the repairs, a fire broke out below decks. Her third captain managed to run into another ship off the Straits of Dover. Her fourth captain ran the ship aground on Cape Breton Island and she was wrecked, nearly beyond repair. After all of that, the *Amazon* was salvaged and repaired. She was given a new name and an experienced captain in Benjamin Briggs and was put back into service.

The investigation in Gibraltar uncovered little more than theories as to what had become of the *Mary Celeste*'s crew. They considered mutiny to be the answer, or perhaps some plot by the American crew to steal the ship's cargo or to sink the ship and recover the insurance. The Admiralty believed that the crew had murdered the captain and his family and then had escaped in the single lifeboat. There was no explanation as to why valuables were left behind on the ship.

The American merchant navy was angry over the finding of mutiny. Captain Briggs was not only a fair and decent man, but he was well liked by all of the men who served with him. He also ran a dry ship. The only alcohol that was aboard the *Mary Celeste* was the cargo and it was crude alcohol and impossible to drink. To do so would cause severe stomach cramps and even blindness.

Finally, in March 1873, the British Admiralty admitted that they had no solution to the mystery. It was the first time that the court had failed to come to a definite conclusion. The owners of the *Dei Gratia* were awarded one-fifth of the value of the *Mary Celeste* as a salvage fee and the ship was returned to the owner. He wasted no time in selling the cursed ship. The *Mary Celeste* earned a terrible reputation and was considered to be haunted. A later captain was even prosecuted for scuttling the ship for the insurance. The courts, knowing the story behind the unlucky ship, suggested leniency rather than hanging, which was the normal penalty of the day. A short time later, the captain committed suicide. The *Mary Celeste* was left to break apart on a reef, scattering the "ghost ship" to the seas.

Over the next decade, no new evidence was discovered about the abandonment of the ship. No one from the crew was ever seen again, and finally interest in the story began to fade. However, in 1882, the strange story of the *Mary Celeste* took an unusual turn. A seemingly unrelated event occurred in England, in the small town of Southsea. This event was the moment that a newly licensed doctor named Arthur Conan Doyle put up a nameplate on the wall outside his office door. Doyle would then spend the days and weeks waiting for patients and prosperity, only to find neither. Instead, he would discover his love of writing and would chase away the boredom of his lackluster medical practice by writing stories. Doyle would go on to become a prolific writer of mystery and horror novels, the creator the legendary detective Sherlock Holmes, and an outspoken proponent of the Spiritualist movement. But, in those days, he was simply a penniless doctor with a taste for strange tales.

In the fall of 1882, he would pen one of these strange stories and it would go on to not only create a sensation, but would also earn a unique place in history. In fact, Doyle's harmless story would jumble the facts of the *Mary Celeste* mystery so badly that many believe that the reason the case was never solved is because of his story.

The story, titled "J. Habakuk Jephson's Statement" appeared in the *Cornhill Magazine* of January 1884. The tale was not only one of Doyle's best, but he used a fictional setting to create a theory about what happened to the crew of the real-life *Mary Celeste*. To do this, he created an entirely different scenario. In the first sentence alone, he changed the location of where the ship was found, the circumstances behind her discovery and even the name of the ship itself from *Mary Celeste* to *Marie Celeste*. Doyle was obviously trying to get the story noticed, and in that, he succeeded marvelously. The public and the popular press immediately seized upon the story. It was published anonymously and accepted as truth with the fictional Jephson claiming to be on board the *Marie Celeste* when she is taken over by a black radical leader with a hatred for whites. No one seemed to notice the obvious errors and changes that Doyle had written into the story. It was taken very seriously and debated by people who should have known better.

The adventures of Jephson created a storm of controversy for the British Admiralty. The chief investigator in Gibraltar, Mr. Solly Flood, was so outraged by the story that he sent a flurry of public telegrams denouncing Jephson's "true account" as an outrageous lie. He followed these (rather embarrassing) telegrams with an official report to the Admiralty pinpointing each of the mistakes in the account. Needless to say, when the real details of the fictional story were learned, the press was delighted, as was Conan Doyle. The story would go on to launch his literary career.

In addition, the story turned out to be the catalyst for a new wave of interest in the mystery of the *Mary Celeste*. In the years that followed, a number of other fraudulent accounts (none as successful) of the last days of the ship emerged, as did stories of strange accidents, giant squids and ghostly tales. In later years, Bermuda Triangle-type theories would be suggested, as would UFO abductions, time warps and mysterious creatures.

However, it would be one small note from Doyle's story that would hamper researchers into the case for decades. In his story, Doyle stated that none of the lifeboats were ever launched from the *Marie Celeste*. In truth, the *Mary Celeste* was missing a single lifeboat when she was found. Somehow, this was forgotten, and fiction and fact were blended together and they became inseparable. Countless books and articles on the subject state that the crew of the ship vanished and no lifeboats were missing. Whether or not the nine people on board could have escaped in a single lifeboat is unknown, but regardless, the fact that one was missing opens many possibilities that were not explored for years.

James Briggs, the brother of the ship's captain, was convinced that the solution to the mystery lay in the ship's last log entry. It stated that the wind had dropped after a night of heavy ocean squalls. It this is correct, it could have meant that the ship lost speed and drifted toward the rocks of Santa Maria Island. The hull of the ship may have been breached, explaining the pools of water below decks, and the crew may have believed the ship was sinking. Another explanation claimed that the ship was struck by a waterspout. This would explain the water below decks and the damage done to the sails. Or the crew may have panicked in the storm and abandoned ship. Author Jay Robert Nash suggested that some of the barrels of crude alcohol on board began leaking and the fumes forced the crew to leave the vessel.

While all of these solutions are certainly plausible, they still never address the question of why only one lifeboat was taken, or why everything was abandoned on board, including clothing, money, food, fresh water and the ship's compass. What really became of the crew of the *Mary Celeste*? We will undoubtedly never know, but without question, the case remains one of the great unsolved mysteries of the sea.

THE LOST DUTCHMAN MINE

The Greatest Hidden Treasure Hoard in American History?

There has been much written over the years, including in my own hand, about the strange history of Arizona's legendary Lost Dutchman Mine. The mine is said to be located east of Phoenix in a rugged, mountainous region that is a place of mystery and lore called Superstition Mountain. It is the West's most celebrated lost mine and while there is a great mythology that surrounds it, there is much truth too. Many have gone in search of it over the years, only to vanish into the rocks and desert, never to be seen again. The history of the mine is filled with danger, death, horror and misconception, and thanks to its mysterious location, it has been the quest of many adventurers and has turned out to be a place of doom for countless others.

What has caused dozens of people who seek the mine to vanish without a trace? Is the answer really as the Apache Indians say-that the "Thunder God" protects this mine, bringing death to those who attempt to pillage it? Or can the deaths be linked to other causes? Are they caused, as some have claimed, by the spirits of those who have died seeking the mine before? The pages that follow will delve into these questions but be prepared—there are far more mysteries here than there are solutions.

Superstition Mountain

Superstition Mountain is actually a collection of rough terrain that has gained the name of a single mountain. The contour of the region takes in thousands of cliffs, peaks, plateaus and mesas and even today much of it remains largely unexplored. Despite the tendency by many to call this a range of mountains, it is, in reality, only one. It is certainly not the highest mountain in the region, but it has the reputation of being the deadliest. Over the course of several centuries, it has taken the lives of many men and women and has perhaps caused a madness in them that has encouraged them to kill one another.

The first inhabitants of the region to set eyes on the mountain were likely the Hohokams, a tribe of ancient Native Americans whose culture and way of life was more advanced than many of the later tribes. The Hohokams numbered in the thousands and the center of their civilization was the Salt River Valley, which is adjacent to Superstition Mountain. They lived in adobe and stone homes and built elaborate irrigation systems to raise crops. They also carried out mining operations and, centuries later, some of their burial grounds have been excavated and have been found to contain ornaments made of gold. This means that they were likely the first to discover the rich vein of gold that is hidden in Superstition Mountain.

The Hohokams are believed to have remained in this region for about 2,000 years but exactly when and why they disappeared is unknown. Some say that they were wiped out by disease, war, or some other disaster or, for inexplicable reasons, simply migrated from the area. What is known is that when the Spanish first came here from Mexico in the 1500s, there was nothing left of the Hohokam civilization but ruins.

In the wake of the Hohokams came the Pima and Maricopa Indians. Their origin has not been definitively established but it is believed they came from the north, although some maintain that they are the descendants of the Hohokams. If so, they were a much more primitive people than their ancestors, growing few crops and existing on what meager rations came from the desert. When they came to the region is unknown but when the Apache came in the early 1400s, the Pima and Maricopa were firmly established; they already held Superstition Mountain in great awe and refused to enter the treacherous peaks and mesas.

The Apaches, according to their tradition, came to the area from Mexico. They had a fierce hatred for the Spanish, who had conquered the lands to the south, and for years had migrated further and further north to escape the bonds of slavery. The Apache were very different from the Pima and Maricopa; they were nomadic, war-like, and had no interest in farming. When they needed food and supplies, they simply raided the villages and dwellings of other tribes. They also had no fear of the mountain—at least not at first—and used the massive tangle of rocks as a fortress. They would launch their raiding parties from the mountain and then vanish back into the valleys, where they knew no other Indians would follow them.

According to legend, there was an event that occurred before the Spanish came to the region that changed the attitude of the Apache toward the mountain. The account has it that the raiding parties of the Apache finally became so unacceptable to the Maricopa that they overcame their fear of the fierce tribe and decided to fight back. They set a trap, and ghe Apaches were turned back and retreated to the mountain, with the Maricopa in pursuit. Their determination to rid themselves of their enemy was even greater than what they feared awaited them on the mountain. However, the Apache outwitted them and ambushed them in the midst of the crags and gulches of Superstition. Many Apache were killed, but the Maricopa were effectively slaughtered. Even so, it was the greatest loss that the Apache had ever suffered. They held council after the battle and decided that the mountain was indeed inhabited by gods who became angry over the battle held in their domain and caused many Apache warriors to die as punishment. In repentance, they set aside the portion of the mountain where the battle occurred as home to their gods—sacred ground. From that time on, this portion of the mountain was home to the Apache Thunder God and forbidden to any intruders.

In 1540 the Spanish conquistadors were the first white men to come to the region. Led by Francisco Vasquez de Coronado, they came north from Mexico to seek the legendary "Seven Golden Cities of Cibola." When they reached the region, the local Indians told them that the mountain held much gold, although they refused to help the Spaniards explore it. They feared the Thunder God, who was said to dwell there, and who would destroy them if they dared to trespass upon his sacred ground.

When the Spaniards tried to explore the mountain on their own, they discovered that men began to vanish mysteriously. It was said that if one of them strayed more than a few feet from his companions, he was never seen alive again. The bodies of the men who were found were discovered to be mutilated and with their heads cut off. The terrified survivors refused to return to the mountain, and so Coronado dubbed the collection of peaks *Monte Superstition*, which explains the origin of the infamous name. The mountain became a legendary spot to the Spanish explorers who followed, and it was regarded as an evil place.

The next important exportant explorer, and the first man to discover the mountain's gold, was Don Miguel Peralta. A member of a prominent family who owned a ranch near Sonora, Mexico, Peralta arrived looking for a new source of income for his family. In the 1600s, his ancestors had been given a huge land grant by the Spanish court, which included a few profitable silver mines, and the Superstition Mountain. After two centuries, the silver mines began to show less and less profit and so Peralta decided to see if there was anything to the stories of gold in the mysterious mountains to the north.

In 1845, he journeyed to the Superstition Mountain and began prospecting for gold. Within six months, he discovered a rich vein of ore and made a map of the area so that he could return to Mexico and come back with men and supplies to begin his excavations. As he mapped out the area, he memorized the surrounding territory. He described the mountain's most outstanding landmark as looking like a sombrero, so he named the cache of gold the "Sombrero Mine." To others, the peak, or spire, looked more like a finger pointing upwards and it has also been referred to as the "Finger of God." However, another explorer, Pauline Weaver, used the rock as a place to etch his name with a knife and subsequent prospectors dubbed the landmark "Weaver's Needle." The name stuck and nearly every reference to what would become the lost mine uses the Needle as a point of origin.

Peralta returned to Mexico and gathered men and material to work the mine. Soon, he was shipping millions of pesos in pure gold back to Sonora. It was obvious that this was a gold strike like no other. He worked for three years, and as time passed, the Apache began to grow angry about the Spanish presence on the mountain. In 1848, the Indians, encouraged by their charismatic leader Cochise, raised a large force to drive Peralta and his men from the area. Peralta soon got word of the impending fight and withdrew his men from the mine. They began to pack up all of the available burros and wagons with the mined ore and go back home. Because he planned to return someday, Peralta took elaborate precautions to conceal the entrance to the mine and to wipe out any trace that they had ever worked there. Early the next day, he assembled his men and prepared to move out, but they never had a chance. Taking them by surprise, the Apache warriors attacked and massacred the entire company of Spaniards. The pack mules were scattered in all directions, spilling the gold and taking it with them as they plunged over cliffs and into ravines.

One of the dead Spanish mules was accidentally found in the late 1850s by two prospectors known as Hurley and O'Connor who were trying to backtrack from the field where Peralta's men were killed. They were hoping to find the entrance to the mine, but stumbled onto the crumbling remains of the burro instead. Strapped to the animal was a leather pack filled with gold ore. Over the course of the next few weeks, they managed to find several other mules and stuffed the gold into their own rucksacks as they continued to search. Then, instead of going to the nearest town to cash in the ore, they made the long journey to the U.S. Government Assay Office in San Francisco and were given $50,000 for it. Needless to say, they returned to the mountain many times over the next several years and retired very wealthy men. Most would agree that they managed to get out just in time for they narrowly avoided the wrath of the Apaches in the area and the desperation of other treasure hunters, who were sure they had found the location of Peralta's lost mine.

Once they retired, Hurley and O'Connor spilled the story of where the gold had come from and the area where the Spaniards were killed was dubbed "Gold Field." It became a favorite place for outlaws and get-rich-quick schemers, who spent days and months searching for the lost gold. The last case of anyone finding the bones of a Peralta mule was in 1914. A man named C.H. Silverlocke showed up in Phoenix one day with a few pieces of badly decayed leather, some pieces of Spanish saddle silver and about $18,000 in gold concentrate.

The next man to profit from the Peralta mine was a man named Dr. Abraham Thorne. He was born in East St. Louis, Illinois and all of his life, he longed to be a doctor to the Indians in the western states. Early in his life, he was befriended by the frontier legend, Kit Carson, and when Fort McDowell was founded in Arizona in 1865, Carson arranged for Thorne to become an army doctor with an officer's rank. At this time, fighting between the whites and the Apache was often fierce. The Indians were besieged by the Army but it would not be long before cooler heads would prevail and President Abraham Lincoln would create a compromise in the area. He proposed a reservation along the Verde River, near Fort McDowell, which could serve as a sanctuary for the Apache. It was here, in an area unofficially known as the "Strip," that Thorne came to live and work amongst the Indians. He soon made many friends and earned respect from the tribal leaders, caring for the sick and injured, delivering babies and teaching hygiene and waste disposal.

In 1870, a strange incident took place in Dr. Thorne's career. Several of the elders in the tribe came to him with a proposal. Because he was considered a good man and a friend of the Apache, they would take him to a place where he could find gold. The only condition would be that he was to be blindfolded during the journey of roughly 20 miles.

64

Dr. Thorne agreed and the Indians placed a cloth around his head and over his eyes. They led him away on horseback and at the end of the journey, the cloth was removed and he found himself in an unknown canyon. He would later write that he saw a sharp pinnacle of rock about a mile to the south of him. Treasure hunters believe this was most likely Weaver's Needle. There was no sign of a mine, but piled near the base of the canyon wall (as if placed there for him) was a stack of almost pure gold nuggets. He picked up as much of it as he could carry and returned home. He later sold the ore for $6,000 and became another strange link in the mystery of the mine's location.

The Dutchman

Of course, the most famous person associated with the lost Peralta mine (and the man who has given the mine its popular name) is a man who has come to be known as "The Dutchman". First of all, I should clear up one popular misconception about Jacob Walz (or Waltz, or Walzer, depending on the story you hear) and it's that he was not a Dutchman. He was actually born in Germany in the early 1800s. He came to America in 1845 and soon heard about the riches and adventures that were waiting in the frontier beyond New York. His first gold-seeking trip took him to a strike in North Carolina; from there he traveled to Mississippi, California and Nevada, always looking for his elusive fortune.

Walz worked the gold field of the Sierra Nevada foothills for more than ten years, never getting rich, but turning up enough gold to get along. By 1868, he was in his fifties and wondering if he was ever going to find his proverbial mother lode. The Indians had nicknamed him "Snowbeard" because of his long, white whiskers and it isn't hard to picture him as one of those grizzled old prospectors who were so common in western films.

That same year, Walz began homesteading in the Rio Satillo Valley, which is on the northern side of Superstition Mountain.

Soon after he arrived, he began to hear stories from the local Indians about supernatural doings around the mountain, about a fierce god—and about vast deposits of gold.

After coming to Arizona, Walz took up with a young Indian woman, and they lived together on the Dutchman's homestead. At that time, Walz was working at the Vulture Gold Mine and rumors say that he was skimming gold from the mine. And he was not the only miner who was doing so either. Things eventually got so bad that the mine operators hired men to raid the homes of the workers who were believed to be stealing. Walz was the only one of them not arrested, but he did lose his job. He had managed to put away enough gold over time that he didn't seem to care. He worked aimlessly at other men's mines and sites and continued to pocket enough wages to keep him going while he searched for his own fortune.

Around 1870, Walz was working a mining claim and he struck up an acquaintance with a fellow German immigrant named Jacob Weiser. Soon, the two Dutchmen struck out on their own and vanished into the land around Superstition Mountain. Not long after, they were seen in Phoenix paying for drinks and supplies with gold nuggets. Some claimed this gold was the stolen loot from the Vulture Mine, while others said that it was of much higher quality and had to have come from somewhere else. Regardless of where it came from, the two men would spend the gold around town for the next two decades.

There have been a number of stories about how the men found the lost mine. According to some, they stumbled upon it by accident. Others say they killed two Mexican miners, who they mistook for Indians, and then realized the men were mining gold. But the most accepted version of the story is that they were given a map to the mine by a Mexican don whose life they saved. The man was said to have been Don Miguel Peralta, the son of a rich landowner in Sonora, Mexico and a descendant of the original discoverer of the mine. The Dutchmen saved Peralta from certain death in a knife fight, and as a reward, he gave them a look at the map to the mine. He was later said to have been bought out of the mine by Walz and Weiser.

At some point in the years that followed, Jacob Weiser disappeared without a trace. Some say that the Apaches killed him, while others maintain that Walz actually did him in. But Walz was always around, at least part of the time. Long periods would go by when no one would see him and then he would show up in Phoenix again, buying drinks with gold nuggets. It was said that Walz had the richest gold ore that anyone had ever seen and for the rest of his life, he vanished, going back and forth to his secret mine, always bringing back saddlebags filled with gold. Whenever anyone tried to get information out of him, he would always give contradictory directions. On many occasions, men tried to follow him when he left town, but Walz would always shake his pursuers in the rugged region around the mountain.

By the winter of 1891, an old Mexican widow named Julia Elena Thomas, who owned a small bakery in Phoenix, befriended the aged miner. Apparently, they became romantically involved and Walz promised to take her to his secret mine in the spring, but she never saw it. He did manage to gasp out some rough directions to her while on his deathbed. According to his story, "the mine can be found at the spot on which the shadow of the tip of Weaver's Needle rests at four in the afternoon. The mine faces west. Near the mine is a hideout cave. One mile from the cave is a rock with a natural face looking east. To the south is Weaver's Needle. Follow to the right of the canyons, but not very far." Walz also went on to tell her that the mine was shaped like an upside down funnel with ledges cut into the sides. The Spaniards also built a tunnel through the hill to remove the gold from the bottom of the shaft. These vague directions were all that he managed to give her. The Dutchman died on October 25, 1891 with a sack of rich gold ore beneath his bed.

On two separate occasions, Julia Thomas attempted to find the mine but failed. She probably now reasoned that there was no harm in making Walz's story public, and there was always the possibility that someone would find the lode and reward her for the information. An article appeared in the November 17, 1894 edition of the *Saturday Evening Review* that claimed to contain the detailed directions that Walz had given to Julia. As soon as word of the article spread, the hunt for the gold, which was already fierce since the Dutchman's death, became frenzied. A number of men who had heard Walz speak about the mine for years rode out for the mountain in search of the mystery.

In the description of the site that Julia gave to the newspaper, she told of a gulch where certain landmarks were located. "There is a two-room house," the report stated, "in the mouth of a cave on the side of the slope near the gulch. Just across the gulch… opposite this house in the cave, is a tunnel, well covered up and concealed in the bushes. Here is the mine…the richest in the world." One prospector, P.C. Bicknell, found the cave with the house but not the the mine. The house was a key landmark in Julia's story, although she failed to find it, and it was said to be in direct line with the mine entrance. After Bicknell found the cave, the search became concentrated in this area and it seemed like it would be only a matter of time before the mine was found, but it never was. Two prospectors, who owned ranches in the area, Jim Bark and Huse Ward, spent the next 25 years searching in vain for what they called "The Lost Dutchman Mine".

The search has since fueled well more than a century of speculation. Theories as to the mine's location have filled dozens of books and pamphlets. Hundreds of would-be prospectors have searched the Superstition Mountain region and most have come home with little more than sunburns. But there are also many who have not come home at all.

The Bizarre Curse that Claims Lives in Search of the Mine

There is no way to guess just how many people have died in pursuit of the Lost Dutchman Mine. Some who have disappeared may have just quietly slipped away, unwilling to admit that they failed to find the treasure, while others may have gone in secretly and never came out, their names recorded as a missing persons case somewhere else.

The original death toll of the legendary Peralta Massacre varies between 100 and 400, and there are the murders attributed to the Dutchman, Jacob Walz, himself. He is alleged to have killed at least two men who found his treasure trove and is blamed for the death of his partner, Jacob Weiser, among others. There are also a number of people slain by the Apaches after they were found searching the mountain for the mine. These deaths, like the victims of the massacre and those killed by the Dutchman, are easy to document and understand. But there are others that are not so easy to explain.

In the summer of 1880, two young soldiers appeared in the town of Pinal. They had recently been discharged from Fort McDowell and were looking for work at the Silver King Mine, operated by Aaron Mason. They also asked him to take a look at some gold ore they had found while crossing Superstition Mountain. Mason was stunned to see a bag of extremely rich gold ore. Where had they found it? The soldiers explained that they had been on the mountain and had flushed a deer into one of the canyons. On their way out, they found the remains of an old tunnel and mine. This small bag of gold was only a little of what could be found there.

Mason asked them if they could find the place again and they believed they could, having been scouts for the Army and very conscious of the details of the landscape. They remembered the mine being in the northerly direction of a sharp peak (which Mason was sure was Weaver's Needle) and in very rough country. A narrow trail had led from the peak and into the valley where they found the mine. The soldiers admitted however, that they knew little about mining. Would Mason go into partnership with them? He agreed and purchased the ore they brought with them for $700, and then helped them get outfitted for their return to the mine. They left Pinal the next day and never returned.

Mason waited two weeks and then sent out a search party. The nude body of one of the soldiers was found beside a trail leading to the mountain. He had been shot in the head. The other man was found the next day and had been killed in the same manner. Apaches? No one would ever find out.

A year later, a prospector named Joe Dearing showed up in Pinal. After hearing about the death of the two soldiers, he began to make searches of Superstition Mountain, looking for the mysterious mine. He was more successful in his search than most, although I don't think I would go as far as to say his luck was any better.

Dearing soon returned to Pinal, seeking a temporary job while he waited for a partner to arrive in the region. He looked for work at the Silver King Mine but since they weren't hiring, he took a job as a bartender instead. He put in his time at a local saloon that was owned by a man named Brown and within a short time, the two men became friends. Dearing confided in Brown that he was anxious for his partner to arrive because he had discovered a mine in the nearby mountains that "was kind of a pit, shaped like a funnel and with a large opening at the top." He said that the pit had been partially filled in by debris and there was a tunnel that had been walled over with rocks. Dearing planned to work until he could make enough money to excavate his find. He did not reveal the location to Brown but his description of the site matched that of Jacob Walz almost exactly. He had found the place after hearing the story of the two soldiers and only told Brown that it was located in an area of extremely rough terrain.

Dearing later went to work at the Silver King Mine, still intent on saving his earnings, and after making friends with his foreman, John Chewning, he told him virtually the same story that he had told to Brown. However, he also produced a piece of mine ore for the foreman that validated his claims. He also added that he had found the mine by following an old trail and remarked that before reaching the mine, the trail became somewhat tricky and that it was necessary to go through a hole. Exactly what he meant by this, no one has been able to discover. Unfortunately, Dearing never made it back to the mine for he was killed in a cave-in just one week after his conversation with Chewning. If he really knew the location of the mine, then he took the secret with him to the grave.

Another story that coincides with the tale of the two soldiers is one reportedly related by an aging Mexican woman named Maria Robles. In her story, she related that when she was a young girl, she went with a lover, Juan Gonzales, from Sonora to a very rich gold mine on Superstition Mountain. To reach the mine, she said that they had followed an inclining trail past a tall peak and from the top, the trail went down over a slope and to the mine. According to Maria, the gold could be taken in small pieces from a deep, vertical, cone-shaped digging.

Not only does Maria's description of the mine match that of the Dutchman and Dearing, but the character of Juan Gonzales shows up elsewhere in Lost Dutchman lore. This story was supposed to have taken place in 1874 and includes the information that he was also known as Juan Peralta Gonzales and that he came to Arizona in search of someone to outfit an expedition into Superstition. He met up with the man who owned the local telegraph office and told his prospective partner that he had a map to a gold mine that had been given to him by his father, Manuel Peralta, just before his death. His father told him of much gold that had been taken from "Canyon Fresco," which was located in the mountains south of Four Peak—mountains that included La Sombrero—and that he now had a map to the spot.

After much haggling, the telegrapher was allowed to see the map briefly and to ascertain that the canyon in question drained from the mountains northwest into the river. An undetermined distance from the river the canyon forked to the east and to the south. At this fork on the map was where the mine was marked. If this story is true, then Canyon Fresco is likely Tortilla Creek. It is the only remarkable tributary that runs from Superstition Mountain and forks in the manner described. This was the first clue as to the location of this elusive canyon.

Gonzales was able to get his grubstake and, after buying supplies, he is said to have traveled up the south bank of the Salt River toward Canyon Fresco. But he never got that far. The story has it that he stumbled on the site of the old Spanish massacre and found several decaying bags filled with gold. Rather than continue the arduous search for the mine, he decided to make do with the bags that he found and, abandoning the quest, returned home to Mexico.

Another prospector connected to the Lost Dutchman Mine and its mysterious deaths was Elisha Reavis, better known as the "Madman of the Superstitions." From 1872 until his death in 1896, he resided in a remote area on the mountain and raised vegetables. The local Apaches never bothered him because they were afraid of him. The Indians held those who were mad in superstitious awe, and Reavis certainly seemed to fit the bill. It was said that he ran naked through the canyons at night and fired his pistol at the stars. In April of 1896, a friend of Reavis realized that he was overdue for his periodic trip into town and went in search of him. His badly decomposed body was found near his home. Coyotes had eaten him and his head had been severed from his body (much like the Spanish conquistadors). It was found lying several feet away.

Around 1900, two prospectors, remembered only as Silverlock and Malm, began an excavation on the northern edge of Superstition. They found some of the gold remaining from the Peralta Massacre, but little else. For some reason, they remained working the area for years after, sinking dozens of shafts and finding nothing. Then, in 1910, Malm appeared at the Mormon cooperative in Mesa. He was babbling incoherently that Silverlock had tried to kill him. Deputies brought the other man in and he was judged insane and committed to the territorial asylum. Malm was later sent to the county poor farm, none too steady himself, and both men died within two years. What was it about Superstition that unbalanced these men?

Also in 1910, the skeleton of a woman was found in a cave,

high up on Superstition Mountain. Several gold nuggets were found with the remains. The coroner judged the death to be of recent date, although no further information about her was ever found. And the gold nuggets were never explained.

In 1927, a New Jersey man and his sons were hiking on the mountain when someone began rolling rocks down on them from the cliffs above. A boulder ended up crushing the legs of one of the boys. The following year, a person rolling huge rocks down drove two deer hunters off the mountain.

In June of 1931, a government employee named Adolph Ruth from Washington, D.C. left for the Superstition foothills with what he claimed was an old Peralta map to the mine. The map had allegedly been given to his son, Erwin, by a prominent Mexican official. The map, which may have been authentic, will turn up again later in this narrative. As it turned out, the map was likely Ruth's undoing, as he told nearly everyone that he met about it. He also made the mistake of going onto the mountain alone and at one of the worst times of the year. After making local inquiries as to the location of a tall peak and being advised that it was likely Weaver's Needle, Ruth was packed into the mountains by a couple of local cowboys. They helped him set up a camp near a water hole in West Boulder Canyon and then left him alone in his search. That was the last time that Adolph Ruth was ever seen alive.

A search party went out looking for him after Ruth had not been heard from in some time but, while they found his campsite to be intact, the old man was nowhere to be found. Six months later, in December, his skull was found on Black Top Mountain with two holes in it. The rest of his skeleton was found a month later, about three-quarters of a mile away. In his clothing was a cryptic note that read "About 200 feet across from cave" and "*Veni, Vidi, Vici*" (I came, I saw, I conquered). The message was written inside a small notebook, along with other material that, had part of it not been missing, might have solved the mystery of the Lost Dutchman years ago.

The notebook implied that it was located just over two miles from Weaver's Needle (no direction was given) in a formation of basalt at approximately 2,500 feet elevation. There was also said to be a "monumented" trail located in the westernmost gorge on the south side of the mountain. It further stated that they followed this trail north and were led over a ridge and down past Sombrero Butte and into a canyon. From this point, they hiked into a side canyon that was dense with brush. At one time, there had been more to the message, but it was at that point where a portion of the page had been destroyed. At the bottom of the page, in Ruth's handwriting, were the mysterious lines mentioned earlier "about 200 feet across from cave" and the Latin notation. Although nothing exists to prove it, it seems that Adolph Ruth must have found the Lost Dutchman Mine about 200 feet away from a cave entrance.

There was no trace of the treasure map that Ruth had taken into the mountains with him. It was not found on his body, nor had it turned up in the earlier search of his camp. It was common knowledge that Ruth had the map with him when he made the ill-fated trip onto the mountain but unless he hid it somewhere that has not been discovered, his killer must have taken it. It is an accepted theory that he was murdered for the map, or that the killer waited until Ruth found the map and then, after murdering him, took the map so that no one else could get their hands on it. Since Ruth's death, there have been a number of people who have claimed to have the map, or at least a copy of it. It seems unlikely that any of them have the original though, unless they are also claiming to be Ruth's killer. The crime has remained unsolved.

Ruth is one of the most famous deaths connected to the Lost Dutchman in the last century but he was far from the only one who was killed or murdered. In December 1936, Roman O'Hal, a broker's clerk from New York City, died from a fall while searching for the mine. It was believed to have been an accident.

In 1937, an old prospector named Guy "Hematite" Frink came down from the mountain with some rich gold samples. And that following November, he was found on the side of a trail, shot in the stomach. A small sack of gold ore was discovered beside him. His death was ruled to be an accident.

In June 1947, a prospector named James A. Cravey made a much-publicized trip into the Superstition canyons by helicopter, searching for the Lost Dutchman Mine. The pilot set him down in La Barge Canyon, close to Weaver's Needle. When Cravey failed to hike out as planned, a search was started and, although his camp was found, Cravey was not. The following February, his body was finally found under mysterious circumstances. Two men were hiking on the mountain when they came upon a rope that had been stretched across the trail in front of them. One end of the rope led into the dense brush at the side of the trail and, when they investigated, they found a headless body that was wrapped in a blanket and bound with the end of the rope. Nearby, they found a jacket and in one of the pockets was a wallet that still held money and identification papers with the name James Cravey on them. Strangely, the trail had been widely traveled during the seven months between when Cravey had vanished and the corpse had been found. It would have been impossible for anyone to have missed the rope that had been stretched across it, which begs the question as to who killed Cravey—and where had his body been during the time when he was missing?

In February 1951, Dr. John Burns, a physician from Oregon, was found shot to death on Superstition. It was said to have been an accidental death.

In early 1952, Joseph Kelley of Dayton, Ohio began his own search for the mine. He had been intrigued by the mystery of the Lost Dutchman for years and came to believe that he had stumbled across the solution. After selling his car, he purchased a gun at a Mesa sporting goods store and then went onto the mountain on foot. He left word with a Mesa motor hotel operator to call his wife and the police in case he did not return within ten days. The calls were placed because Kelley never returned and was never heard from again. He was never seen again—until his skeleton was discovered near Weaver's Needle more than two years later, in May of 1954. He had been shot directly from above and, according to the coroner's jury, "by accident."

Two California boys hiked onto Superstition Mountain the same year as Kelley. Nothing further was ever seen of them. Some have suggested that they met the same fate as the three Texas boys who had also disappeared a few years before.

Bernardo Flores, a prospector from Coolidge, also went onto the mountain in search of the mine. According to his relatives, he left one summer day and just never returned. His headless skeleton was found nearly a year later.

Charles Massey came from Tucson to do some javelina hunting with friends in 1954, but while on the mountain, he became separated from the others and was never seen alive again. His skeleton was found in February 1955 at the bottom of a cliff; he had been shot directly between the eyes. A coroner's jury later ruled that it was an accident.

In January 1956, a Brooklyn man reported to police that his brother had been missing for several weeks. It was believed that he had gone in search of the mine. The body of Martin Zywotho was discovered with a bullet hole above his right temple. A coroner's jury was undecided as to whether it was the result of an accident or suicide.

In April 1958, a deserted campsite was found on the northern edge of the mountain. There was a bloodstained blanket, a Geiger counter, cooking utensils, a gun-cleaning kit (but no gun), and some letters from which the names and addresses had been torn. No trace of the camp's occupant was ever found.

In April 1959, two friends traveled to Arizona from Hawaii in a search for the mine. They came equipped with a map of dubious origins and were eager to search for the gold. However, they did not hunt for long. One night, as he lay in his sleeping bag, Stanley Fernandez was shot and killed by his companion and best friend,

Benjamin Ferreira. The accused later took a guilty plea to a manslaughter charge and was sentenced to serve time in Florence, Arizona. No explanation was ever given as to why he killed his friend. After he was released on parole, he headed back to Hawaii and after a brief time at home, shot his mother-in-law.

In November 1959, Robert St. Marie was shot and killed on Superstition Mountain. His killing was not mysterious, and stemmed from another case of senseless madness, the kind that has long plagued the mountain. He had been murdered by a prospector named Ed Piper, who had gotten into a disagreement over "claim jumping" with St. Marie. The dead man had been part of a group led by a singer named Celeste Marie Jones, who had come seeking the Lost Dutchman on a tip from a Los Angeles astrologer. The two parties ran into one another on the mountain and got involved in a shoot-out over who had the right to be there. Norman Teason, the justice of the peace at Apache Junction, ordered all of the rifles from both parties confiscated. Despite the order, Piper later testified that he saw St. Marie approach him with a rifle in his hand, so Piper shot and killed him. Piper was released after the judge agreed that it had been a shooting in self-defense.

In October 1960, a group of hikers found a headless skeleton near the foot of a cliff. The skull was found four days later and it was determined that it belonged to an Austrian student named Franz Harrier. Five days later, another skeleton was found, and in November, police identified the body as William Richard Harvey, a painter from San Francisco. His cause of death was unknown.

In January 1961, a family picnicking near the edge of the mountain discovered the body of Hilmer Charles Bohen buried beneath the sand. He was a Utah prospector who had been shot in the back. Two months later, another prospector, Walter J. Mowry from Denver, was found shot to death in Needle Canyon.

That fall, police began searching for Jay Clapp, a prospector who had been working on Superstition on and off for about fifteen years. He had last been seen in July and, after several weeks, the search was eventually called off. His headless skeleton was finally discovered three years later. He was identified by two cameras with the initials "JC" scratched on them.

And with that, my personal record of mysterious deaths comes to an end, although the death of Jay Clapp was reportedly far from the last. I've been told there have been many others who have sought the gold of the Dutchman and who never returned.

There have been many who have searched for it and, according to their reports, many who have found the mine as well. In fact, the Lost Dutchman may just qualify as the most found lost mine in the world! The finding of the Lost Dutchman just might constitute an entire saga of disappointment, fraud and disillusionment all its own. Most of the time the perpetuation of the mine's discovery can be blamed on the press and its search for a good story and the mine has been allegedly found many times in the past and undoubtedly will be found many times in the future. These stories have become almost as an important a part of the story as Jacob Walz himself. Arizona newspapers, from the 1800s to the present, contain many stories of finding the Lost Dutchman Mine but no one ever has. It is still out there somewhere in the rugged hills of Arizona, just waiting for someone to return and claim its prize.

The first public acknowledgment of the mine's discovery came right after the turn of the last century, in September 1901, when it was thought to have been found by Charlie Woolf, a prospector and cowboy, who accidentally stumbled onto an 80-foot shaft that was surrounded by abandoned mining equipment and human skeletons. The paper soon retracted the story, stating that the mine that Woolf supposedly found was not in the right area to have been the Lost Dutchman.

The famous mine was discovered again in 1920 and, according to a publicity report from Dr. R.A. Ailton, the secretary and treasurer of the Lost Dutchman Mine, it was the greatest gold strike in Arizona history. The story was carried in many regional newspapers but to many, the wording of the publicity release was little more than a phony scheme to bilk investors in the new mine out of their money. The public wanted to believe that the mine had been found and many readers simply couldn't wait to become a part of the company.

Using the newspaper's thirst for a good story, the new owners of the Lost Dutchman neatly laid out their snare. They spoke of the many prominent men who had approved of the company and their plans without saying who these men actually were. And it also happened that the Lost Dutchman Company planned to set up offices in downtown Phoenix and conveniently planned to offer stock to the public. On the company's application for stock, they even stressed their 90 day credit plan. Hundreds of people invested but, not surprisingly, the company vanished and the subsequent development of the mine never took place.

In January 1935, sheriff's deputies in Phoenix were puzzled over a note that had been found in a bottle floating in the Salt River. It read: "Lost up Salt River. Broken Leg. I've found the Lost Dutchman Mine, I think. Come up and I'll reward you. By Blue Point. Please come quick. Jake Lee." Since no one believed the writer had actually found the mine, no one bothered to go up onto the mountain to look for the supposedly injured "Jake Lee." He was never heard from again.

Another of the stranger findings of the mine came in 1936. But in this case, the man who claimed it did not get rich-it actually cost him money. One day, a man stumbled down from Superstition with a sack of pure gold, claiming that it had come from the lost mine. The gold was very fine and pure—too pure in fact—and it aroused the suspicions of the authorities. Police investigators launched an investigation and it was discovered that the gold was actually manufactured from gold meant to be used to fill teeth. The gold, worth about $5,000, turned out to be stolen and was confiscated by the United States Mint authorities.

Years later, according to Frank Edward's 1961 book *Strange People*, the well-known psychic Peter Hurkos also reportedly found the mine. He and several associates came to Arizona without the amount of fanfare that usually accompanied the psychic's outings. It was announced that he planned to find the Lost Dutchman using ESP. Little was heard about his progress until a somewhat belated report appeared to say that he had found the mine and was now very rich. The report added that it had not been found where the stories normally claimed it would be. There was no fanfare and no fuss and not much more was learned about the search. The statement was made and after a brief flurry of interest—as well as denials by every-one not involved—it was dismissed as another eccentric tale.

When Edwards reported the find in his book, he wrote of Peter Hurkos: "Today he lives in Milwaukee, happily married and with a substantial income assured, for Hurkos used his weird tal-ents to locate for himself and a small group of associates the fabu-lous Lost Dutchman gold mine in Arizona, one of the legendary treasures of the West." But did he really? It's true that Hurkos had established an excellent reputation for himself, especially among law enforcement professionals, for having fabulous psychic powers but was he able to use them to find the mine, as he had done for missing and murdered people? Only Hurkos can answer that for sure but there were many claims of finding the mine that came after him, so most have to wonder.

Some 45 years after the demise of the Lost Dutchman Mining Corporation in 1920, another company formed with an amazingly similar name, the Lost Dutchman Exploration Company. Except this time, it was for real—the Lost Dutchman Mine had finally been found. Glenn Magill, a private investigator from Oklahoma City, and a group of associates had laid claim to Jacob Walz's mine. They had incorporated and were in the process of developing it. The publicity ran rampant and included not only newspaper and magazine reports but also a book by Curt Gentry called *The Killer Mountains*. Wild statements by Magill flashed across the newswires. "We don't think we have the right mine, we know we do," he stat-ed without hesitation.

A Tucson radio station, learning of the discovery, received permission from Magill to do live broadcasts from the site. Adding more credence to the discovery was a statement from Sidney Brinkerhoof of the Arizona Historical Society in Tucson. The statement said in effect that Magill's mine certainly matched the legendary aspects of the story and that the "significance of this discovery is in close parallel with descriptions of the mine left to us in years past. If in the weeks ahead, they are to hit pay dirt, it will be because they have gone at this project with a conscientious and scientific approach. Certainly they've put a lot of hard work into the project. And in the end they will probably come closer to the truth than any group in the past."

Brinkerhoff had been careful to make his statement so that it was not an outright confirmation of Magill's claims and this was likely for the best because something here was not right. Brinkerhoff had wondered "if in the weeks ahead, they are to hit pay dirt," but Magill was already claiming that they had hit pay dirt. He confirmed in press releases that he had discovered the Lost Dutchman Mine and had even talked of gold being taken out. But if this was the case, where was the gold?

Not everyone, including some newspapers, was taken in by Magill's assertion. His filing of a claim that included the location of the mine was met with skepticism by locals who were long familiar with the stories of the mine. They also noted the absence of any hard evidence to corroborate the discovery, namely the gold. Magill claimed to find nuggets of pure gold in the mine, and yet he had not produced them, or even produced photographs of the mine that he claimed to have showing his men removing a seal on the entrance that had been placed there by the Apache.

It later turned out that Magill had found the mine using maps that had originally belonged to Erwin Ruth, whose father, Adolph Ruth, had been killed looking for the mine in 1931. This would cause many to wonder what may have gone wrong, as Adolph Ruth remains one of the only people in the history of the mine to have ever really discovered its location. Perhaps Magill read them wrong. The Lost Dutchman find never turned up any gold. A few pieces of quartz, flecked with gold—a common find for even amateur prospectors—was the extent of the so-called fabulous bonanza. After being questioned, Magill finally admitted that perhaps some of his previous statements had been premature.

On June 7, 1967, the Oklahoma Securities Commission filed a "cease and desist" order against the Lost Dutchman Exploration Company. The officers had been selling stock in the company and failed to first register it with the Securities Commission. Magill abandoned Superstition Mountain and went back to Oklahoma.

In April 1975, Robert "Crazy Jake" Jacob held a press conference to announce to the world that he and another prospector had found the Lost Dutchman. It was on Superstition Mountain and within view of Weaver's Needle, as the legends had always stated. Jacob reported that the entrance to the mine was covered by "only 18 inches of dirt and some two by fours and rocks." The article from the Associated Press added one more ingredient, which seems to be common on all Dutchman discovery stories—that Jacob failed to present any gold at the press conference to substantiate their claim of finding the mine.

Two more Dutchman discoveries were announced within weeks of one another in 1980. In January of that year, Charles Kentworthy, head of a treasure-hunting corporation said that he had his group had found a number of gold and silver "glory holes" on Superstition Mountain. He said that they had used aerial photography, the infamous "Peralta Stone Maps" (a set of carvings later shown to be phony carved stone markers), a proton magnetometer and an optical sensing device to find the mine. In this case, Kentworthy was a bit more cautious than some of his predecessors about claiming outright that it was Walz's mine. When asked by a reporter if he thought it was the Lost Dutchman, he replied, "Who can tell? Nobody ever put a sign on it."

A few weeks after the Kentworthy discovery, Charles

Crawford announced that he had found the Lost Dutchman mine. He added a new twist by confessing that he had found it by dowsing. He told reporters that this time "there was no doubt about it." He had found the mine in La Barge Canyon, exactly where the old maps said it would be, but Crawford claimed he was the first to interpret these maps correctly. The mine had been sealed by tons of rock and an old tailing dump nearby, Crawford said, had assayed at three ounces of gold per ton. By his estimate, this pile alone would contain more than $20 million in gold and he had not even gotten into the mine yet.

What happened to it though? As opposed to most Lost Dutchman claimants—who vanished within days and weeks of achieving publicity—Crawford remained in the area until 1982, giving slide presentations about his find for $5 per person. He also conducted horseback tours to the mine, where visitors were allowed to pan for gold. These seem to be unusual activities for someone who claimed just two years before to have found the "richest mine in the world."

And so it continues today. Although prospectors who come looking for the Dutchman's gold today find a much different place than most who came before. Superstition Mountain is now a part of the great Tonto National Forest and falls within an area that has been designated as the Superstition Wilderness Area. Most of the land, with Weaver's Needle as its center, was set aside as a public landmark and recreation area and mining claims are no longer allowed. There are no roads permitted here, which is unchanged from the past, but Forest Service trails now beckon to the adventurous and are so clearly marked that one can navigate to as far as Weaver's Needle without hesitation. Thousands of people come here every year, lured by the mystery, but the days of lost mines— at least here—are now largely forgotten.

The legends of the place remain strong, at least for as long as we want to remember them and they keep the link to the past alive and well. There is a mine out there somewhere, still waiting to be found and perhaps the prospector named Joe Dearing said it best when he described the mine as "the most God-awful rough place you can imagine... a ghostly place."

What brought so many to it, to fight and die for an enigma? Was it merely the lure of wealth, or a madness they could not explain? That answer is as mysterious as the location of the Lost Dutchman Mine itself.

Chapter Two

WITHOUT A TRACE

Those Who Walked to the Edge and Never Came Back

American history is dotted with personages who, although long since gone, are far from forgotten. They are people who brushed the edge of the unexplained, the unsolved and the mysterious and sometimes their paths took them so far over the edge of it that they vanished completely, without a trace. Where did they go? How did they die? And why do so many unanswered questions trail after them in their wake?

Dorothy Arnold

On the cold morning of December 12, 1910, a young woman named Dorothy Arnold left her parent's home in Manhattan to go shopping for a dress to wear to her younger sister's coming out party. It was the holiday season in New York and a time for festivities, galas and balls; this particular party was a much-anticipated one for Dorothy, a young and beautiful graduate of Bryn Mawr, and the daughter of a prosperous and socially prominent clan.

After she left the house that morning, several acquaintances stopped and spoke with her as she walked along Fifth Avenue, and others saw her going toward a bookstore on 27th Street. They all said that she seemed cheerful. A clerk who sold Dorothy a box of chocolates said that she seemed very carefree, and friends who ran into her outside the bookstore said that they noticed nothing unusual about her. Strangely, these acquaintances would be the last people to ever see the girl who came to be known as the "vanishing heiress" alive. Despite an international search, she disappeared without a trace.

At first, the Arnold family kept her disappearance a secret, conducting discreet investigations through a friend of the family and with the Pinkerton Detective Agency. Her parents spent thousands with the Pinkertons, who had no more success than family friend John S. Keith did. Keith was the attorney for the family and he had often escorted Dorothy to social functions, so he took her disappearance especially hard. For weeks, he searched hospitals, morgues and jails in New York, Boston and Philadelphia. He inspected patients, inmates and corpses before finally giving up in despair.

The secret investigations continued for six weeks, before the Arnolds finally turned to the police and the newspapers. Her father, Francis Arnold, summoned reporters to his office and announced his belief that Dorothy had been "attacked in Central Park" on her way home and that her body had been thrown into the reservoir. As grim and hopeless as this sounds, the rigid and proper Arnold would rather his daughter be dead than the alternative—that she had run away with a man with whom she had spent a clandestine week several months before.

The man's name was George Griscom, Jr. but, when questioned

by detectives and by the police, he denied any knowledge of Dorothy's whereabouts. Her brother John was so suspicious of the rich bachelor that he throttled him and threatened to kill him if he didn't reveal where Dorothy was hiding. Griscom insisted that he had nothing to do with her disappearance, but he did turn over a letter that she had recently written to him concerning her depression over a story she had written being rejected by a magazine. She concluded the letter with "All that I can see ahead is a long road with no turning." Griscom feared that she had been so distraught over this that she had taken her own life. Or so he said. A few friends believed that if Dorothy had committed suicide, she had done so because Griscom refused to marry her.

Another theory was that Dorothy was in a hospital some where, suffering from amnesia. It was thought that perhaps she had slipped on an icy sidewalk that chilly morning and had fallen, striking her head on the pavement. A check of the hospitals in Manhattan revealed no one matching her description though.

As the publicity began to spread, reports of "Dorothy sightings" began coming in from all over the country. She was "recognized" in hundreds of cities but all of the reports turned out to be false. Francis Arnold spent more than $100,000 trying to recover his daughter, but it all amounted to nothing. He died in 1922 and his wife passed on in 1928, never knowing what became of the young woman. In Arnold's will though, a provision stated that he had left nothing for Dorothy "for I am satisfied that she is not alive."

George Griscom also continued to search, spending huge amounts of money on "Come Home Dorothy" ads in major newspapers. But could this have been an act to throw off a trail that may have led to his own door? Six years after the girl had disappeared, a Rhode Island convict released a story to the press that claimed he had been paid $150 to dig a grave for the murdered heiress. The description that he gave of the man who paid him was strikingly close to that of Griscom; however he never learned the man's name. The convict stated that Dorothy had died after a botched abortion and that she had been buried in the cellar of a house near West Point. Police unearthed cellars all over the area but they found no sign of a corpse. And no one ever found any sign of Dorothy Arnold.

Judge Joseph F. Crater

Perhaps no disappearance in American history has created as much speculation as that of New York Supreme Court associate justice Joseph F. Crater. For many years, he was known simply as "the most missingest man in New York." He was last seen on the evening of August 6, 1930, walking out of a New York restaurant. Crater was a tall heavyset man and an avowed clotheshorse. He was especially dapper that evening as he stepped out of the restaurant, waved goodbye to a couple of friends and then climbed into a taxicab. His friends would remember his double-breasted brown suit, gray spats and high collar for it was the last suit they ever saw him wear. After that final glimpse, Crater was never seen again. But how was it possible for a man as powerful and prominent as a Supreme Court judge to disappear forever?

Judge Crater's career was unquestionably successful. He was born and raised in Easton, Pennsylvania and later graduated from Lafayette College and the Columbia University Law School. In 1913, he began practicing law in New York and got mixed up in local politics. He soon became president of the Democratic Party club in Manhattan and saw his law practice flourish, thanks to his connections to the corrupt Democratic leadership at Tammany Hall. In April 1930, he was appointed to the New York Supreme Court. He had withdrawn $20,000 from the bank just days before his appointment. The sum was close to a year's salary but was the standard Tammany payoff for the lucrative post. It was not a poor investment, according to investigators who later looked into his role as a receiver of a bankrupt hotel. Crater sold it to a bond and mortgage firm for $75,000 and two months later, the city agreed to buy it back for a planned street widening for a condemned property price of almost $3 million. Crater did just as well in his private life. In 1916, a woman named Stella Wheeler retained him in a divorce trial and the next year, right after her divorce became final, Stella married her attorney. By all accounts, they appeared to be a happy and devoted couple.

In the summer of 1930, Judge Crater and his wife were vacationing at their summer cabin at Belgrade Lakes, Maine. In late July, he received a telephone call and he offered no information to his wife about the content of the call, other than to say that he had to return to the city "to straighten those fellows out." The following day, he arrived at his Fifth Avenue apartment but instead of dealing with business, he made a trip to Atlantic City in the company of a showgirl. On August 3, he was back in New York. On the morning of August 6, he spent two hours going through his files in his courthouse chambers. He then had his assistant, Joseph Mara, cash two checks for him that amounted to $5,150. At noon, he and Mara carried two locked briefcases to his apartment and he let Mara take the rest of the day off.

Later that evening, Crater went to a Broadway ticket agency and purchased one seat for a comedy that was playing that night called "Dancing Partners" at the Belasco Theater. He then went to Billy Haas' chophouse on West 45th Street for dinner. Here, he ran into two friends, a fellow attorney and his showgirl date, and he joined them for dinner. The lawyer later told investigators that Crater was in a good mood that evening and gave no indication that anything was bothering him. The dinner ended a little after 9:00 (a short time after the curtain had opened for the show for which Crater had a ticket), and the small group went outside. As mentioned, Crater waved goodbye to his friends and entered a cruising taxi that he hailed. His next and likely final location remains a mystery.

Strangely, there was no immediate reaction to Judge Crater's disappearance. After he did not return to Maine for ten days, his wife began making calls to their friends in New York, asking if anyone might have seen him. Only when he failed to appear for the opening of the courts on August 25 did his fellow justices become alarmed. They started a private search but failed to find any trace of him. The police were finally notified on September 3, and after that, the missing judge was front-page news.

The story captivated the nation and a massive investigation was launched. Had Crater been killed, or had he simply disappeared on his own? That was the question to which everyone wanted the answers, from police detectives to shady business partners to the average man on the street. The official investigations started off with a bang, but quickly slowed down. Detectives discovered that the judge's safe-deposit box had been cleaned out and the two briefcases that Crater and his assistant had taken to his apartment were missing. These promising leads were quickly bogged down by the thousands of false reports that were coming in from people who claimed to have seen the missing man.

In October, a grand jury began looking into the case, calling 95 witnesses and amassing 975 pages of testimony. After all of that, the conclusion was: "The evidence is insufficient to warrant any expression of opinion as to whether Crater is alive or dead, or as to whether he has absented himself voluntarily, or is the sufferer from disease in the nature of amnesia, or is the victim of crime."

The investigation was at a standstill and most assumed that the judge had ducked out just one step ahead of someone who was looking for him. For decades after his disappearance, his name was a slang term for dodging one's responsibilities and "to pull a Crater" was to slip away permanently. But if the judge did go into hiding with a trunk load of cash, how do we explain what Sally Crater discovered in her apartment in January 1931? Hidden in a bureau, she found several uncashed checks, stocks, bonds, three life insurance policies and a note from Judge Crater himself. The note listed his financial assets and then added: "I am very whary (weary). Joe." If the judge had simply run off, wouldn't he have cashed in these checks and stocks? And why would he have made his disappearance seem like a depressed man was carrying it out?

Better yet, why would he disappear at all?

There have been many theories put forward to answer the mystery of Judge Crater. Mrs. Crater and many of his close friends believed that he was the victim of foul play. Sally Crater stated that he was murdered "because of something sinister connected to politics." And she may have been right, given his involvement in bribery, back door dealing with Tammany Hall politics, and questionable real estate deals. She also did not believe that the judge would have voluntarily vanished. "Joe Crater would not run away from anybody but would meet his problems directly, whatever they were."

In 1937, Mrs. Crater sued the three insurance companies for double indemnity on her husband's life insurance policies. During the trial, her attorney, Emil K. Ellis, advanced her murder theory, but left politics out of the mix. He claimed that Judge Crater had been blackmailed by a Broadway showgirl and had cashed the checks for $5,150 to pay her off. When she demanded more money and Crater refused to pay it, a gangster friend of the showgirl had killed him, perhaps accidentally. The attorney's theories did not impress the court and they denied the double indemnity claims.

On June 6, 1939, Judge Crater was officially declared dead but sightings continued for years, as did the theories as to what happened to him. Possible exits of the judge have included his murder by political cronies just before he could testify against them in a graft investigation and a cover-up of his death in the arms of his mistress or a prostitute. Some believe he was killed in a dispute over a pay-off or that he decided to drop out and start a new life in Quebec, Europe of the Caribbean. One thing that is sure is that it's unlikely we'll ever really know what happened to the "missingest man in New York."

John Dillinger

On the evening of July 22, 1934 a dapper-looking man wearing a straw hat and a pin-striped suit stepped out of the Biograph Theater in Chicago, where he and two girlfriends had watched a film called *Manhattan Melodrama* starring Clark Gable. No sooner had they reached the sidewalk than a man appeared and identified himself as Melvin Purvis of the FBI. He ordered the man in the straw hat to surrender. Several shots rang out and the fleeing man in the straw hat fell dead to the pavement, his left eye shredded by one of the shots fired by the other agents who lay in wait. And so ended the life of John Herbert Dillinger, the most prolific bank robber in modern American history and the general public's favorite Public Enemy No. 1—or did it?

On the evening that he was allegedly killed, Dillinger left the theater in the company of Anna Sage (the famed "Lady in Red") and his girlfriend, Polly Hamilton. He had been hiding out in her North Halstead Street apartment but for months he had been pursued diligently by Melvin Purvis, the head of the Chicago branch of the FBI. Purvis had lived and breathed Dillinger (and would, after the robber's alleged death, commit suicide) and had narrowly missed him several times before. It was finally at the Biograph where Purvis caught up with Dillinger and put an end to his career.

The criminal life of John Dillinger started in 1925 when he was arrested after holding up a grocery store in his hometown of Mooresville, Indiana. Pleading guilty, he was sentenced to serve 10 to 20 years in prison, while his accomplice, who pleaded not guilty, only received a sentence of two years. Dillinger spent the next eight years in jail but when he was released in May of 1933, he robbed three banks in three months and netted more than $40,000. Thus began Dillinger's wild crime spree.

Dillinger was captured in September 1933 and imprisoned in Lima, Ohio. Three weeks later, his gang sprung him in a dangerous escape and he was back to bank robbing. In January 1934, Dillinger shot and killed a police officer in East Chicago, for which he was arrested in Arizona and then jailed in Crown Point, Indiana to await trial. He escaped a month later, using a fake gun that he had carved from a bar of soap (or a piece of wood) and blackened with shoe polish. He eluded the police for another month, shooting his way out of an ambush in St. Paul, and dodging the FBI near Mercer, Wisconsin. Dillinger arrived in Chicago in late June and proceeded to rob a South Bend, Indiana bank and kill a police officer and four civilians. In just over a year, Dillinger had robbed six banks, killed two cops and two FBI agents, escaped from jail twice, and escaped from police and FBI traps six times.

In the process of all of this violence, Dillinger managed to become an American folk hero. It was the time of the Great Depression and here was a man striking back at poverty by taking from those who could afford losing their money the most. Stories began to circulate about Dillinger giving away much of his stolen money to the poor and the needy. Were these stories true? The American public believed it, which was more than the government could stand. Dillinger had to be taken, and soon. He had become J. Edgar Hoover's Public Enemy No. 1—and the heat was on.

Dillinger knew that his luck could only hold out for so long and in May 1934, he contacted a washed-up doctor who had done time for drug charges named Loeser. He paid him $5000 to perform some plastic surgery on his recognizable face, removing three moles, a scar, the cleft of his chin and the bridge of his nose. The doctor agreed to the surgery and left Dillinger in the care of his assistant to administer the general anesthetic. An ether-soaked towel was placed over Dillinger's face and the assistant told him to breathe deeply. Suddenly, Dillinger's face turned blue and he swallowed his tongue and died. Dr. Loeser immediately revived the gangster and proceeded to do the surgery. Dillinger would have no idea how close he had come to death. Ironically, just 25 days later, he would catch a bullet in front of the Biograph Theater, or so they say.

When Dillinger walked into the theater that night he had been set up by Anna Sage, who had taken him there at the request of the FBI. She promised to wear a red (actually bright orange) dress for identification purposes. Sixteen cops and FBI agents waited over two hours outside the theater, watching for the unknowing Dillinger to exit. They even walked the aisles of the theater several times to make sure that he was still there. Finally, Dillinger left the theater and was met by Melvin Purvis. He stepped down from the curb, just passing the alley entrance and tried to run. He reached for his own gun, but it was too late. Four shots were fired and three hit Dillinger. The gangster fell, dead when he hit the pavement.

Purvis ordered Dillinger rushed to nearby Alexian Brothers Hospital. He was turned away at the doors as he was already dead, and Purvis and the police waited on the hospital lawn for the coroner to arrive. A mob scene greeted the coroner at the Cook County Morgue where curiosity-seekers filed in long lines past a glass window for a last look at Dillinger. Little did they know that the man they were looking at might not have been the famed gangster at all.

And it is at this theater where the final moments of John Dillinger have left a lasting impression. It would be many years later before people passing by the Biograph on North Lincoln Avenue would begin to spot a blue, hazy figure running down the alley next to the theater, falling down and then vanishing. Along with the sighting of this strange apparition were reports of cold spots, icy chills, unexplainable cool breezes, and odd feelings of fear and uneasiness. Local business owners began to notice that people had stopped using the alley as a shortcut to Halstead Street. The place certainly seemed haunted. But is the ghost of the man who has been seen here really that of John Dillinger?

Ever since the night of the shoot-out at the Biograph, eyewitness accounts and the official autopsy have given support to the theory that the dead man may not have been Dillinger. Rumors have persisted that the man killed by the FBI was actually a small-time hood from Wisconsin who had been set up by Dillinger's girlfriend and Anna Sage to take the hit.

There are many striking errors in the autopsy report. The dead man had brown eyes while Dillinger's were blue. The corpse had a rheumatic heart condition since childhood while Dillinger's naval service records said that his heart was in perfect condition. It's also been said that the man who was killed was much shorter and heavier than Dillinger and had none of his distinguishing marks. Police agencies claimed that Dillinger had plastic surgery to get rid of his scars and moles, but also missing were at least two scars on Dillinger's body.

And there is more conflicting evidence to say that the FBI killed the wrong man. On the night of the shooting, a local man named Jimmy Lawrence disappeared. Lawrence was a small-time criminal who had recently moved from Wisconsin. He lived in the neighborhood and often came to the Biograph Theater. He also bore an uncanny resemblance to John Dillinger. In addition, a photograph taken from the purse of Dillinger's girlfriend shows her in the company of a man who looks like the man killed at the Biograph. The photo that was taken before Dillinger ever had plastic surgery. Could Dillinger's girlfriend have made a date with Jimmy Lawrence to go to the Biograph, knowing that the FBI was waiting for him there?

Some writers have suggested this is exactly what happened. Respected crime writer Jay Robert Nash, an expert on Dillinger, reported in his book *The Dillinger Dossier* that Sage and the girlfriend rigged the whole affair. According to Nash, Sage was a prostitute from England who was in danger of being deported. To prevent this, she went to the police and told them that she knew Dillinger. In exchange for not being deported, she would arrange to have Dillinger at the Biograph, where they could nab him. She agreed to wear a bright red dress so she would be easily recognized. While FBI agents waited, "Dillinger" and his girlfriend watched the movie and enjoyed popcorn and soda. When the film ended, the FBI agents made their move. Nash believes that they shot Jimmy Lawrence instead of Dillinger. He also believes that when they learned of their mistake, the FBI covered it up, either because they feared the wrath of J. Edgar Hoover, who told them to "get Dillinger or else," or because Hoover himself was too embarrassed to admit the mistake.

So, what happened to the real John Dillinger? Nobody knows for sure, but some claim this American Robin Hood married and moved to Oregon. He disappeared in the late 1940s and was never heard from again.

Jimmy Hoffa

Another famous American figure who inexplicably disappeared was Jimmy Hoffa, the famed president of the Teamsters Union from 1957 until he went to prison in 1967. There was no question that Hoffa had a lot of enemies in his day, and perhaps none as powerful as Robert F. Kennedy, the president's brother and the Attorney General from 1961 to 1964. Hoffa's ties to organized crime landed him in prison but it would not be until those same gangsters turned against him that those ties would lead to his disappearance and likely murder. And while Hoffa's body has never been found, there is little question about whether or not he is dead. One way or another, Hoffa is not coming back!

For many years, Hoffa was the controversial leader of the Teamsters Union, which boasted strong connections to organized crime. Despite his underworld dealings, Hoffa was immune to prosecution through the 1950s. In the early 1960s, he became the chief target of Bobby Kennedy, chief counsel to the Senate Select Committee on Improper Activities in the Labor or Management Field (popularly called the McClellan Committee), and later, the Attorney General. In 1961, Kennedy made Hoffa the top priority of his administration and his efforts resulted in the labor leader's 1962 trial for extorting illegal payments from a firm that employed Teamsters. The proceedings ended in a hung jury, but then Hoffa was arrested for attempting to bribe one of the jurors. He was sentenced to eight years in prison.

In 1964, Hoffa was convicted of misappropriating $1.7 million in union pension funds but managed to stay out of prison until 1967. He ended up serving 58 months, and had his sentence commuted by

President Nixon with the condition that he stay out of union politics until 1980, which would have been the full term of his prison sentence. Hoffa didn't take this condition seriously and he started legal action to get it set aside. In addition, he went ahead with efforts to regain control of the union from his former right-hand man, Frank Fitzsimmons. This maneuver did not sit well with mob leaders, as Fitzsimmons was much easier to manipulate than the stubborn Hoffa and could always be counted on to look the other way. He was also welcome at the White House, which Hoffa was not, and was infinitely more desirable as the head of the union. Hoffa was warned several times by mobsters to stop interfering and trying to regain his position but, not surprisingly, he refused to listen.

On July 30, 1975, Hoffa went to a restaurant outside of Detroit to allegedly meet three men: a Detroit labor leader, an important local mobster and a powerful figure in New Jersey Teamster politics. Hoffa arrived first, around 2:00 in the afternoon, but after waiting nearly 30 minutes, none of the others had arrived. Annoyed, he called his wife and told her that he was going to wait for a few more minutes before giving up. This was the last time that she ever spoke with her husband.

At 2:45, Hoffa was seen getting into a car in the restaurant parking lot with several other men. Investigators are pretty sure that he never got out of the car alive. According to FBI investigators, Hoffa had been brought to a peace conference with mobster Anthony "Tony Pro" Provenzano and then killed. Provenzano was just one of the long list of suspects in Hoffa's disappearance, although he had a good alibi at the time the union leader vanished. In fact, some would say that it was too good. Tony was apparently touring with a number of union officials around Hoboken, New Jersey on July 30. He may not have actually done the deed but that didn't mean he wasn't involved.

Provenzano was far from alone on the suspect list. The number of possible killers grew as investigators probed their underworld connections and spoke with convicts who were looking for reductions in their sentences. The main suspects were Provenzano, Russell Bufaliano, and two Hoffa cronies, Thomas Andretta and Gabriel Briguglio. Another suspect, Briguglio's brother, Salvatore, was believed to be an FBI informant when he was shot to death in March 1978.

As the investigation continued, loose ends began to unravel everywhere. One of the most obvious mysteries was why Provenzano would have linked himself to a meeting with Hoffa if he planned to kill him. This seemed almost as odd as why the men who were supposed to kill Hoffa showed up 45 minutes late! This was not the usual for mob hitmen, who find punctuality certainly makes the job easier. These questions notwithstanding, the authorities were able to track down the auto that Hoffa got into and they did find traces of blood and hair inside. They were convinced that Hoffa got into the car and then was garroted from behind. But was he really killed? Some insisted that he was not. One union official, after long bouts of questioning by the FBI, swore that Hoffa had skipped off to Brazil with a "black go-go dancer." Supposedly, this was the inside story among union members!

In all reality, it is unlikely to be the truth. In the years since 1975, Hoffa has been declared legally dead, and most of the suspects in the case are dead themselves or have gone to prison on other charges. Any convictions for the murder of the vanished union leader would depend on testimony from an inside source—and don't look for that anytime soon! As one unidentified union official stated: "We all know who did it. It was Tony and those guys of his from New Jersey. It's common knowledge. But the cops need a corroborating witness, and it doesn't look like they're about to get one, does it?"

And so, officially, Jimmy Hoffa walked away from a Detroit restaurant one day and vanished into the ether. He was never seen or heard from again. Whether or not his body is hidden away in a landfill or beneath the concrete of a football stadium is anyone's guess—but we'll certainly never see him again.

Dorothy Forstein

Many American disappearances are not only mysterious, but are also tinged with tragedy and despair as well. The case of Dorothy Forstein is among the saddest of these stories and is also one of the most unusual in this collection of the unsolved.

Mrs. Forstein vanished from her Philadelphia home in 1950, having been married for nine years to her childhood sweetheart, Jules Forstein, a clerk for the Philadelphia City Council at the time of the wedding. Dorothy was a happy, outgoing young woman and the devoted mother of two children. Marcy, an infant, and Merna, age 10, were children from Mr. Forstein's first marriage. His wife had died in childbirth not long before he and Dorothy had gotten together again. This second marriage was a happy one and Forstein's professional life began to prosper when he was made a magistrate in 1943. Another child, Edward, was born a little later.

That idyllic life was shattered on January 25, 1945. Dorothy left the children with neighbors and went out to do some shopping. She reportedly joked with the butcher and chatted with friends as she went about her errands. Later, her neighbor saw her return home and thought that someone was with her, or walking behind her, as she made her way through the evening shadows to her front door. It was getting dark and the neighbor, Maria Townley, admitted that she didn't look too close.

Just as Dorothy was entering her three story brick home, the stranger (or whomever it might have been that Mrs. Townley saw) jumped out of the darkness at her. He began beating her with his fists and some sort of blunt instrument. Dorothy fell to the ground and was pounded into unconsciousness. As she tumbled into the house though, her arm dislodged the hall telephone. In those days of live operators, the voice on the other end of the line heard the commotion and quickly summoned the police. The attacker fled at the sound of approaching sirens.

Police officers arrived moments later and found a battered Dorothy on the floor of the hallway. She had suffered a broken jaw, a shattered nose, a fractured shoulder and a brain concussion. She was rushed to the hospital and when she awakened, she could only weakly explain that "someone jumped out at me. I couldn't see who it was. He just hit me and hit me," she said.

Investigators labeled the attack an attempted murder and Captain James A. Kelly of the Philadelphia Homicide Division began trying to put the pieces together. He concluded that it could have only been someone trying to kill Dorothy since no money, jewelry or anything else had been taken from the Forstein home. Jules Forstein himself was investigated but he had an unimpeachable alibi, and the children were too young to have been involved. The case was complicated by the fact that Dorothy had no known enemies and, in fact, was one of the most well-liked residents in the neighborhood.

Captain Kelly could find no reason for the attack and no suspects were ever arrested. Before long, almost everyone had forgotten about it, except for Dorothy, who was so shaken by what happened that she was never the same again. Her happy and carefree personality was gone and had been replaced by a woman who was nervous and upset, jumping at every noise in the house and checking and rechecking the locks on the doors and windows. She was sure that someone was out to get her, but who?

Jules Forstein was perplexed. He was sure that no one he had come into contact with as a magistrate would bear him enough of a grudge to hurt his wife or his family, and yet he could not explain Dorothy's attack either. He seldom left his wife and children alone but on the night of October 18, 1950, he made plans to attend a political banquet. As he was leaving the office, he called his wife to check on her, explaining that he didn't plan to be home too late. Dorothy replied that everything was fine at home and she joked with him for a moment, finally seeming more like her old self. "Be sure to miss me!" she reportedly said just as she was hanging up.

Tragically, her words would turn out to be prophetic ones.

Around 11:30 that night, Forstein came home to be greeted by the wails of his two youngest children, Edward and Marcy. They were huddled on the floor, crying and shrieking. Their sister, Merna, was away at a friend's house, and Dorothy was nowhere to be found. While surprised that she would have left the children at home by themselves, Forstein assumed that Dorothy was visiting with friends or neighbors. He telephoned for several hours but no one had seen her. Finally, he called Captain Kelly again and the detective soon had his men checking hospitals, morgues and hotels all over Philadelphia. They worked frantically but no clues were discovered. Kelly went door-to-door in the neighborhood but no one had seen anything. Wherever she was, Dorothy had left her purse, money and keys at home.

The only lead came from Marcy Forstein, but her story was so wild that detectives at first dismissed it as nothing more than her frightened and overactive imagination. She told Captain Kelly that she had been awakened and had left her room to see a man coming up the stairs. He went into her mother's room and through a crack in the door, Marcy stated that she could see Dorothy lying facedown on the rug. "She looked sick," the little girl offered. Then, the man, who she described as wearing a brown hat and jacket with something sticking out of the pocket, picked up her mother and put her over his shoulder. Dorothy was wearing red silk pajamas and red slippers at the time. Marcy asked the man what he was doing and he replied: "Go back to sleep, little one, your mommy has been sick, but she will be all right now." The man carried Dorothy downstairs and out the front door. He locked the door behind him and vanished. Marcy awakened her brother and they waited together for their father to come home. The little girl told the detectives that she had never seen the man before and had no idea who he was.

As bizarre as this sounded, it was the only possible explanation the police had for Dorothy's disappearance. Nothing was disturbed in the house. There was no sign of a struggle and also no sign that anyone else had been there. There was not a single fingerprint in the house that did not belong and the investigators wondered how a man could have walked down the street with a woman in pajamas over his shoulder without someone noticing. And how did he get into the locked house anyway? It seemed impossible that the girl's story could be true and yet it had to be. If she had walked away on her own, why had she not taken her purse or keys with her?

Dorothy Forstein was never seen again. There were no leads, no suspects and no explanations as to who might have taken her or why. She simply had vanished—gone without a trace.

Ambrose Small

If one can have a favorite case of a person who disappears without explanation, then the case of Ambrose Small is undoubtedly mine. Although Small was actually a Canadian entertainment figure, I couldn't help but include him in this section of mysterious vanishings. His disappearance on December 2, 1919 was so sensational and mystifying that it made a permanent mark on North American history. The marvelous and controversial showman would have undoubtedly wanted it no other way.

Ambrose Small was born in 1863 and at the age of 13, went to work in his father's modest establishment, Toronto's Warden Hotel. As he grew older, he began managing the hotel bar and booking entertainment for the customers. Working with these minor musical acts, he realized that show business was to be his life's work. In addition to working for his father, Small also took a part-time job as an usher at the Grand Theater. He slowly worked his way up the ranks to assistant manager and then booking manager, arranging for florid and spicy melodramas for the venue. These programs met with much success and Small began to prosper. He also began to buy interests in small theaters in and around Toronto. His ambition was to own the Grand Opera House, but his offers to buy it were frequently refused. This made him all the more anxious to own it and he began to work ever harder to amass the necessary wealth.

Small also began to acquire a couple of different reputations. One of them was as a daring gambler. He was never afraid to bet huge sums on races and, while he always paid off when he lost, he was not above being involved in fixed races either. He managed to win $10,000 in one race that was said to be fixed and not surprisingly, he was said to have been the one who fixed it. He started to gain a number of enemies in racing circles and in his romantic life as well. The short but handsome Small, with his luxuriant walrus mustache and fancy clothes, was a notorious womanizer. He was often seen squiring young and beautiful women about town, especially the gorgeous showgirls who worked the local theaters. He left many a hopeful starlet feeling both used and disappointed when he moved on to another attractive lady.

This is why it must have come as a great surprise when the rakish Small, just before his fortieth birthday, suddenly married Teresa Small, the wealthy heiress to a brewing fortune. What did not come as a surprise though was when Small began to use Teresa's money to purchase scores of small theaters and to book the biggest-named talent that he could find.

Small now had his fortune and he finally realized his dream of owning the Grand Opera House. Within a few years, Small began to grow tired of his marriage and secure business life, and he began gambling and seeing women again. In order to conduct his affairs discreetly, he ordered that a secret room be constructed to adjoin his office at the opera house. The room was fitted with heavy drapes to muffle sound, a deep Oriental carpet, a well-stocked bar and a gigantic bed with satin sheets and pillows. Many a beautiful young woman was willingly ravished in the clandestine chamber.

As his fortunes grew, Small continued to make enemies. He made his prejudices well known to anyone who would listen, even strangers. He disliked children, Catholics, and the poor, and felt that giving anything to a charity was foolish. His continued gambling didn't help most to like him either, but as he grew more and more daring with his wagers, he began to win more and more. Small was able to keep informed of the races at every track in the United States and bet on most of them. He became more interested in gambling than in running his theatrical empire, which now included almost every theater in eastern Canada. He spent huge sums of money and treated his employees and business associates with disdain. Small placed much of his business dealings in the hands of his private secretary, John Doughty, who was well aware of his employer's dark and secret habits. Doughty though, had secrets of his own.

By the late 1910s, the high life began to take its toll on Small. His hair had started to gray and recede and his face was always reddened by broken blood vessels, the result of too much drinking. While he was still gambling, his wagers began to be tamed somewhat and his womanizing was mostly confined to his long-time mistress, Clara Smith. He was also beginning to tire of the theater business and wanted out.

In 1919, Small and his wife began negotiating the sale of the Small chain of theaters to a British-owned firm, Trans-Canada Theaters Limited. The deal was concluded on December 2, 1919 and the Small's received a check for $1 million, with an additional $700,000 to be paid to them in installments over the next five years. The husband and wife endorsed the check and deposited it in their account at the Dominion Bank at 11:45 in the morning. That afternoon, Small told his lawyer, E.W.M. Flock that he planned to inform his secretary John Doughty that not only had Doughty been retained by the new firm as a secretary and booking manager, but he would see a substantial increase in salary.

Attorney Flock saw Small again later that evening around 5:30 at the Grand Opera House. Small was in a fine mood, laughing and smoking cigars to celebrate the sale of the chain. He spent a few minutes with Small but then left to catch a train. As he walked out of the front foyer of the opera house and into a driving snowstorm, he looked back and waved at the smiling Small. It was the last time that he would ever see his client.

A short time later, Small also left the opera house. Bundled up against the biting wind, cold and snow, he made his way to the corner of Adelaide and Yonge, ducking into the shelter of a newsstand operated by Ralph Savein. The newsstand owner knew Small well as he habitually checked the racing results in the paper each day. Small always picked up the paper around 5:30 when it arrived by train, however on this day, the papers had not been delivered because the train had been delayed by a terrible snowstorm in New York. Savein said that Small cursed bitterly over the lack of the paper, which was something that he had never heard him do before. Small then trudged off into the snow and as he made his way down the block, Savein saw his form fade away into the blowing storm. He was the last person to report speaking with Ambrose Small.

Several days passed before anyone realized that Small had disappeared. His wife and friends were so used to his dalliances and gambling that they guessed he had simply gone out of town for a few days. They wanted to ignore his shortcomings so badly that they never dreamed he could have met with foul play. Once his disappearance became official, the authorities launched the biggest manhunt in Canadian history. Teresa Small offered a staggering $50,000 reward for information on her husband, inspiring every amateur sleuth and crackpot to join the hunt with the legitimate detectives already on the case.

Meanwhile, the police were also seeking John Doughty, who had vanished on the same day as Ambrose Small. The authorities learned that Doughty had not taken kindly to losing his position with Small and before leaving town, he had gone to the Dominion Bank and, using Small's key to his safety-deposit box, had absconded with $100,000 in negotiable Victory bonds. Doughty was found one year later, working in a Portland, Oregon paper mill under the name Charles B. Cooper. He was arrested and sentenced to five years in prison for the theft of the bonds but was cleared of having anything to do with Small's disappearance.

As the hunt for Ambrose Small continued, many began to fear that the theater magnate had been murdered. A man named George Soucy, a publishing house employee, reported that he had seen Small being forced into a car on the evening of December 2. Also, on that same night, a caretaker named Albert Elson insisted that he had seen four men burying something in a ravine just a short distance from Small's home. A cleaning woman, Mary Quigley, swore to police that she had seen a notice pinned to the wall in the Convent of Precious Blood, located on St. Anthony Street, which requested "prayers for the repose of the soul of Ambrose J. Small" several days before the public or the press knew that he had vanished.

These turned out to be some of the best leads that the police had, but they were among the hundreds that came in. The authorities conducted a painstaking search for the missing man. Every business in Toronto was searched and all six cities where Small had theaters were scoured for clues. Toronto Bay was dredged several times and the basement of the Small mansion on Glen Road was excavated. The search continued for years and even as late as 1944, investigators were still digging up the basement of the Grand Opera House, hoping to find Small's bones.

Teresa Small was interrogated several times about her husband's disappearance. She was convinced that he had been done in by one of the countless women he had been involved with over the years. She knew all about his affairs but had ignored them for a long time. Finally, she had demanded that he stop seeing all of them, including his mistress Clara Smith, after Teresa discovered several obscene letters that Clara had written to Small. She had placed the letters on the dining room table so that he would know that she had seen them. Small came upon the correspondence and destroyed it all, assuring his wife that his cheating days were over. This occurred in 1918 but Teresa did not know that her husband had continued seeing Smith up until the day that he vanished. In fact, he even had dinner with her on December 1. The police concluded that Smith knew nothing of her lover's fate.

By 1920, the police had become desperate and had resorted to following ridiculous stories and what turned out to be frequent hoaxes. That same year, Sir Arthur Conan Doyle, the writer who created Sherlock Holmes and was known in England for helping the authorities with a number of seemingly unsolvable crimes, was touring the United States. A reporter asked him what he thought of the Small disappearance and he admitted that he was intrigued and had been following the story in the papers. He was asked if he might help out with it and Doyle agreed that if asked, he would consult on the case. Within days, newspapers in Canada and the United States were running headlines that cried "World's Greatest Detective to Solve Small Case" and "Sherlock Holmes to Reveal Toronto Mystery." For some reason, Doyle was never asked to consult and his interests turned to other things.

And while the famous author was never asked to look into the case, the authorities were desperate enough in 1926 to contact a Vienna criminologist named Dr. Maximilian Langsner and to hire him to delve into the rapidly cooling affair. Langsner claimed that he was able to use psychic "thought processes" to find the missing man. While he was put up the finest Toronto hotel, conducting seances and "astral trips," he sent the police out to follow his divinations, digging up half the countryside and finding nothing. When the detectives complained, he replied that the policemen were clouding his vision and he would have to look more later. Public outcry sent Langsner packing and the police department was left with the huge bills that he had run up on the official tab.

Since 1919, Ambrose Small has been spotted in hundreds of places, from owning a hotel in South America to living it up in France with a girl on each arm and a champagne bottle gripped in each fist. A psychic envisioned him buried in the Toronto city dump. An old friend claimed to catch a glimpse of him on the street in London. The magician Harry Blackstone swore that he spotted Small gambling in a Mexican cantina. Despite these sitings, the courts pronounced him officially dead in 1923, making Small gone, but not forgotten from that point on.

Missing in Vermont's Green Mountains

The historic Green Mountains of Vermont have been described as being part of the most beautiful stretch of wilderness in New England. The warm weather months make this a place of tranquil shade, soaked in a warm array of greens and browns. In the autumn, the hills come alive with a symphony of breath-taking color. But at other times, a darker side emerges from these rugged mountains, when the shadows grow long and the snow starts to fall, finally covering the landscape in a monotonous blanket of white. There are places, like this place some say, where the fabric of time and space is stretched a little bit thinner. Places where things that aren't supposed to do so slip through into our world. And occasionally things from our world sometimes slip out.

This is one of the treacherous secrets of the Green Mountains near Bennington, Vermont. The area has always had a reputation for strangeness. It is a spot that is almost inaccessible and remote, and since colonial days, it has been plagued with reports of mysterious lights and sounds, ghostly tales and unknown creatures. The local Native Americans shunned the place and according to tradition, used it as a place to bury the dead. And while stories of spook lights and Indian curses may stretch the limits of the imagination, there is no denying that nearby Glastonbury Mountain, and its scenic Long Trail, has been the site of a great American mystery. This unsolved puzzle involves the disappearance of a number of people who have never been found. Thousands of hours were spent searching for them, but not a single clue was ever discovered.

The bizarre disappearances began on November 12, 1945 with the vanishing of Middie Rivers, a 74 year-old hunting and fishing guide. He was reportedly in perfect health and knew the area well, having been a native of the region for most of his life. The day that he disappeared was unusually mild for late fall and Rivers led four hunters up onto the mountain. After spending the day away from camp, they packed up to return with Rivers leading the way. He got a little bit ahead of them and literally vanished around a bend in the trail. One minute he was there and the next he wasn't. The old man simply disappeared.

The hunters searched frantically and then notified the authorities. State police, soldiers, boy scouts and local residents combed the woods for hours. They refused to lose hope, knowing that Rivers was an experienced outdoorsman and could survive in the woods, even under icy cold conditions. When no sign of him turned up, efforts were expanded and the search continued for a month. It was eventually called off, and Middie Rivers was never seen again.

On December 1, 1946, the second person vanished from the Long Trail. Her name was Paula Welden from Stamford, Connecticut; she was a sophomore at Bennington College. Paula was the daughter of Archibald Welden, an industrial engineer at Revere Copper & Brass Co., and had come to Bennington College because of the excellent reputation the school had for progressive teaching. Paula was described as blue-eyed, blond and pretty. Her features were "regular and slightly heavy and she had a clean, well-scrubbed look." Paula stood 5-foot-5 and weighed about 123 pounds. Descriptions of her from 1946 speak of her being soft-spoken, polite and well behaved, like the average girl of her background. She was a fair student whose favorite subject was botany. Her interest in trees and plants gave her an excuse for solitary walks along the local forest trails.

On the afternoon of Sunday December 1, she announced to her roommate, Elizabeth Johnson, that she was going out for a short afternoon hike. Paula changed into outdoor clothing, blue jeans, white sneakers and a red parka with a fur-trimmed hood, but failed to take into account the miserable conditions outside. It was a particularly gloomy day, her roommate later recalled, and a cold rain had make the ground slippery and muddy and it seemed a much better day to stay indoors and study than to go out. Elizabeth, knowing her friend's affinity for being outside, made no effort to dissuade her from going.

Paula's actions from the moment that she left her roommate cannot be traced exactly. Against the drab December day, she made a conspicuous figure with her bright red coat but only a handful of people were out to notice her. An attendant at a gas station across Route 67A from the Bennington College gates saw her hitchhiking a short distance from the gas station at around 3:15 in the afternoon.

Shortly, a car appeared on the highway driven by Louis Knapp, a contractor who lived about 15 miles east of the college, in the direction of Glastonbury Mountain and the Long Trail. The trail was Paula's goal that day and during the summer, the picturesque trail was one of the area's greatest attractions, with thriving tourist cottages and cabins lining it. In the winter, it was barren and neglected. Only four families lived along it in the winter months, which made Paula's choice for her hike that day a strange one. Nevertheless, Knapp agreed to take her up the highway as far as to where he lived in Woodford Hollow, just three miles from the start of the Long Trail. When Knapp stopped the car at his driveway, Paula asked him the distance to the trail and then she got out and started walking. She soon vanished into the mist that had replaced the cold rain of the early afternoon.

About an hour later, close to 5:00, she encountered another resident of the area, Ernest Whitman, a night watchman for the *Bennington Banner* newspaper. Whitman was surprised to see a young girl sloshing along the desolate and now growing dark road. He spoke with her for a few minutes and gave her directions. After that, other witnesses spotted her on the trail itself and remembered her distinctly because she had been wearing a bright red parka. It was very visible, even though the sun was setting by this time. They would be the last people to see her alive.

Paula did not return to wait on tables at the Commons, the Bennington College dining hall, that evening, nor had she appeared by her usual bedtime. Although worried, Elizabeth Johnson decided to wait until morning to report her absence. After a sleepless night, she left her room at dawn and made her way to the Dean's residence. The Dean offered the opinion that Paula might have made a last minute application to stay away from the college all night but a quick check of the sign-out records showed that this was not the case. The two of them hurried across campus to the home of Bennington president Lewis Webster Jones. He had no solution to the problem, except to make a careful telephone call to the Welden home in Stamford to see if Paula had unexpectedly turned up there. She had not, and Jones next called the local Sheriff Clyde W. Peck, who came straight to the college. He was later joined by Vermont State Police detective Almo Fronzoni, a veteran of more than 25 years with the department.

Fronzoni took charge of the investigation and started by questioning Elizabeth Johnson. He accompanied her to the dorm room that she shared with Paula and saw that there was no sign that she had taken any clothing with her. Nor, apparently, had she taken any extra money either. He found $8.26 on her bureau, along with an uncashed check for $10. Elizabeth told him that Paula rarely ever had more cash than that on hand.

Fronzoni next drove to the local bus and railroad stations. Here, he ran into a taxi driver who told him that he had driven a Bennington girl to the bus station that day but this later turned out to be untrue. At the railway station, Fronzoni mentioned Stamford and the ticket seller perked up. On Sunday afternoon, three hunters had purchased tickets to New York and then at the last minute, had changed their destination to Stamford. The ticket seller remembered this because it required quite a bit of adjustment on his part. No matter how Fronzoni tried, he was unable to see a connection, other than coincidence, between the three hunters and Paula. All it did, like the false statement from the taxi driver, was slow down the investigation and lessen his chances of finding the missing girl.

The detective returned to the Bennington campus and began questioning other students who knew Paula. Since she had not told anyone where she was going that day, only that she was going for a hike, no one knew where she was headed when she left campus. However, several of her friends mentioned her fondness for a place called Everett's Cave on Mount Anthony. It was three miles south of the college. If Paula had hiked there, it was suggested, she might have fallen and been injured. Fronzoni, Sheriff Peck and several deputies immediately drove to Everett's Cave but Paula, injured or otherwise, was not to be found there.

By this time, word was beginning to spread of the disappearance and when newspaper reporters from the *Bennington Banner* picked up the story, night watchman Ernest Whitman heard about the missing student. He immediately reported to Fronzoni that he had met Paula near the entrance to the Long Trail. After the story hit the newspapers on Tuesday, the authorities would hear from the gas station attendant who saw Paula hitchhiking and from local resident Louis Knapp as well. The officials now realized that Paul had been heading for the Long Trail when she vanished and an immediate search was started. It was feared that the young woman had met with an accident while hiking on the trail in the dark and not being dressed for the bitterly cold nighttime temperatures, she could be dead or badly injured. There was hope that, injured or lost, she could have broken into one of the empty summer cottages on the trail and that she could have found food or at least a fire.

The search commenced on Monday afternoon, headed by Bennington game warden Jesse Wilson. He was assisted by five other game wardens, some sheriff's deputies and several search dogs. It was hurriedly put together and badly organized but they believed that if Paula was injured, time was crucial. Besides that, many of the men in the area were expert woodsmen and they had the best chance of finding her quickly.

As they searched along the trail, Detective Fronzoni questioned members of the families who lived on Long Trail all year long. He found two leads. One person stated that he had seen a half-ton truck driving along the trail late Sunday evening at a time when Paula might have been on it. The other lead was more definite. A female resident had been walking along the trail on Sunday and had been forced to step aside to permit a maroon colored car to pass by. She saw a young couple inside and the girl had been a blonde. She had not looked very closely at the couple but it did raise the question as to whether or not someone had given Paula a lift. If they had though, what had happened to her?

On Tuesday, December 3, a more comprehensive search for Paula Welden was organized. Classes at Bennington College were suspended and nearly 400 students took part in the effort. Faculty members, Williams College students, Boy Scouts, trappers, woodsmen, local residents and search dogs joined deputies and law enforcement officials as they scoured the area. The group was joined by a number of employees from Revere Copper & Brass, and the huge contingent was organized into smaller search teams by expert mountain climbers from the National Guard. The United States Navy also sent nine Marine search planes from the air base at Squantam, and a helicopter was brought in to fly low over isolated areas.

As the National Guard climbers worked their way up Glastonbury Mountain, the army of searchers sloshed in long lines up and down the foothills. The weather was drab and drizzling, soaking everyone to the skin. It was cold, wearying work along the trail and elsewhere, other work was being accomplished too. The Bennington student body and friends of the Welden family had started a reward-for-information fund, which soon made it to $5,000. The offer of a reward brought in even more volunteers and the search continued for two full days. On December 5, it was called off due to overhanging clouds that had grounded the search planes, followed by several inches of snow that obliterated the landscape.

By this time, the Welden family and most of the volunteers were exhausted. The fact that Paula had written no farewell note and no ransom letters had been received indicated that whatever happened to her must have been spontaneous—she was a victim of amnesia, an accident or someone's murderous madness. Many feared that Paula was now dead but her parents refused to give up hope, insisting that their daughter had been kidnapped. With no evidence of this, the FBI refused to get involved. When the official refusal became public knowledge, well-known novelist Dorothy Canfield Fisher, a Bennington College trustee, wrote letters to J. Edgar Hoover and several political figures in Washington. "Paula is not in these hills," she stated. "She was taken away against her will."

Others felt the same way and made determined appeals but all were turned down. The governor appealed to both New York and Connecticut for skilled investigators to assist them but only Connecticut responded, sending two state detectives who had proven expert at missing persons cases in the past. Their laborious investigations still failed to produce the missing girl. One of the investigators, Robert Rundle, agreed with Detective Fronzoni when he had declared Paula's case to be the most perplexing of his career. "We have not a single clue," Rundle admitted. Paula was simply gone. In the end, helicopters, aircraft, bloodhounds and as many as 1,000 people combed the mountain for the young woman but no evidence was found—no blood, no clothing, nothing.

On December 16, the Weldens returned to Connecticut and took all of Paula's belongings from her dorm room with them. Even they had given up hope of seeing their daughter alive again. Classes resumed at Bennington College and after the shock of Paula's disappearance passed, students began to think more of going home for the holidays than about the missing girl. The townspeople still talked and speculated, but few were still willing to spend time combing the hills for her. Detective Fronzoni moved on to other cases and Paula Welden began to become a part of Bennington's past.

But over the next few months, Archibald Welden urged a second organized search, once the winter snows had thawed. On May 23, several hundred volunteers assembled and spent two days in the rain, crisscrossing more than 24 square miles between Glastonbury and Bald Mountains. When the search ended, it had accomplished nothing. When Bennington College reconvened again the following autumn, Paula Welden seemed a forgotten, shadowy figure. People still walked the Long Trail and wondered about her sometimes but few spoke of her again—until the next person vanished into the mountains.

On December 1, 1949, three years to the day of Paula Welden's disappearance, an elderly man named James E. Tetford also vanished near Bennington. Tetford had been visiting relatives in northern Vermont and his family had placed him on a bus in St. Albans for the journey back to where he lived, the Bennington Soldier's Home. For some reason, he never arrived. Where he actually disappeared is just part of the mystery. Witnesses recalled him getting on the bus and several were sure that he was still on board at the stop before Bennington. At some point, he apparently got off along the road. He left no clues behind. No one saw him disappear (including the bus driver) and he was never seen again.

Another disappearance took place near Bennington in October 1950. An eight-year-old boy named Paul Jepson vanished from the town dump, where his parents were caretakers. Paul was waiting in the family's truck while his mother relocated some pigs. She was gone for only a moment but when she looked up, the boy was gone. It was between 3:00 and 4:00 in the afternoon of a sunny day. Paul was wearing a bright red jacket and should have been easily spotted—but he was nowhere to be seen. Mrs. Jepson searched frantically and called for him and after a little while, went for help.

Volunteers assembled to start another search and hundreds of local residents joined police officers in combing through the dump, walking the roads and scouring the mountains. They even instituted a double check system so that after one group searched an area, another would follow them and check it again. But even with the search parties and aircraft brought in by the Coast Guard, there was no sign of the boy. The only clues came from a group of bloodhounds that were borrowed from the New Hampshire State Police. The dogs managed to follow Paul's scent, only to lose it at the junction of East and Chapel Roads, just west of Glastonbury Mountain. According to locals, this was the same spot where Paula Welden had last been seen. The search was eventually called off and another person was lost to the mountains.

About two weeks later, on October 28, the mountain claimed another victim. Her name was Freida Langer, and she was on a hike that day with her cousin, Herbert Elsner. The 53 year-old Langer was described as a rugged outdoor person with long experience in the woods and a skill with firearms. She was also very familiar with the region and like Middie Rivers before her, was an unlikely person to simply get lost or to wander off the trail. At about 3:45 that after-noon, Freida slipped and fell into the edge of a stream, soaking her boots and pants. Since she and her cousin were only about a half-mile from camp, she said that she would run back and change clothes and then catch up with him. Elsner sat down to wait but after Frieda had been gone for a while, he began to grow concerned. After an hour or so, he started back up the trail to their camp. When he got there, he discovered that no one had seen her come back and from the looks of her gear, she had never returned to change her wet cloth-ing. He immediately contacted the authorities.

Alarmed by another disappearance in the same area, local offi-cials quickly launched another massive search. Again, hundreds of volunteers combed the woods, tracing and re-tracing what should have been Freida's footsteps between the stream where she had fall-en and the camp. On November 1, General Merritt Edson, the state director of public safety, started a second search. He vowed that they would find Freida, dead or alive, and he ordered his men to keep looking around the clock. More helicopters, aircraft, officers and volunteers were brought in, but once again, they found no clues.

Another search was started on November 5 and the volunteers divided into groups of 30. They lined up and marched side by side along trails and through the forest, scanning every inch of ground. There was still no sign of the missing woman. On November 11, the largest search was organized. Over 300 people joined police officers, fire fighters and military units as they scoured the woods. A few days later, Frieda's family gave up hope and the search was called off.

Strangely though, Freida Langer would be the only person to go missing here that would later be found. On May 12, 1951, seven months after she had vanished, the body of Freida Langer was discovered lying in some tall grass near the flood dam of the Somerset Reservoir. It was nowhere near the spot where she had vanished and this site had been thoroughly searched during the hunt for the missing woman. The volunteers swore that the body had not been there during the initial search. The site where the corpse was found was an open and visible area and it was simply impossible that the searchers could have missed it. Unfortunately, no clues could be gathered from Frieda's body and no cause of death could ever be determined by the medical examiner. Her remains were too decomposed and the newspaper stated they were in "gruesome condition."

Could someone have placed the body there much later? Rumors swirled about a killer who was hiding on Glastonbury Mountain, claiming victims that were chosen from those who vanished into the woods. In those days, the term serial killer had not come to public attention and later examinations of each case do suggest that a killer might have been at work. The disappearances occurred over a limited length of time (five years) and in one central area, around the mountain and the Long Trail. Perhaps the killer was someone who came to Vermont each fall, committed his crimes, and than left. That might explain why no one ever became a suspect in the vanishings but why was no body, save for that of Freida Langer, ever found?

What happened in the mountains near Bennington, Vermont between 1945 and 1950? Was a madman preying on lone hikers or were darker and more mysterious forces at work? Could these people have simply gotten lost or were they carried off against their will, to a place that none of us can imagine? Hopefully, no one else will ever discover the answers to those questions.

CAN SUCH THINGS BE?

The Mysterious Life and Death of Ambrose Bierce

On the cold evening of November 8, 1878, a sixteen-year-old boy named Charles Ashmore walked out the back door of his family's farm house near Quincy, Illinois. He carried with him a bucket with which to fetch fresh water from the spring a short distance away. When he did not return, his family became uneasy, and Christian Ashmore and his oldest daughter, Martha, took a lantern and went in search of the boy. A new snow had just fallen and Charles' footprints were plainly visible as they went out the back door and started across the yard. His father and sister followed his trail for a short distance but after going about 75 yards, they saw that the trail abruptly ended. Beyond the last footprint was nothing other than smooth, unbroken snow—the boy's tracks simply came to an end, with nowhere for him to go.

Ashmore and his daughter made a wide circle around the tracks, careful not to disturb them, then walked to the spring. They found the water covered with a layer of unbroken ice and it became apparent that Charles had gotten no closer to the spring than his tracks had indicated. The boy had vanished without explanation.

But the story does not end there. Four days later, the grief-stricken mother of the young man went to the spring for water and insisted that she heard the voice of her son calling to her when she passed the spot where his footprints had ended. She wandered the area, thinking that the voice was coming from one direction and then another. Later, when questioned about the voice, she said that the words were very clear, and the voice definitely that of her son, and yet she could make out no message from them. For months afterward, the voice was heard every few days by one family member, or sometimes many of them. It seemed to come from a great distance and yet was entirely distinct, although none of them could determine its message or repeat its words. Soon, the intervals of silence grew longer and longer and the voice much fainter and by mid-summer of 1879, it was heard no more.

Those with an interest in the strange and the unusual have likely heard of this story before. Or perhaps the reader may have run across a slightly different variation of it, with the name of Charles Ashmore being changed to that of David Lang and the location being moved from Illinois to Gallatin, Tennessee. Or the reader may have heard another version (enhanced by the young man crying for help before vanishing) that changes the boy's name to Oliver Larch and moves the location to South Bend, Indiana. It should not be surprising if you have read any one of these stories for they have all appeared in various books on ghosts, unsolved mysteries and the unexplained over the years.

The problem with each of these stories is that not a single one of them is true. The story of Charles Ashmore first appeared in the writings of a journalist named Ambrose Bierce, who penned not only newspaper articles, but also several books, scores of stories about ghosts and the Civil War and a number of acerbic and cutting essays over the course of his career. Bierce's style and journalistic background gave his stories of war and strange disappearances such an uneasy realism that many mistook them for being true. Such was the case of the Charles Ashmore story. As time has passed, his stories have been changed and presented as being real disappearances that took place years ago. It seems obvious to all of us that no one could simply walk out their door one day, start walking, and then simply vanish into space. So it may surprise the reader to learn that the fictional stories of the disappearance of Charles Ashmore and others were based on a real experience that Bierce investigated during his journalistic career.

Ironically, the author of such chilling tales of disappearance also vanished without a trace in 1914. No clue has ever been found to explain what may have become of one of America's most famous writers of that time. But Bierce was an eccentric man and his life was riddled with many mysteries. In the San Francisco of 1900, Ambrose Bierce reigned as the unchallenged literary king of the city and was considered the best-known writer west of the Rocky Mountains. But a long road led from the beginnings of his career to his mysterious disappearance, and there were many who believed that if anyone actually deserved to disappear, it should be the man known by many as "Bitter" Bierce.

Ambrose Gwinnett Bierce was born in Meigs County, Ohio in 1842. As a young man, he was an ardent abolitionist and worked for an anti-slavery newspaper in northern Indiana. As he began writing, he realized his life's work and spent the next number of years as a journalist. He briefly attended the Kentucky Military Institute but left in 1859 without a degree. This lack of education would dog him through his life as critics always complained of his poor grammatical skills. Bierce never let this stop him, and as a born storyteller, he was able to achieve success with those who mattered, his readers. Bierce was always considered cynical and aloof, but he reveled in the unknown. His writings on war and adventure as well as his ghost and horror stories were influenced by events in Bierce's life. And it's possible that his interest in weird disappearances stemmed from an event that he wrote about in 1854.

One hot day in July of that year, a planter named Orion Williamson from Selma, Alabama was sitting on the front porch of his farm house with his wife and child. As he squinted into the bright sunshine, his gaze fell on the field where his horses were grazing. Williamson stood up and announced to his wife that he was going to put the animals into the shade of the barn. She later remembered him stepping down from the porch and walking out into the field. He picked up a small stick in his hands and he absent-mindedly swished it back and forth as he walked across the ankle-high grass.

At that same time, a neighboring farmer, Armour Wren, and his son were returning from Selma in a buggy and they were passing by the field on a road on the far side of it. They stopped when they saw Williamson approaching, and Wren stood and waved to him. At that split second, with four sets of eyes upon him, Williamson abruptly disappeared. A moment earlier, he had been walking away from his family and waving at friends, and the next moment, he had vanished into thin air. Stunned, Wren and his son jumped from their wagon and ran into the field, where they soon met Mrs. Williamson and her child. They breathlessly searched the area where Williamson had vanished but saw nothing but bare ground and sparse grass. It seemed impossible but the man was gone.

For two hours, the Wrens and the Williamsons searched the field. They found nothing and as Mrs. Williamson realized what had happened, she collapsed in shock. She was taken to Selma and hospitalized. When news spread of the disappearance, 300 men from town gathered at the field. They formed three hand-to-hand ranks and moved across the field inches at a time, stopping every few feet to kneel down and to search for openings or holes. They searched the field dozens of times, and when night fell, they used torches and lanterns to light up the area. Bloodhounds were brought in, but no trace of the farmer could be found. The following morning, hundreds of other volunteers arrived from nearby communities, along with a team of geologists. They began digging at the point where Williamson disappeared but a few feet below the surface, they hit solid bedrock. There were no cave-ins, crevices or holes to explain where he had gone. He had simply vanished.

And while what happened to Orion Williamson was certainly strange, it did not prepare anyone for what happened next. The following spring revealed an odd circle that appeared in the field at the exact spot where Williamson was last seen. The grass within the circle died, and this curious event was pointed out to Mrs. Williamson by investigators who were still interested in the mystery. By this time, Mrs. Williamson was still so traumatized by the vanishing that she was reluctant to mention her husband's name or to consider what had become of him. Her strange behavior brought many questions from volunteers and the authorities alike. Why was the woman still in such a state of shock? True, the disappearance of her husband was undoubtedly bizarre, but why did she refuse to talk about him?

In a quavering and fearful voice, Mrs. Williamson finally explained. She told the searchers that in the days following her husband's disappearance, she and her child distinctly heard Williamson's voice calling for help from the spot where he had vanished. They had run to the spot each time they heard him, but there was no one and nothing there. The calling continued for almost two weeks with Williamson's voice becoming weaker and weaker as the days passed. On the last night he was heard, the family slept outside on the edge of the vanishing spot. They heard Williamson's whispers and then he was heard no more.

The sensational word of Williamson's disappearance attracted the attention of journalists from around the South and Midwest. One of those was Ambrose Bierce, whose own fascination with the unknown brought him to look into the case. Bierce would interview not only the searchers in the Williamson affair, but experts who claimed to have theories as to where the farmer had gone. One of them, Dr. Maximilian Hern, was a scientist who had written a book called *Disappearance and Theory Thereof*. He stated that Williamson had walked into "void spot of universal ether." These spots, he explained, only lasted for a few seconds but were capable of destroying any and all material elements that happened into them. Other scientists stepped forward with theories as well. One of them said that he believed Williamson walked into a periodic "magnetic field" that disintegrated his atomic structure and sent him into another dimension.

None of these theories helped to discover the missing Orion Williamson though, and he now seemed to be gone for good. His story refused to die though. Williamson was immortalized in one story and provided the inspiration for many other tales by Ambrose Bierce. In addition, his story would be plagiarized numerous times over the years, starting in 1889.

In that year, a traveling salesman from Cincinnati named McHatten was trapped by a snowstorm in Gallatin, Tennessee. With nothing to do but sleep, eat and drink, McHatten decided to rewrite the Orion Williamson story and sell it to a newspaper as an original report. He changed Williamson's name to David Lang and the site of his disappearance to Gallatin. He also altered the date of the occurrence from 1854 to 1880. McHatten's story, except for the basic facts, was a complete fabrication. It has since been accepted and rewritten to appear in many reputable journals and books, but research has revealed that no one named David Lang ever lived in Gallatin. The same research however does show that Orion Williamson was no figment of anyone's imagination, and that in 1854, he was a real resident of Selma, Alabama.

The story of Orion Williamson almost surely provided the inspiration for Bierce's works on the unknown, but it would be his service during the Civil War that would provide inspiration for his gritty tales of death and adventure. Bierce always considered the war to be his finest hour. He enlisted three times and rose through the ranks to brevet major. He saw horrific action as well, fighting at Shiloh, Chickamauga, Murfreesboro, Kennesaw Mountain, Franklin, Nashville, Lookout Mountain and along Sherman's March to the Sea. The war took a physical toll on him as he wounded twice, but he always returned to the battlefield. He seemed to love the war, but his brother always believed that it changed him in terrific ways. He stated that Bierce was never the same after he was wounded in the head on one occasion. "Some of the iron of the shell seemed to stick to his brain," he said, "and he became bitter and suspicious."

Following the war, Bierce joined a military expedition that fought its way through Indians to reach the Pacific. He settled in wild San Francisco, among the miners, gamblers and prostitutes. Times were changing in the West and a good newspaperman was needed.

Bierce was determined to fit the bill and he soon became popular. He earned a reputation as a witty writer but was considered as unpredictable and as odd as many of the people he wrote about.

He was a tall and handsome man with a fair complexion, blue eyes, blond hair and a luxuriant mustache that was said to have attracted almost every woman who looked in his direction. Despite his good looks, Bierce was a failure with women. He simply worshipped them too much, placing them on a pedestal from which they were guaranteed to fall. When he discovered their flesh and blood failings, his love turned to dislike and hatred. His tirades against women were infamous and they became even worse after he destroyed his marriage to lovely society belle Ellen Day. He was married to her long enough to father two sons and a daughter but never stopped hating his wife for having failed him. Strangely, he never had much contact with his sons, both of whom died young, and yet he maintained a loving relationship and voluminous correspondence with his daughter and secretary, Carrie Christiansen.

And Bierce made many enemies outside of his family as well. His writings contained a level of viciousness and brutality that were unrivaled in journalism of the day and he received scores of threats. Bets were placed on how long he might live and he took to carrying a pistol with him on the streets. He was not subtle in his criticisms, but he was impartial about how he handed out the abuse. Bierce and his family traveled widely in the 1870s, journeying to London for a time, where his reputation as a bitter curmudgeon took hold. His writings became even more acidic, perhaps because of his dislike for England, and yet people seemed to love what he published. He published a number of sardonic pieces in British papers and magazines and put together a volume of his early journalism.

In 1874, Bierce returned to San Francisco and became one of the star writers in the spreading editorial empire of William Randolph Hearst. Their partnership became an arrangement that would last for more than 20 years, despite frequent arguments and resignations. Bierce and Hearst eventually came to hate one another, and yet Bierce's writings appeared in the *New York Journal*, the *New York American* and the *San Francisco Chronicle*, as well as in Hearst's tremendously popular magazine, *Cosmopolitan*. His name became a household word and between his sharp attacks on everyone from clergymen to politicians, he wrote short stories of the Civil War and of the bizarre and the curious. Curious collections such as *Fantastic Fables* and *Can Such Things Be?* began to appear. Many of the stories were based on real-life happenings, or claimed to be, and Bierce's mixing of fact with fiction continues to thrill readers today. In many of his stories, he wrote about unsolved disappearances and seemed obsessed by them. On several occasions, he conducted interviews at the sites where people had vanished and while many of them expressed skepticism about the supernatural nature of the vanishing, they did draw attention to the events. Oddly, Bierce began to joke about the possibility of his own disappearance, which would no longer be a jest in 1914.

As time passed, Bierce became increasingly erratic and eventually he grew tired of fighting with Hearst and began to rekindle memories of his Civil War glory days. In 1913, he made two important decisions. One of them was that he would retrace the paths that he had taken on battlefields of the war and the second was that he then would go to Mexico, where revolutionary forces were fighting to overthrow the federal troops of dictator Victoriano Huerta. Bierce did make his sojourn to the battlefields of his youth in early October 1913 and stayed for a short time in New Orleans. While he was there, a reporter managed to land an interview with him, and Bierce made the claims that he had never amounted to much after the Civil War. Then he told the reporter "I'm on my way to Mexico because I like the game. I like fighting. I want to see it."

On December 16, 1913, he wrote a letter to his daughter from Laredo, Texas. In the note, he stated that he was crossing the border into Mexico "with a pretty definite purpose which is not at present disclosable." From there, Bierce crossed the border into Juarez, which had recently been liberated by popular bandit leader,

Pancho Villa. The bandit, now turned general, issued Bierce credentials that would allow him to accompany Villa's army.

Bierce sent a last letter home to his daughter and it was dated December 26. He said that he had ridden four miles to mail the letter and that he had been given a sombrero as a reward for picking off one of the enemy with a rifle at long range. He also told her that he was leaving with the army for Ojinaga, a city under siege, the following day. Here, the facts behind the disappearance of Ambrose Bierce end and the speculation begins.

George F. Weeks, a friend of Bierce's from California, set out on a personal search for the author in February 1919. No word had come from his old friend since the last days of 1913 and while most assumed that he had long since died, answers were still being sought about his final destination. In Mexico City, Weeks managed to track down an officer who told him that Bierce had been killed during a campaign in January 1914. He had collapsed during the attack on Ojinaga and had died from hardship and exposure.

Other rumors, clues and leads suggested that Bierce was killed by a firing squad, conducted by federal soldiers. He was also said to have been killed by the volatile Pancho Villa after the two of them had quarreled. Or that he was killed by guides or by Villa's men after one too many insults from his sharp tongue. Some have suggested that Bierce did not go to Mexico and instead committed suicide over his failing health. (At this time of his disappearance, Bierce was 70 years old.) It was also theorized that he might have been murdered and buried in secret.

Others theorized that Bierce had never really gone to Mexico but had actually crossed back into the United States to live and die in obscurity and have a last laugh at those who puzzled over his mysterious disappearance. While this sounds like something Bierce might have done, most would agree that the lure of war would have been too strong for him to be able to resist going to Mexico. Odo B. Slade, a former member of Pancho Villa's staff, recalled an elderly American with gray hair who served as a military advisor to

Villa. The American called himself "Jack Robinson" and he criticized the Mexican's battle strategies with the eye of a military expert. Slade later stated that "Robinson" quarreled violently with Villa and was shot to death when he announced his intention to leave and ally himself with the enemy.

But what really happened to Bierce remains a mystery. He vanished, as he wrote in his own words, into a space "through which animate and inanimate objects may fall into the invisible world and be seen and heard no more." And that's just the way that Bierce would have liked it.

WANTED DEAD OR ALIVE

Billy the Kid and Pat Garrett

The outlaw known as Billy the Kid, although both colorful and legendary, may be one of the most overrated outlaws of the Old West. The Kid was an accomplished rustler and horse thief, but his prowess with the gun has been exaggerated greatly by dime novels and modern day entertainment. Billy was credited for killing as many as twenty-one men, one for each year of his life, it is difficult to find that he actually killed more than four or five. In spite of this, Billy did become a major part of the conflict that came to be called the Lincoln County War, a volatile series of events that claimed many lives and wreaked havoc in New Mexico.

According to the history books, Pat Garrett killed Billy the Kid on the night of July 14, 1881 in Fort Sumner, New Mexico. In truth, an impressive amount of evidence exists to say that Billy actually wasn't killed that night at all. This evidence shows that he vanished and managed to live for another 69 years, longer than Pat Garrett and all of the other participants in the Lincoln County War.

In March 1878, former friend of Billy the Kid, Pat Garrett, became the sheriff of Lincoln County. One of his campaign promises had been to rid the county of the notorious outlaw. Garrett handily won the election and soon had the Kid locked up. He had been captured at Stinking Springs and arrested for the murder of Sheriff William Brady. He was found guilty and sentenced to hang on April 28 in Lincoln. But to Garrett's embarrassment, Billy escaped from jail, killing two deputies in the process. Eventually, Garrett and his men tracked the Kid to Fort Sumner.

Garrett allegedly killed Billy around midnight on July 14, 1881. According to his story, Garrett was visiting with rancher Pete Maxwell in his bedroom when a stranger stepped through the doorway. Wearing only a pair of socks and carrying a knife, the stranger whispered *"Quien Es?"* (Who is it?). Garrett, believing the stranger was Billy the Kid, raised his pistol and shot the man in the chest. A moment later, Garrett ran out the door and shouted to his deputies outside, "Boys, that was the Kid, and I think I have got him!" One of the lawmen, John Poe, leaned in the doorway and looked at the body on the floor and then turned to Garrett. "Pat, the Kid would not come to this place. You have shot the wrong man!"

The word quickly spread through Fort Sumner that the dead man was not Billy. Of the three officers present, only Garrett had ever seen the Kid before, but the other two men quickly went along with his identification. With Billy officially dead, Garrett could claim the reward as well as the fame and prestige of killing the outlaw. But things would not go smoothly for Garrett after that.

Strangely, two different inquests followed the killing, one of them on that same night and the other the following morning. The inquests only made things more confusing. The account of the first was lost and the second appears to have been slanted by Garrett to make himself look good. Some have even claimed the second inquest documents are forgeries. According to one author, only three of the six witnesses who signed the report could even identify the body, and one of these later stated that it was not the Kid. Neither document was ever recorded and according to W. C. Jameson, "there exists no legal proof of the death of Billy the Kid at the hands of Pat Garrett."

The burial of the dead man was as controversial as the shooting and the inquest. The body of the man who was buried had dark skin and a beard, in spite of the fact that Billy had been described by newspaper editor J. H. Koogler as "a mere boy, with the traditional silky fuzz on his upper lip" with "light hair and complexion." Who Pat Garrett actually killed that night is unknown, but it seems likely that it wasn't Billy the Kid.

As time passed, things grew much quieter in Lincoln County— almost quiet enough to hear the whispers and rumors that circulated about how Billy the Kid was not actually dead and that someone else had been killed in Fort Sumner. In the years that followed, many of those who knew Billy reportedly saw him. In addition, many claimed to be him, especially on the sideshow circuit of the early 1900s. Most of them were not taken seriously, had the wrong look or were clearly imposters. Now and then, one would come along that had to be looked at a little closer. One of them was a man named John Miller, who died in Ramah, New Mexico in 1933. Many of the old-time residents of the area believed that Miller was the Kid, but there was little evidence to support the idea. And Miller's claims would pale when compared to another man, who came to public attention in 1948. His name was William Henry Roberts and there is a very good chance that he was the missing Billy the Kid.

In 1948, an attorney named William Morrison was working on an estate settlement in Florida when he accidentally learned about a man in Texas that some people claimed was Billy the Kid. Morrison became intrigued and set out to find him, driving across several states and interviewing dozens of people. He eventually found Roberts in a small town called Hamilton. He arranged an interview with the man and told him that he was believed to be Billy the Kid. Roberts immediately denied it but did admit that the Kid was his half-brother and that he was alive and living in Mexico. After the two men talked for a few minutes, Morrison thanked him for his time and got ready to leave. Roberts walked him to the door and stepped outside into the sunshine with the attorney. As he shook his hand,

Roberts leaned forward and whispered to Morrison. He didn't want his wife to hear him, but he wanted to invite the attorney to come back the next day and speak to him in private.

The next morning, Morrison returned to the house and Roberts sent his wife out on an errand. When the men were alone, he confessed that he was Billy the Kid. He said that he did not want his wife to know about it, but he was anxious to be pardoned for the crimes that he had committed in New Mexico. The governor had long ago promised him a pardon but he had never received it. Even though it was 1948, Roberts stated that he believed he was still under the death sentence that he had been given for the murder of Sheriff William Brady.

Morrison explained that he would try to help if he could, but that he would need some proof to show that Roberts was actually the Kid. He told him that he knew of some bullet wounds that had been suffered by the real Billy the Kid and he asked Roberts to show him any scars that he had. Roberts obliged him by removing his shirt and trousers and by showing Morrison not only the scars that he knew about, but about 20 others as well. Morrison also reminded the man that the Kid was known for being able to slip out of a pair of locked handcuffs. Roberts never hesitated to show how it was done. He held out his hands and in a double-jointed move, tucked each thumb inside his palms and made his hands narrower than his wrists.

While Morrison could still not be certain, he was growing to believe that Roberts really might be Billy the Kid. He made arrangements to take the old man to Lincoln County, New Mexico where he could question him in detail about certain aspects of the Lincoln County War and ask him about the people, places and incidents from the time. Amazingly, Roberts was able to come up with information that was unknown to historians at that time and much that could be confirmed as accurate, although not general knowledge.

Morrison then asked Roberts to recount what had occurred on the night of July 14, 1881. Roberts explained that it was not he who had gone to Pete Maxwell's house, but a friend named Billy Barlow.

Barlow was about the same age as the Kid, but was half-Mexican and so while he was about the same size, was darker skinned. Barlow, along with Roberts (the Kid), Saval Guiterrez and a woman stopped at the home of Jesus Silva after a dance that night. As Silva prepared a meal for his guests, he mentioned that a freshly cut beef was hanging near Maxwell's room. He sent Barlow to bring some back and the young man left in his stockinged feet, carrying only a knife. It was Barlow, Roberts said, that Garrett mistook for the Kid.

When Roberts heard the shooting, he grabbed his guns and ran towards Maxwell's. He was fired on by Garrett and his deputies and was struck in the lower jaw and in the back of his shoulder and the top of his head was grazed. He was stunned and bleeding badly but managed to make it to the home of a Mexican woman who kept him hidden while she tended his wounds. In the early morning hours, a friend brought him his horse and told him that Garrett had killed Barlow and had passed the body off as the Kid. He and his friend rode off into the darkness and Billy the Kid vanished for the next 67 years.

The famous outlaw was gone and William Henry Roberts took his place. During the next several decades, Roberts told Morrison that he worked on ranches in Mexico and in the United States, served in Roosevelt's Rough Riders during the Spanish-American War, rode with Pancho Villa in the Mexican Revolution, worked for a couple of small-time Wild West shows and even served as a law officer for awhile. He married three times but never had children and was 88 years old when Morrison found him in Texas.

On November 15, 1950, Morrison filed a petition for a pardon for William Henry Roberts, a.k.a. Billy the Kid, with then New Mexico governor Thomas J. Mabry. The governor agreed to meet with Roberts and Morrison on November 30, assuring them that the meeting would be kept private and away from the press. That all turned out to be a farce however for the meeting was anything put private. Mabry invited the press, along with descendants of Pat Garrett and other figures from the Lincoln County War.

Questions were asked of Roberts that had nothing to do with seeking the truth and it was clear that Mabry never really intended to consider the petition filed by Morrison. The pardon was ultimately denied. Heartbroken, Roberts returned home to Texas and died from a heart attack two months later. He had tried to make amends, but forgiveness had eluded him.

Could William Henry Roberts have been Billy the Kid? Researchers who were skeptical of Roberts' claims admit that the existing history of Billy the Kid is badly flawed and contradictory, especially when it comes to his alleged death in 1881. It had long been determined that what most people believe they know about Billy the Kid comes from a single source: Pat Garrett. Garrett himself spent time on both sides of the law and as a born politician, had little use for the truth. Even his book (used by many of the subject's foremost researchers), *The Authentic Life of Billy the Kid*, was written by someone else, an alcoholic newspaperman named Ashmon Upson. Time has not been kind to Garrett's book and dozens of errors and outright lies have been discovered in it. But for some reason, it is considered the best reference on the life of Billy the Kid.

In 1998, authors W.C. Jameson and Frederic Bean began unraveling the many problems with Garrett's book and digging into the story told by William Henry Roberts. They found some pretty amazing evidence to show that Roberts may have really been the Kid, including a genealogy reconstructed from a family Bible owned by relatives that, among other things, shows that Roberts was related to people named McCarty, Antrim and Bonney. These were all names that Billy the Kid used as aliases and prior to Jameson and Bean's research, the origin of the name Bonney had eluded researchers. They also tracked elements of Roberts' story, starting with his escape from Fort Sumner, and where documents could be found, were able to follow his trail for years. In the end, it turned out that Roberts' credibility far exceeded that of Pat Garrett.

Even after all of this, some questions do remain. One of the most important is whether or not Pat Garrett knew that he had not killed Billy the Kid? If he did, why did he pass off another body as Billy, knowing that the Kid might return? It's possible that Garrett's quest for fame and glory caused him to throw caution to the wind in this situation. Or perhaps he believed that if the Kid escaped, he would feel safe enough with people believing him dead that he would leave and not come back. Or perhaps, as many believe, Garrett and the Kid concocted the scheme and Garrett knew all along that Billy had gotten away.

We'll probably never know the answers to these questions, but we still have to wonder why Garrett's deputies, Poe and McKinney, backed up Garrett's version of events if they knew it was not the Kid who had been gunned down. The truth is, the statements attributed to Garrett, Poe and McKinney do not agree with each other at all. It was Poe who first informed Garrett that he had shot the wrong man and in 1933, he published a book called *The Death of Billy the Kid*. While supportive of Garrett, Poe referred to the circumstances of Billy's death as a mystery. According to a cousin of McKinney, he often spoke of that July night in his later years and admitted that the Kid got away and that Garrett had fabricated the events that he claimed happened that night.

But will you find a conservative history book that admits Billy the Kid was not killed by Pat Garrett in 1881? It's unlikely, but believe it or not, the death of Billy the Kid remains one of the great unsolved mysteries of the West.

The President's Assassin

As related in the previous tale, history books are not always accurate. According to history, President Abraham Lincoln was killed on April 14, 1865 by an assassin named John Wilkes Booth. A short time later, Booth was trapped on a farm in Virginia and gunned down. There has never been any doubt that Booth was the killer of Lincoln as dozens of people were in attendance at Ford's Theater that night who knew Booth and who witnessed the horrific assassination.

However, the subsequent nine-day pursuit, and the capture and death of John Wilkes Booth remains one of the most controversial, contradictory and, according to some, conspiratorial events in American history. As the years have passed and the mysteries surrounding Booth unravel, many researchers have become convinced that Booth was not killed. These same researchers insist that the assassin vanished instead and that a Confederate officer and Booth look-alike was killed in his place. But what happened to John Wilkes Booth?

After shooting President Lincoln, John Wilkes Booth escaped from Washington on horseback across the Anacostia Bridge, passing a sentry who had not yet learned of the assassination. He made it to a farm in Virginia with the help of his fellow conspirators, only stopping to rest because of a broken leg that he suffered jumping from the seating box where he had shot Lincoln.

Soon, the hunt for Lincoln's assassin was on, and by morning, more than 2,000 soldiers were looking for Booth. On April 26, a detachment of 25 men finally tracked down Booth, and his comrade David Herold, at a tobacco farm near Port Royal, Virginia. The barn where they were hiding was surrounded, and Herold decided to surrender. He was manacled and tied to a tree. Booth decided to die rather than be taken alive—or so we are told to believe.

In the darkness outside, a decision was made to try and smoke Booth out. The barn was set on fire and in a few moments, the interior was engulfed in flames. Booth came to the door and raised his weapon, apparently looking for a target among the soldiers outside. One of the soldiers, a Sergeant Boston Corbett, saw Booth through the slats of the barn and, ignoring Edwin Stanton's specific orders to bring Booth back alive, shot him in the back of the head. Booth fell to the floor and the soldiers rushed to subdue him. He died two hours later, whispering instructions to tell his mother that he "died for his country and did what he thought best." A search of the dead man's pockets turned up a few items, including a compass, a diary and photographs of several women, along with one portrait of Booth's fiancée, Lucy Hale.

Booth died on the porch of the farm house as light was beginning to show in the sky. The dead man was sewn into a burlap bag and was taken to Alexandria on a steamer. Booth's body was then placed on a carpenter's bench and identified from a crude tattoo of the actor's initials, by dental fillings and by a scar on the back of his neck. Others claimed that the body only resembled Booth, but that it actually wasn't him at all. Regardless, the corpse was taken to the Old Penitentiary in Washington and, using a gun case for a coffin, was buried under the floor of the old dining room. The door to the room was locked and the body stayed there for another four years. Finally, pleas from Edwin Booth convinced President Andrew Johnson to allow the body to be exhumed and buried in an unmarked grave in the family plot in Baltimore. But was it really the body of John Wilkes Booth in the grave?

Shortly after the assassin was gunned down, the word began to spread that it might not have been Booth in that barn after all. The government's handling of the body in question and of the witnesses who were present did not add much credence to the official version of the story. The Union soldiers had certainly killed a man. The War Department and the newspapers told a breathless nation that the man had been John Wilkes Booth. But from the day the body was brought back to Washington, there were already people on the streets saying that the body wasn't Booth's. They believed the assassin had long since escaped and that the government was offering a secret substitution for the real killer.

The Secret Service and the War Department took a firm position: the corpse belonged to Booth. In their possession were items that belonged to him and other evidence that proved they had the right man, including the left boot that Booth had abandoned to put his broken leg in splints and the revolver he had been carrying when killed. They also had affidavits from the soldiers who brought the body back, swearing that the face of the corpse matched the photos of Booth they had been given. The investigators studied these, but they were never shown to the public. The government refused to even consider the idea that the body might not be that of Booth.

The mystery continued for many years. More than twenty-two men would later claim to be Booth—with books, anecdotes and sworn testimony. The newspapers got hold of each story and fanned the flames of doubt. By June 1865, stories spread that witnesses had seen Booth on a steamer to Mexico, or to South America. It was said that several people saw him in the West and others recognized him in the Orient, England, India, Rome, Paris and Vienna. In Ohio, a man claimed that Booth had stopped in his tavern on the way to Canada. In the Southwest, several people who claimed to know Booth said that he owed his escape to Union troopers because of his membership in a fraternal order. They had spirited him away rather than see him hanged. It was no wonder that before long, dark-haired, pallid men who walked with a limp began to be pointed out all across the country as John Wilkes Booth.

The story became so popular that in July 1867, Dr. John Frederick May, who had identified the body as Booth, felt that it necessary to make an emphatic denial of his once positive identification. He now stated that he could have been wrong when he said the dead man had been John Wilkes Booth. It seems that two years before the assassination, May had removed a tumor from the back of Booth's neck. The surgery had left a jagged scar and this scar was how the doctor had identified the remains. May said the body he saw did not resemble Booth, but since he found a scar on the back of the neck, he assumed it must be him.

His new testimony continued, bringing to light a more damning bit of evidence. May explained in detail his examination of the corpse in question, noting its broken right leg. But the witnesses at Ford's Theater said that Booth had broken his left leg when he jumped from the theater box. Did this mean the body was not Booth's or that Dr. May was a careless observer and did not make an accurate identification?

Suspicion thrived across the country, and by 1869 President Johnson decided to dispel all the rumors and allow the assassin's brother to bury the disputed corpse in his family's cemetery plot. On February 15, 1869, government workers exhumed the body. Many believed the mystery of the body would be settled once and for all by Edwin Booth, but he simply added to the confusion by bungling the whole thing. First, he attempted to keep the exhumation a secret and then decided that he couldn't bear to look upon the face of his dead brother. He remained outside of the undertaker's room while friends went inside to examine the corpse. Not surprisingly, they decided the body belonged to John Wilkes Booth.

Needless to say, the public had a good mystery and they weren't about to let it go. A reporter for the *Baltimore Gazette* was soon claiming that he had been present at the exhumation and that the body had a broken right leg and no bullet holes in it. Modern historians believe this reporter had either a vivid imagination or lied about being at the exhumation at all, still in those days, the story looked like new evidence that Booth was still alive.

The mystery continued into the twentieth century and, while Booth's skull was supposedly on display in a number of different traveling carnivals, there remained a question as to his eventual fate. Historians looked for answers in the early 1900s as many of the people involved in the case were still living. Statements were taken from surviving soldiers who aided in Booth's capture and all information was thoroughly researched. They even checked out the claims of men still posing as Booth and found all of them transparently fraudulent. Could Booth have survived the days after the assassination? The question nagged at historians, although logic would say that he had been killed. Still, it is interesting that after all of the conflicting evidence, there was not a single eyewitness, sufficiently impartial to be above suspicion, which had seen the corpse in 1865 and could say, with certainty, that it was John Wilkes Booth.

As mentioned, almost every single claim that Booth was alive was quickly exposed as a hoax, however there were a few of them that weren't as easily dispelled, and perhaps the most intriguing of these was the case of a man named David E. George, who died in Oklahoma in 1903.

Author W.C. Jameson explains that in order to understand the case of David George, the reader must also understand the history of Finis L. Bates, a young lawyer from Granbury, Texas. Bates was struggling to earn a living in the early 1870s and must have been happy when a man who called himself John St. Helen strolled into his office one day and asked the attorney to defend him. The charge was operating a saloon without a license in the nearby town of Glen Rose, and the man admitted he was guilty of the charge but that he did not want to appear in federal court. John St. Helen was not his real name, he confessed, and he feared that his true identity might be exposed in court. Bates became the man's lawyer and got to know him quite well. He stated that St. Helen seemed to have more money than his status should have allowed and that he had an intimate knowledge of the theater and of the works of Shakespeare, most of which he could recite from memory.

Then, late one night in 1877, Bates was summoned to the sickbed of his client. He was seriously ill and he told Bates that he did not expect to live much longer. He told Bates to reach under his pillow and the attorney took out an old tintype that showed a much younger St. Helen. The sick man told the attorney that if he died, he was to send the photograph to an Edwin Booth in Baltimore with a note that said the subject of the tintype had passed away. In between coughing fits, St. Helen explained to the stunned attorney that his name was actually John Wilkes Booth and that he had assassinated former President Abraham Lincoln.

Bates was shocked and dismayed at the revelation but he knew that he could not betray his client's confidence. He replied that he would send the photograph if needed and he sat next to St. Helen's bed throughout the rest of the night. However, St. Helen did not die. He remained sick for several weeks but eventually began to recover. Once he was mobile again, he met with Bates and again confessed to being John Wilkes Booth. He begged for the attorney to keep the secret, and Bates had no ethical choice but to agree. He did demand some answers though, knowing full well that John Wilkes Booth was reportedly dead.

Booth explained that Andrew Johnson, the Vice President, was the principle conspirator behind the assassination. (Interestingly, many theorists agree with this and a number of scenarios exist to explain Johnson's motives.) St. Helen said that he had met with Johnson just hours before Lincoln was killed, and Johnson told him that General Grant was away from Washington so Booth would have an easy escape route into Maryland. St. Helen then provided details of the assassination plot, the actual event, his escape from Ford's Theater and flight into the countryside. According to Bates, his descriptions seemed to have intricacies that only someone intimately involved with the assassination plot would have known. Most of all, they were different enough from the already published accounts of the events that Bates began to give some credibility to St. Helen's version of the story.

St. Helens told the attorney that he had escaped into Kentucky in late April and eventually made his way west of the Mississippi and into the Indian Territory. After spending some time here, he disguised himself as a priest and entered Mexico. In 1867, he traveled to California and met with his mother and older brother Junius in San Francisco. Later, he drifted to New Orleans, where he taught school, and then moved to Texas. Here, he assumed the name John St. Helen and opened a tavern.

He was, he insisted, the assassin known as John Wilkes Booth; Bates humored St. Helen with friendly skepticism and eventually the two men parted ways. Several months after St. Helen's confession, Bates moved to Memphis and established what became a very successful law practice. As the years passed, he developed a deep interest in Abraham Lincoln, especially the events surrounding his death. In his spare time, he read everything that he could get his hands on about Lincoln and Booth—and the more he studied, the more convinced that he became that his old client was telling the truth. John St. Helen, he realized, really had been John Wilkes Booth.

The story of John Wilkes Booth and Finis Bates took another turn in January 1903. On the 13th of that month, the corpse of a man named David E. George arrived at the undertaking parlor of W.B. Penniman in Enid, Oklahoma. George, who had been working in Enid as a handyman and house painter, had apparently committed suicide by ingesting a large dose of strychnine. He was already known as a heavy drinker and was thought to have been depressed of late. As Penniman's assistant, W.H. Ryan, was embalming George's body, the Reverend E.C. Harper stopped by the funeral parlor. Harper stepped into the embalming room, and surprised to see the body there, asked Ryan if he knew who the man was. He explained that the dead man was none other than John Wilkes Booth and that he had confessed his identity to the minister's wife in 1900. Mrs. Harper was summoned and she identified the corpse of David E. George as the man who had told her that he was Booth. She later wrote out and signed a statement, swearing that the confession had taken place.

Over the course of the next few days, a number of newspapers carried the story that a man believed to be Booth had died in Oklahoma. One of the stories caught the attention of Finis Bates in Memphis and he wondered if the late David E. George might be the man that he had once known as John St. Helen. Curious, he decided to go to Enid and see. Bates arrived in Oklahoma on January 23, and the next morning, went to the undertaker's to compare the face of the dead man with the tintype photograph that he still possessed. He placed it next to the face of the corpse and compared them. It was, Bates stated without a doubt, the same man.

The body remained on display at Penniman's parlor and after it went unclaimed for some time, it was eventually moved into a back room and stored for several years. Eventually, Bates pur-chased the body. In October 1931, the mummy was examined by a group of seven doctors at Chicago's Northwestern University. It was studied, x-rayed and dissected and the team did find evidence of a broken leg, although the report did not state whether it was the right or the left. The most compelling discovery was that of a ring that had somehow become embedded in the flesh of the body cavity. Digestive juices had damaged it over time, but the researchers present believed that the initials "JWB" could be discerned on the surface of it. Dr. Otto L. Schmidt, who was present and who was the president of the Chicago Historical Society at that time, subsequently wrote, "I can say safely that we believe Booth's body is here in my office."

The fate of this intriguing mummy remains a mystery. At one point, Bates tried to sell it to the *Dearborn Independent* for $10,000 and at another time, offered it to Henry Ford for $100,000 but it was declined both times. During the 1920s and 1930s, Bates leased the mummy to a carnival promoter who charged 25 cents to view "The Assassin of President Abraham Lincoln." The mummy was still being displayed into the 1940s but after the promoter went bankrupt and moved to Idaho, he placed the mummy in a chair on his front porch and charged visitors a dime to look at it. Eventually, the mummy disappeared, and to this day, no one knows what became of it. It is rumored to be in a private collection somewhere but no one knows for sure.

The final resting place of the mummy is just as mysterious as the questions that linger about John Wilkes Booth. Was Booth and St. Helen/George the same man? Although many feel that Bates tried too hard to make Booth and St. Helen appear to be the same, it can't be ignored that they possessed many of the same characteristics: heavy drinking, an intimate knowledge of Shakespeare, a penchant for the theater, the same style of dress, and the fact that the men were well-educated. In addition, studies of physical characteristics between George and Booth showed many striking similarities, including the shape of their heads, jaw lines and the bridges of both men's noses.

There are many problems with the theory as well. Skeptics

state that the color of George's eyes was enough to debunk his claims. His eyes, according to the undertaker, were blue-gray, while government documents say Booth's were black. On the other hand, Asia Booth, the actor's sister, wrote that they were hazel. However, Bates wrote that George had a broken right leg, not the left leg that Booth broke jumping from the theater box. Of course, the government's own records stated that the body that was dug up from beneath the floor of the Old Penitentiary had a broken right leg as well. So, which records were accurate? Bates showed photographs of St. Helen and George to a number of people who had known Booth, including those who had seen him perform many times. All of them stated that the men in both photos were John Wilkes Booth.

Another mysterious piece of evidence involved the signet ring worn by Booth. The actor was seldom seen without the ring, which was inscribed with his initials, and he was photographed wearing it many times. The ring was not on the finger of the man who was killed in Virginia. David E. George wore a similar ring, many recalled. Some weeks before his death, George told one of his neighbors that he was being followed. One afternoon, when he saw two sheriff's deputies coming his way, George was so afraid that he would be identified that he removed the ring from his finger and swallowed it. This strange anecdote would provide startling evidence to researchers in 1931 that the body they were examining (with a ring inside of the body cavity.) was that of John Wilkes Booth.

But was it? The evidence for the man from Oklahoma being John Wilkes Booth is certainly plausible but unfortunately, so much time has passed, and so much evidence lost, that the answers will likely never be known.

Chapter Three

AMONG THE SPIRITS

Unsolved Mysteries From the Other Side

The Spiritualist movement, like jazz, was purely an American invention. Although the idea that man was able to communicate with spirits had existed already for centuries, modern belief in such a practice came about in March 1848 in Hydesville, New York. The movement would remain strong for nearly a century, enjoying its greatest revival after World War I. The practice was founded on the belief that life existed after death and that the spirit existed beyond the body. Most importantly, it was believed that these spirits could (and did) communicate with the living.

Spiritualism was born at the home of the Fox family in Hydesville, but legend holds that the beginnings of the movement actually came about a few years before the Fox family took up residence in their cottage. In those days, between 1843 and 1844, a couple named Bell occupied the cottage. In the last few months of their occupancy, a young local woman named Lucretia Pulver handled the household chores.

One day, a young peddler came to the door of the house. He was a friendly young man, and he brought with him a case of merchandise. These goods consisted of pots, pans and other useful items for the home. Strangely, Lucretia would later recall that Mrs. Bell seemed to know the young man. The peddler was greeted warmly and asked to dine with the family. In fact, Lucretia remembered that he stayed on with them for several days. The nature of his and Mrs. Bell's relationship has never been clearly established, but it seems obvious that some sort of friendship existed.

Nevertheless, Lucretia soon found herself fired from her position in the house. No explanation was ever given but apparently, there were no hard feelings about her dismissal. Mrs. Bell took the girl home in her wagon, but before Lucretia left the house, she purchased a small kitchen knife from the peddler's selection. She left him instructions to deliver the item to her father's farm, but the knife never arrived.

Barely a week later, Lucretia was surprised to find that Mrs. Bell was again requesting her services. Thankful to have her job back, she reported for duty the next morning. Once again, she would have some unusual recollections later on. For one thing, she found that the peddler who had been staying with the Bells had departed. No one mentioned when he might have left and Lucretia never asked. She also found that a number of the articles that the peddler had carried in his case were now in the possession of Mrs. Bell, including her own knife. She remembered seeing these items in the case, but simply assumed that Mrs. Bell must have bought them before the young man left for parts unknown. Nothing seemed to be out of the ordinary, but that would soon change.

Shortly after returning to the house, Lucretia began to speak of an unsettling feeling that seemed to hang over the place. She also began to notice some particularly strange things had begun to occur. Unaccountable noises, like knocking and tapping, came from the room that the peddler had once occupied. On several occasions, she also heard footsteps pacing through the house and then descending the stairs to the cellar. Not surprisingly, Lucretia began to feel frightened and nervous when left alone in the house. She would often send for her brother, or a friend, to come and stay with her, and usually the strange sounds would cease. However, on one occasion, they continued for hours and scared Lucretia's brother so badly that he left the place and refused to return.

One afternoon, while in the cellar, Lucretia found herself suddenly up to her knees in a patch of freshly turned dirt. Her scream brought Mr. Bell racing down the stairs and when she asked him why the cellar had been dug up the way that it had, he laughed and replied that he had been covering up rat holes.

A short time later, the Bells moved out, and the Weekman family moved in, along with a relative, Mrs. Lafe. The length of their residence in the house would prove to be a short one. One day, Mrs. Lafe entered the kitchen, and as she closed the door behind her, she spotted the apparition of a man in a black frock coat standing across the room. She screamed in terror and the figure vanished. Soon, they all began to hear the rappings and footsteps in the house. They would come during the daylight hours, but mostly they were heard at night. Finally, the odd happenings proved to be too much for them and they abandoned the place.

Then in 1848, the Fox family moved into the house. John Fox and his wife had two young daughters, Margaret and Kate, and they settled temporarily into the cottage. Fox was a farmer who had come to New York from Canada and had purchased land nearby. A home was being built on the new property and he moved his family into the cottage until the other house could be completed. Their stay would turn out to be very eventful.

Within days of moving in, the noises began. The banging and rattling sounds pounded loudly each night, disturbing them all from their sleep. At first, John Fox thought nothing of the sounds that his wife and children were so frightened by. He assumed that they were merely the sounds of an unfamiliar dwelling, amplified by active imaginations. Soon however, the reports took another turn. Kate woke up screaming one night, saying that a cold hand had touched her on the face. Margaret swore that rough, invisible fists had pulled the blankets from her bed. Even Mrs. Fox swore that she had heard disembodied footsteps walking through the house and then going down the wooden steps into the dank cellar.

Fox, not a superstitious man, was perplexed. He tried walking about the house, searching for squeaks and knocks in the floorboards and along the walls. He tested the windows and doors to see if vibrations in the frames might account for the sounds. He could find no explanation for the weird noises and his daughters became convinced that the house had a ghost. On the evening of March 31, Fox began his almost nightly ritual of investigating the house for the source of the sounds. The tapping had begun with the setting of the sun and although he searched the place, he was no closer to a solution. Then, Kate began to realize that whenever her father knocked on a wall or door frame, the same number of inexplicable knocks would come in reply. It was as if someone, or something, was trying to communicate with them.

Finding her nerve, Kate spoke up, addressing the unseen presence by the nickname that she and her sister had given it. "Here, Mr. Splitfoot," she called out, "do as I do!" She clapped her hands together two times and seconds later, two knocks came in reply, seemingly from inside of the wall. She followed this display by rapping on the table and the precise number of knocks came again from the presence. The activity caught the attention of the rest of the family and they entered the room with Kate and her father. Mrs. Fox tried asking aloud questions of fact, such as the ages of her daughters and the age of a Fox child who had earlier passed away. To her surprise, each reply was eerily accurate.

Unsure of what to do, John Fox summoned several neighbors to the house to observe the phenomenon. Most of them arrived very skeptical of what they were hearing from the Fox family, but were soon astounded to find their ages and various dates and years given in response to the questions they asked.

One neighbor, and a former tenant in the house, William Duesler, decided to try and communicate with the source of the sounds in a more scientific manner. He asked repeated questions and was able to create a form of alphabet using a series of knocks. He also was able to determine the number of knocks that could be interpreted as "yes" and "no." In such a manner, he was able to determine the subject of the disturbances. The answer came before an assembled group of witnesses: the presence in the house was the spirit of a peddler who had been murdered and robbed years before.

As it happened, one of the neighbors who had assembled in the house was the former maid of the Bell family, Lucretia Pulver. She came forward with her story of finding the dirt that had been unearthed in the cellar. The story now took on a more sinister tone. John Fox and William Duesler went to the area that Lucretia described and began to dig. After more than an hour, they had little to show for their trouble but an empty hole and sore backs. That was until Fox noticed something odd beneath the blade of his shovel. He prodded at the object and then picked it up. It appeared to be a small piece of bone with a few strands of hair still clinging to it. Spurred on by the gruesome discovery, he and Duesler began to dig once more. They found a few scraps and tatters of clothing, but little else. They were far from disappointed, as a local doctor determined that the bone appeared to be a piece of a human skull. They were convinced that the presence in the house was indeed the ghost of the luckless peddler.

Shortly after, the story of the Fox family took a more dramatic turn. The two daughters were both purported to have mediumistic powers and the news of the unearthly communications with the spirit quickly spread. By November 1849, they were both giving public performances of their skills, and the Spiritualist movement was born. The mania to communicate with the dead swept the country and the Fox sisters became famous. Regardless, both of them were doomed to unhappy lives and despite amassing great wealth, both died penniless in the 1890s. Some would say that they died just a few years too soon.

Over the years, the credibility of the Fox family was often called into question. As no real evidence existed to say that any peddler was actually killed in the house, many accused the family of making up the entire story to support their claims of supernatural powers. Margaret, at the lowest point in her career, even confessed to having faked the early manifestations. She later retracted the confession, claiming that she had done it for the money, having been drunk at the time. It comes as no surprise that the Spiritualist movement was riddled with fraud, but was the story of the murdered peddler merely a ruse to prove the powers of the Fox sisters?

It's possible that Margaret and Kate, had they not died broken and poor years before, would have been vindicated in 1904. By this time, their former home had been deserted for some years. A group of children were playing in the ruins one day when the east wall of the cellar collapsed, nearly killing one of them. A man who came to their aid quickly realized the reason for the wall's collapse. Apparently, it had been a false partition, hastily and poorly constructed in the past. Between the false brick wall and the genuine wall of the cellar were the crumbling bones of a man and a large box, just like the ones that had been carried by peddlers a few decades before. A portion of the man's skull was missing.

Dead men, as they say, really do tell tales. Or do they? That's been the mystery behind Spiritualism since it was first conceived. Were those involved with the movement really communicating with the dead? Skeptics, even of those times, were convinced they were not, but the public was not so easily discouraged. In fact, they were fascinated with the reports coming from New York as news of these "spirited communications" quickly spread and the Fox Sisters became famous. In November 1849, the girls were giving public demonstrations of their powers in contacting the spirit world and drawing crowds that numbered into the thousands. Seemingly overnight, Spiritualism became a full-blown religious movement, complete with scores of followers, its own unique brand of phenomena and codes of conduct for everything from spirit communication to seances.

The Spiritualists believed that the dead could communicate through individuals known as mediums. These were sensitive persons who were in touch with the next world, and while in a trance, they could pass along messages from the other side. Besides these "message mediums," there were also practitioners who could produce physical phenomena that was said to be the work of the spirits. This phenomenon included lights, unearthly music, the levitation of objects, disembodied voices and even actual apparitions.

All of this was produced during seances (or sittings), which were regarded as the most exciting method of spirit communication Any number of people could attend and the rooms where the seances took place often contained a large table that the attendees could sit around, smaller tables that were suitable for lifting and tilting, and a cabinet where the mediums could be sequestered while the spirits materialized and performed their tricks. The sessions reportedly boasted a variety of phenomena, including musical instruments that played by themselves and sometimes flew about the room, glowing images, ghostly hands and messages from the dead.

While each seance was different, most had one thing in common in that they were always held in dark or dimly lighted rooms. Believers explained that the darkness provided less of a distraction to the audience and to the medium. They also added that since much of the spirit phenomena were luminous, it was much easier seen in the darkness. Those who were not so convinced of the validity of the movement offered another explanation. They believed the dark rooms concealed the practice of fraud. These early questioners would go on to become the first paranormal investigators of the era.

But while the Spiritualist movement brought the study of ghosts and spirits into the public eye, it also provided fame (and sometimes infamy) to many of those involved. Not only did the mediums gain notoriety, but so did many of the investigators, and in many cases, the movement led to their ruin. Even the Fox Sisters, who had known such early fame and fortune, drank themselves to death and died penniless. The downfalls of many of the mediums came about because of their exposure as fakes. It was obvious that Spiritualism was riddled with cases of deliberate fraud. It seemed easy to fool the thousands of people who were looking for a miracle and many of the mediums began lining their pockets with money that they had swindled from naive clients.

Of course, that's not to say that all of the Spiritualists were dishonest. Many of them, like famous author Sir Arthur Conan Doyle, truly believed in the validity of the movement. At the very worst, many of these believers were good-hearted but gullible and at best, there do remain a few of the mediums for which no logical explanations have been suggested. As William James said about the medium Lenora Piper: "to upset the conclusion that all crows are black, there is no need to seek demonstration that no crows are black; it is sufficient to produce one white crow; a single one is sufficient." Piper, James believed, was the "one white crow."

The Man Who Could Fly

If there was a single word that best fit Daniel Douglas Home (pronounced "Hume"), it was arrogance. Considered by many to be the most gifted medium who ever lived, Home avoided contact with other Spiritualists, declaring that he had nothing to learn from them. And perhaps he was right, or perhaps it was because he chose not to mingle among the common people, for Home used his purported paranormal powers to mingle among the rich, the royal and the famous. Regardless of what he did with these skills, he remains an enigma to many researchers today, especially those who consider Spiritualism to have been nothing more than entertainment and illusion for the masses. Home stands unique in that many of the feats that he allegedly performed have yet to be duplicated by anyone.

Home was born in Edinburgh, Scotland in March 1833 and his psychic talents, said to have been inherited from his mother, began to show themselves when he was only an infant. His aunt reported that his cradle would rock by itself, as though moved by an unseen hand, and at age four, Home accurately foretold the death of a cousin. He was a sickly and strange child and believed by his family to have remarkable powers. When he was just nine years old, Home moved to America to live with an aunt in Connecticut. His health continued to decline and he was diagnosed with tuberculosis. Unable to exert himself as most boys could, he spent most of his time walking in the woods and reading his Bible. He came to believe that the spirits of the dead constantly surrounded him.

Shortly after he turned 15, the Fox sisters created a sensation with their table rapping and Spiritualism was embraced by the public. Not long after, Home's own paranormal talents began to increase. His aunt Mary Cook grew to believe that the eerie events were the work of the devil and she threw him out. For most of the rest of his life, Home had no place of his own to live. Staying in various households as a guest, he traveled about, holding seances for those who were interested. His seances however, were different than most others as he always held them in brightly lit, rather than darkened, rooms. Home had attended many other seances in the past and regarded most mediums as frauds. He decided to do the opposite of what was being done elsewhere, showing the public that he had nothing to hide.

During these sessions, he produced spectral lights, rappings, and ghostly hands which shook hands with audience members. He also moved tables, chairs and other objects, played spectral music, spelled out messages from the dead using lettered cards and amazingly seemed to be able to shrink his body in size. While he was doing these things, he would ask the sitters to hold his hands and feet to prove that he was not somehow manipulating the objects with secret devices or wires. He claimed that all of his feats were made possible by friendly spirits over whom he had no control.

In August 1852, Home moved beyond what many would consider to be parlor tricks (although darn clever parlor tricks!) and first accomplished the feat that would make him famous. To put it bluntly, Home managed to fly. The seance took place in the Connecticut home of Ward Cheney, a wealthy businessman. Also present that night was a local journalist, F.L. Burr, whose assignment it was to find something incriminating against Spiritualism in general and especially about Home, who had debunkers in an uproar with his excellent reputation. However, instead of writing an expose of the evening, Burr instead wrote:

> *Suddenly, without any expectation of the part of the company, Home was taken up into the air. I had hold of his hand at the time and I felt his feet-they were lifted a foot from the floor. He palpitated from head to foot with the contending emotions of joy and fear which choked his utterances. Again and again, he was taken from the floor, and the third time he was taken to the ceiling of the apartment, with which his hands and feet came into gentle contact.*

But how was this accomplished? Home claimed not to know himself. He stated that an "unseen power" simply came over him and lifted him into the air. Needless to say, most readers who came upon this article (and it was re-printed many times) were skeptical, as are most who come across it today. Full-body levitation is, and always has been, considered impossible. Throughout history, only a few saints had ever been alleged to be able to lift themselves from the ground in such a manner, although some practitioners of strict meditation techniques claim to be able to manage a few inches from the floor today. But back in America of the middle 1800s, there was only one man, Daniel Douglas Home, who could levitate without the aid of mirrors, ropes or even a safety net.

In 1855, Home traveled to Europe, where he began associating with the rich and famous. He conducted seances in England and on the Continent, gaining supporters and wealthy patrons. In 1858, he was married to the daughter of a Russian nobleman with whom he had a son, Gregoire, but his wife passed away in 1862.

In 1866, the Spiritual Anthenaeum was founded with Home as the Secretary and soon after, he became embroiled in a scandal involving a wealthy widow who would later claim that Home tried to bilk her out of a large sum of money. Home maintained that the money was freely given for his "spiritualistic services" and the widow did not demand the return of the fortune until he refused her sexual advances. The trial became an embarrassing affair and many of Home's supporters abandoned him. When it was over, he was forced to return the money.

During the scandal, Home was at his best when it came to producing incredible phenomena. In December 1868, his most famous feat took place at the home of Lord Adare. During the evening, Home reportedly went into a trance and floated out of the window on the third floor, then floated back in another window—all before the eyes of a number of stunned witnesses. The event occurred in front of three irreproachable members of London's high society, Lord Adare, his cousin Captain Charles Wynne, and the Master of Lindsay.

Skeptics contend the event was a mass hallucination or was somehow accomplished through trickery. They base this on the fact that there are slight discrepancies in the accounts of Adare and Lindsay, mostly concerning the size of the windows that Home floated out of and how high they were off the ground and whether or not the night outside was dark or moonlit. The debunkers ignore the statement of Captain Wynne, which was simple and straightforward. "The fact of Mr. Home having gone out of one window and in at another I can swear to," he wrote. "Anyone who knows me would not for a moment say I was a victim of a hallucination or any other humbug of the kind."

It should again be noted that during Home's entire spectacular career, he was never seriously accused of fraud (all of those accusations have come much later) and he was never caught cheating, as so many of the mediums of the day were. It is also worth noting that this feat, like his other levitation, was accomplished in the home of someone that he was visiting for the first time and was among people of limited acquaintance. Any opportunity that he had to rig up elaborate machinery or engage the services of an accomplice to do so was nonexistent. There is no evidence to say that he ever resorted to such tricks.

And who can say that he could have even if he had wanted to? When not "entranced by the spirits," Home was not exactly a robust character, thanks to his tubercular condition. It seems that he would be the last person to have gone fumbling about on ropes and pulleys outside of the window of Lord Adare's mansion on a cold December night. And how could he have rigged them in place anyway? Of course, if we listen to the debunkers, it never happened at all. Home was nothing more than a hypnotist and cheap conjurer who convinced everyone present that he floated out the window. But isn't it often the case that the incredible claims of the debunkers is harder to believe than accepting that the paranormal may have occurred?

In 1871, Home married again and that same year began a series of tests with Sir William Crookes, a scientist interested in Spiritualism. To determine if Home could somehow manipulate electro-magnetic energy, Crookes wrapped an accordion in copper wire and then placed it in a metal cage. He ran an electrical current through the wire, which he believed would block any magnetic energy coming from Home. The medium was still able to make the accordion play, leading Crookes to believe that he possessed an independent psychic force.

In 1873, after two years of testing with Crookes, Home announced that he was retiring. Tired and in poor health, he traveled with his wife and son until his death from tuberculosis in 1886. After his death, dozens of explanations were given about how Home accomplished his feats through trickery, but not a single one of these theories was ever proven. In addition, the most prominent stage magicians in the world all claimed they could duplicate his stunts on stage but, for some reason, they never did.

Home was a shadowy figure in the annals of history and soon became forgotten by all but the most stalwart Spiritualists. He is remembered today largely because of the sheer variety of phenomena he was said to have produced and for his alleged ability to fly. Whether or not Home could actually do the things that he and his followers claimed remains a mystery but most believe that it is worthy of continued research.

Most debunkers would dismiss the idea of any research into Home (or mediums of his day altogether) and say that what he claimed to do was impossible. These debunkers may be those who profit in some way from exposing the unexplained or may simply have an obsession with the paranormal and a desperate need to try and destroy it before it disrupts their otherwise orderly world. Theses pundits for the rational defy the true meaning of the word skeptic by closing their minds to anything they don't personally agree with instead of considering everything until proven impossible. In this way, Daniel Douglas Home, whose feats made him a foe of rationality, had many enemies in his time and still has them a century and a half later.

The Watseka Wonder

As we have already established, the era of Spiritualism was riddled with unexplained mysteries. While it is true that many of the strange occurrences that took place during this period are easily dismissed as nothing more than the hysterical remembrances of true believers in the movement, there are a number of cases that seem to defy rational explanation. The strange sensation that became known as the "Watseka Wonder" was just such a case.

The unexplained came to the small Illinois town of Watseka in

July 1877. It was at this time that a 13-year-old girl named Lurancy Vennum first fell into a strange, catatonic sleep during which she claimed to speak with spirits. The attacks occurred many times each day and sometimes lasted as long as eight hours. During her trance, Lurancy would speak in different voices but when she awoke, she would remember nothing. News of the unusual girl traveled about the state and during this time of popularity for the Spiritualist movement, many visitors came to see her.

Finally, doctors diagnosed Lurancy as being mentally ill and they recommended that she be sent to the State Insane Asylum in Peoria, Illinois. In January of 1878, a man named Asa Roff, also from Watseka, came to visit the Vennum family. He claimed that his own daughter, Mary, had been afflicted with the same condition as Lurancy. He was convinced that his daughter had actually spoken to spirits. In addition, he was also convinced that his daughter's spirit still existed. Little did he know, but it would soon become apparent that his daughter's spirit was now inside the body of Lurancy Vennum.

To understand the strange and fantastic events that took place in Watseka, we must first start at the beginning of the tale. Mary Roff died on the afternoon of July 5, 1865 while hospitalized at the State Mental Asylum in Peoria. She had been committed there after a bizarre incident when she began slashing at her arms with a straight razor. It was the final tragedy in Mary's descent into madness and insanity. In the beginning, it had only been the strange voices that seemed to come from nowhere. Next she experienced the long periods when she stayed in a trance-like state. Then came her moments of awakening, when she spoke in other voices and seemed to be possessed by spirits of other people. Finally, she developed an obsession with blood. Mary was convinced that she needed to remove the blood from her body, using pins, leeches and at last, a sharpened razor.

After that final incident, her parents discovered her on the floor of her room, no longer conscious and lying in a pool of blood.

Broken-hearted, they took her to the asylum and here, Mary endured more tragedy as the "cures" for insanity in those days were hardly up to the standards of psychiatric hospitals of today. A favored treatment in the 1860s was the Water Cure, where a patient would be immersed naked in a tub of icy water and then taken to a tub of scalding water. And there was more horror. Female patients, like Mary, received a cold water douche, administered with a hose and then wet sheets were wrapped tightly around them to squeeze the blood vessels shut. This was followed by vigorous rubbing to restore circulation. These treatments were administered several times each week. Not surprisingly, such techniques brought little success and most patients never improved. Mental hospitals at that time were merely cages to store the insane and it would be some years to come before any real progress was made in mental health care. Like most others, Mary showed no improvement and soon died.

At the time of Mary Roff's death, Lurancy Vennum was a little more than one year old. In just over a decade, their lives would be forever connected in a case that remains today one of the strangest, and most authentic, cases of possession ever recorded. Lurancy Vennum had been born on April 16, 1864 and she and her family had moved to Watseka when she was seven years old. Since they arrived long after Mary Roff's death, the Vennum family knew nothing of her strange illness, nor did they know the Roff family, other than to speak to them on the streets of the small town.

Then on July 11, 1877, a series of strange events would begin. On that morning, Lurancy complained to her mother about feeling sick and then collapsed onto the floor, passed out cold. She stayed in a deep, catatonic sleep for the next five hours but when she awoke, she seemed fine. But this was only the beginning. The next day, Lurancy once again slipped off into the trance-like sleep but this time was different, as she began speaking aloud of visions and spirits. In her trance, she told her family that she was in heaven and that she could see and hear spirits, including the spirit of her brother, who had died in 1874.

From that day on, the trances began to occur more and more frequently and would sometimes last for up to eight hours. While she was asleep, Lurancy continued to speak about her visions, which were sometimes terrifying. She claimed that spirits were chasing her through the house and shouting her name. The attacks occurred up to a dozen times each day and as they continued, Lurancy began to speak in other languages, or nonsense words that no one could understand. When she awoke, she would remember nothing of her trance or of her strange ramblings.

The stories and rumors about Lurancy and her visions began to circulate in Watseka. People were certainly talking and even the local newspaper printed stories about her. No one followed the case more closely than Asa Roff, the father of Mary Roff. In the early stages of Mary's illness, she too had claimed to communicate with spirits and would fall into long trances without warning. He was sure that Lurancy Vennum was suffering from the same illness as his poor daughter. But Roff said nothing until the Vennum family exhausted every known cure for Lurancy. It was not until the local doctor and a minister suggested that the girl be sent to the State Mental Hospital that Roff got involved. He refused to see another young woman end up in the hands of the doctors who had so tortured his Mary.

On January 31, 1878, he contacted the Vennum family. They were naturally skeptical of his story but he did persuade them to let him bring a Dr. E. Winchester Stevens to the house. Stevens, like Asa Roff, was a dedicated Spiritualist and the two men had become convinced that Lurancy was not insane. They believed that Lurancy was actually a vessel through which the dead were communicating. Roff only wished that he had seen the same evidence in his own daughter years before.

The Vennum's allowed Dr. Stevens to "mesmerize" the girl and try to contact the spirits through her. Within moments, Lurancy was speaking in another voice, which allegedly came from a spirit named Katrina Hogan. Then, the spirit changed and claimed to be that of Willie Canning, a young man who had committed suicide. She spoke as Willie for over an hour and then suddenly, she threw her arms into the air and fell over backward. Dr. Stevens took her hands and soon Lurancy calmed and gained control of her body again. She was now in heaven and would allow a gentler spirit to control her. She said the spirit's name was Mary Roff.

The trance continued on into the next day and by this time Lurancy apparently was Mary Roff. She said that she wanted to leave the Vennum house, which was unfamiliar to her, and go home to the Roff house. When Mrs. Roff heard the news, she hurried to the Vennum house in the company of her married daughter, Minerva Alter. The two women came up the sidewalk and saw Lurancy sitting by the window. "Here comes Ma and Nervie," she reportedly said and ran up to hug the two surprised women. No one had called Minerva by the name Nervie since Mary's death in 1865.

It now seemed evident to everyone involved that Mary had taken control of Lurancy Vennum. Although she looked the same, she knew everything about the Roff family and treated them as her loved ones. The Vennums, on the other hand, although treated very courteously, were seen with a distant politeness. It was as if their own daughter only knew them as friendly strangers.

On February 11, Lurancy, or rather Mary, was allowed to go home with the Roffs. Mr. and Mrs. Vennum agreed that it would be for the best, although they desperately hoped that Lurancy would regain her true identity. The Roffs however, saw this as a miracle, as though Mary had returned from the grave. Lurancy was taken across town and as they traveled, they passed by the former Roff home, where they had been living when Mary died. She demanded to know why they were not returning there and they had to explain that they had moved a few years back. Further evidence that Lurancy was now Mary Roff?

For the next several months, Lurancy lived as Mary and seemed to have completely forgotten her former life. She did tell her mother that she would only be with them until "some time in May." As days passed, Lurancy continued to show that she knew more about the Roff family, their possessions and habits, than she could have possibly known if she had been faking the whole thing. Many of the incidents and remembrances that she referred to had taken place years before Lurancy had even been born.

Of course, not everyone in Watseka believed that Mary had taken possession of Lurancy's body and ridiculed the very idea of it. Several of the doctors who had attempted to treat Lurancy started scathing rumors about Dr. Stevens, and the Vennum's pastor pleaded with them to have Lurancy committed. He predicted a time when they would wish that they had followed his advice.

In early May, Lurancy told the Roff family that it was time for her to leave. She became very sad and despondent and would spend the day going from one family member to the next, hugging them and touching them at every opportunity. She wept often at the thought of leaving her real family. Over the next couple of weeks, a battle raged for control of Lurancy's physical body. At one moment, Lurancy would announce that she had to leave and at the next moment, Mary would cling to her father and cry over the idea of leaving him. Finally, on May 21, Lurancy returned home to the Vennums. She displayed none of the strange symptoms of her earlier illness and her parents were convinced that somehow she had been cured, thanks to intervention by the spirit of Mary Roff. She soon became a happy and healthy young woman, suffering no ill effects from her strange experience.

She also remained in touch with the Roff family for the rest of her life. Although she had no memories of her time as Mary, she still felt a curious closeness to them that she could never really explain. During occasional visits to their home, Lurancy would sometimes allow Mary to take control of her so that she could communicate with her family.

Eight years later, when Lurancy turned 18, she married a local farmer named George Binning and two years later, they moved to

Rawlins County, Kansas. They bought a farm there and had 11 children. Lurancy died in the late 1940s while she was in California visiting one of her daughters. Lurancy's parents stayed on in Watseka for many years but after the death of her husband, Lucinda Vennum moved to Kansas to live with Lurancy and her children.

Asa Roff and his wife received hundreds of letters, from believers and skeptics alike, after the story of the possession was printed on the front page of the Watseka newspaper. After a year of constant hounding and scorn from neighbors, they left Watseka and moved to Emporia, Kansas. Seven years later, they returned to Watseka to live with Minerva and her husband. They died of old age and are buried in Watseka.

Dr. Stevens lectured on the Watseka Wonder for eight years before dying in Chicago in 1886, and Mary Roff was never heard from again.

So what really happened in Watseka? To all accounts, Lurancy had the memories and personality of a girl who had been dead for more than twelve years. She knew things about the family that no one could have possibly known. There has been some suggestion that perhaps Lurancy acquired her knowledge of the Roff's to use for her own purposes. A rumor said that she had fallen in love with one of the Roff sons and wanted to be close to the family. This claim was never taken seriously and it seems unlikely that he could have coached her well enough for her to pull off what she did. Others have suggested that Lurancy was psychic and somehow picked up the memories of Mary Roff from the minds of the Roff family themselves. Again, this is also unlikely as Lurancy had never, and would never again, exhibit any signs of psychic powers.

So, what did happen? No one will ever know for sure but it's safe to say that something very strange did occur in Watseka. Although what that something may have been is up to the reader to decide. As for this author, I've begun to think that anything might be possible.

The Riddle of Patience Worth

One of the greatest unsolved mysteries of all time dates back to the year 1913 and the city of St. Louis, Missouri. It was a strange case, wrapped up in the elements of Spiritualism, but so otherwise bizarre that no one really knew what to make of it then—and still can't comprehend it today.

From the start of the movement in the late 1840s, Spiritualists believed that ghosts could communicate through mediums. Those persons passed along messages that were relayed while the mediums were in a trance state. This could be done through a variety of ways, including speech, automatic writing (when the spirit allegedly controlled the writing hand of the medium), or devices like Ouija boards, which spelled out the spirit messages. While most professional mediums contacted the spirit world during seances, dark room sessions where the ghosts supposedly manifested in various ways, many people all over the country began arranging what were called "home circles." These were really just small gatherings of family and friends who attempted to communicate with the spirits on an amateur level. Such sessions usually involved table tipping, where the ghosts would knock or cause a table to tilt in reply to a question, or the Ouija board, which was the most popular.

Ouija, or "talking boards," were wooden trays that had been painted with the letters of the alphabet arranged in two long lines across the board. Below these letters were the numbers 1 through 10 and the words "yes" and "no." According to those who used them, the boards allowed ordinary people to communicate with the spirits as the ghosts were allowed to cause the pointer (planchette) on the board to move about. This occurred when sitters placed their fingertips very lightly on top of it. Allegedly, the ghosts who were present would then work through the sitters to spell out messages. Controversy has raged since the inception of the Ouija board as to whether or not the messages that come from them are real, clever hoaxes, or simply hidden thoughts that are dredged up from the unconscious mind of the sitter. No real consensus on how the Ouija board actually works has ever been reached even to this day. Which is why what happened to a St. Louis housewife in 1913 remains an enigma.

Pearl Curran had little interest in the occult prior to 1913. She was born Pearl Leonore Pollard in Mound City, Illinois in February 1883. She grew up in Texas, playing outdoors and exploring the countryside. Her parents, George and Mary, were easy-going and never really demanded much from Pearl, which probably made her an indifferent student. She left school after the eighth grade and began to study music in Chicago, where her uncle lived. She also played the piano at her uncle's Spiritualist church, where he was a medium. But Pearl and her parents were not Spiritualists and had no interest in the movement at all. Pearl had attended Sunday School as a child but few of the teachings ever stuck with her. She did not attend church and never read the Bible.

In fact, she rarely ever read anything at all. She had enjoyed books like *Black Beauty* and *Little Women* as a child and was always entertained by fairy tales but, thanks to her education, she had little interest in books or writing. Her only creative desires were to learn the piano and perhaps act on stage, but she gave up that idea at age 24 when she married John Curran.

Her marriage was an uneventful as her childhood had been. The Currans were not rich, but they did make a comfortable living. Pearl had a maid to take care of the household chores and she and her husband enjoyed going to restaurants and to the theater. They were a social couple and enjoyed meeting friends and playing cards with neighbors in the evening. They seldom read anything, other than the daily newspaper and some periodicals of the day; they never really had an opportunity to associate with well-educated writers or poets. They were happy and content in their middle-class home with their close friends and acquaintances. Never could they have imagined the changes that were coming to their lives.

In the afternoons, while their husbands were at work, Pearl would often have tea with her mother and a friend who lived nearby, a neighbor named Mrs. Hutchings. It's not clear if the three women had used if before, but it's likely that the Ouija board that was in the house on the afternoon of July 8, 1913 actually belonged to Mrs. Hutchings, who was curious about the contraption. It's likely that Pearl had seen one of the boards before, and had even experimented with it at her uncle's home, but she professed to have no interest in it at all. In fact, she believed that Ouija boards were a boring and silly pastime, having seen the pointer spell out nothing but gibberish.

Then, to the ladies surprise, the message on the board seemed to make sense. "Many moons ago I lived. Again I come. Patience Worth is my name," it spelled out. The three women were startled. They certainly knew no one by that name. Who could Patience Worth have been? Pearl was the most skeptical that the dead could make contact by way of a wooden board. However, at her friend's urging, she asked the sender of the message to tell them something about herself. Replies to her queries began to come through the message board and were recorded by Pearl's mother. According to the spirit who called herself Patience Worth, she had lived in Dorsetshire, England in either 1649 or 1694 (the pointer included both dates) but even that information was difficult to obtain. Patience spoke in an archaic fashion, using words like "thee" and "thou" and sometimes refusing to answer their questions directly. When Mrs. Hutchings pushed for more information, the spirit first replied by saying "About me ye would know much. Yesterday is dead. Let thy mind rest as to the past." Eventually, the ladies would learn that Patience claimed to come to America, where she was murdered by Indians.

The initial contact with Patience Worth came through the Ouija board when Pearl and Mrs. Hutchings controlled it. But it was soon evident that Pearl was mainly responsible for the contact, for no matter who sat with her, the messages from Patience would come. The messages continued to be very strange in that whoever was speaking had an extensive knowledge of not only 17th century vernacular but of clothing, mechanical items, musical instruments and household articles of the period. "A good wife keepeth the floor well sanded and rushes in plenty to burn. The pewter should reflect the fire's bright glow," said one message from the Ouija board, "but in thy day housewifery is a sorry trade."

Pearl was fascinated with the messages that they were receiving and began devoting more and more time to the Ouija board. Eventually, the messages began coming so fast that no one could write them down and Pearl suddenly realized that she didn't need the board anymore. The sentences were forming in her mind at the same time they were being spelled out on the board. She began to dictate the replies and messages from Patience to anyone who would write them. She would first employ a secretary, but later Pearl would record the words herself, using first a pencil and then a typewriter. For the next 25 years, Patience Worth dictated a total of about 400,000 words. Her works were vast and consisted of not only her personal messages, but creative writings as well. She passed along nearly 5,000 poems, a play, many short works and several novels that were published to critical acclaim.

Shortly after Patience made her presence known, the Curran house in south St. Louis began to overflow with friends, neighbors and curiosity-seekers. When word reached the press, Casper Yost, the Sunday editor of the *St. Louis Post-Dispatch*, began publishing articles about Pearl Curran and the mysterious spirit who seemed to be dictating to her. In 1915, he even published a book called *Patience Worth, A Psychic Mystery* and the housewife from St. Louis became a national celebrity.

People came from all over and the Currans, always gracious and unpretentious, welcomed visitors who wanted to witness the automatic writings sessions where Pearl received information from Patience Worth. Authorities in the field of psychic investigation came, as well as people from all over the country who had begun to read and admire the writings attributed to Patience. The Currans never charged any admission to the house and all the writing sessions were conducted with openness and candor. There were no trappings of Spiritualism here with darkened rooms and candles. Pearl would usually just sit in a brightly lit room with her notebook or typewriter and when the messages began to come to her, she would begin to write.

In addition to the stories and novels, Patience produced thousands of poems through Pearl Curran. One of her unusual abilities was to present poems that would suit any topics suggested by the company present. On January 12, 1926, at Straus's Studio in St. Louis, during a meeting of the Current Topics Club, suggestions were made by some of the members and Patience composed two poems called "Lavender and Lace" and "Gibraltar." Each poem was presented with no noticeable delay and without change of word. Neither poem had ever been produced before. The famous poet, Edgar Lee Masters, was asked if anyone could actually write poetry that way, instantly and to topics suggested by a group, and he replied, "There is only one answer to that—it simply can't be done!"

Not surprisingly, many questioned the reality of the spectral Patience Worth. Witnesses were hard put to get Patience to offer much detail about her past. She seemed to think that her origins were unimportant; however she did mention landmarks and scenery around her former home in England. The newspaperman Casper Yost, who was one of the spirit's greatest defenders, took a trip abroad during the height of the phenomenon and, when he reached Patience's alleged home in Dorset he did find the cliffs, old buildings, a monastery and scenery just as Patience had described it. And while this is interesting, it is hardly proof.

Perhaps the most convincing evidence that Patience Worth was not the conscious or unconscious creation of Pearl Curran is the material that she dictated for her books and stories. Patience seemed to be able to pass between old English dialects at will or could write in a semblance of modern English, as she did with most of her poetry.

The Story of Telka was one of her novels and it is a poetic drama of medieval life in rural England, written mostly in Anglo-Saxon words. It was composed during a series of sittings and as with other Patience Worth dictations, there were no revisions and no breaks where sentences left off and began again. The only comparable work to this novel is the Wickcliffe's Bible of the 14th Century, which is also composed of almost pure Anglo-Saxon. However, the language in The Story of Telka does not resemble the language in this particular Bible. In the novel, there are few words that the modern reader cannot understand, as if the desire by the writer was to create something that seemed old but could still be comprehended. Many argued that it would be impossible for a person living in turn-of-the-century St. Louis to create such a dramatic work and then limit the vocabulary in the work to only easily understood words in an ancient form of their own language.

And this was far from Patience's only book. The Sorry Tale was a lengthy novel that was set in the time of Christ; in it, the author brought to life the Jews, Romans, Greeks and Arabs of the period. The book was also filled with an accurate knowledge of the political, social and religious conditions of the time. Critics hailed it as a masterpiece. It had been started on July 14, 1915 and two or three evenings a week were given over to the story until it was completed. The tale proceeded as fast as John Curran could take it down in abbreviated longhand and as long as Pearl was physically able to receive it. Professor W.T. Allison of the English Department of the University of Manitoba stated that "No book outside of the Bible gives such and intimate picture of the earthly life of Jesus and no book has ever thrown such a clear light upon the manner of life of Jews and Romans in the Palestine of the day of our Lord." At the same time that The Sorry Tale was being produced, The Merry Tale was started as a relief from the sadness of the previous book. For a time, work was done on both novels during a single evening.

When the first words of the next book, Hope Trueblood,

appeared, the sitters gathered at the Curran home were astonished. For the first time since Patience Worth's arrival, then four years before, the material was in plain English. Her previous stories had dealt with ancient Rome, Palestine and Medieval England. This book told the story of a young girl's effort to find her family in Victorian England. When the book appeared in Great Britain, no clues were given as to its mysterious origins and reviewers accepted it as the work of a new and promising British author. Once critic stated that "the story is marked by strong individuality, and we should look with interest for further products of this author's pen."

While critics were impressed with the works she produced, those who witnessed Pearl taking dictation from the spirit were even more astounded. For instance, *The Story of Telka*, which came in at over 70,000 words, was written over several sessions but was completed in just 35 hours. This type of speed was fairly typical. Once, in a single evening, 32 poems were delivered, along with several short stories. Sometimes, in the course in one evening, Patience dictated portions of four novels, always resuming the work on each one at the same place she left off. Pearl took down all of the words, usually in the presence of a number of witnesses, and never made any revisions.

Those who came to investigate the strange events often made requests of Patience in order to test her. She never hesitated to respond to questions or tasks they put to her. When asked to compose a poem on a certain subject, she would deliver the stanzas so quickly that they had to be taken down in shorthand. Weeks later, when asked to reproduce the poem, she could do so without any changes or errors. One night, author and psychic investigator Walter Franklin Prince, who was a regular visitor to the Curran house, posed an unusual task for Patience. Could she deliver a poem about the "folly of being an atheist" while simultaneously producing a dialogue that might take place between a wench and a jester at a medieval-era fair? He asked that she alternate the dialogue every two or three lines. Not only could Patience accomplish this, but she did it so quickly that dictation was given to Pearl within eight seconds after the request was made. When she finished, Pearl stated that she felt as if her head had been placed in a steel vise.

It should come as no surprise to learn that Pearl Curran's life was permanently changed by the arrival of Patience Worth. While the alliance was undoubtedly a wondrous affair, as Pearl often stated, it also demanded a lot from her, both physically and mentally. She never allowed herself to become obsessed with Patience either and the Currans never attempted to exploit the partnership for material gain. Pearl continued, with the help of her maid, to do all her own shopping, cooking and housework and she continued to visit with friends as she had always done. Two or three nights each week were set aside for writing sessions and Patience always dictated to Pearl, no matter how many people were in the house. She only stopped when frightened by loud or sudden noises or when Pearl halted to converse with the guests.

Pearl explained that as the words flowed into her head, she would feel a pressure and then scenes and images would appear to her. She would see the details of each scene. If two characters were talking along a road, she would see the roadway, the grass on both side of it and perhaps the landscape in the distance. If they spoke a foreign language, she would hear them speaking but above them, she would hear the voice of Patience as she interpreted the speech and indicated what part of the dialogue she wanted in the story. She would sometimes even see herself in the scenes, standing as an onlooker or moving between the characters. The experience was so sharp and so vivid that she became familiar with things that she could have never known about living in St. Louis. These items included lamps, jugs and cooking utensils used long ago in distant countries, types of clothing and jewelry worn by people in other times, and the sounds and smells of places that she had never even heard of before.

On once occasion, Pearl was shown a small yellow bird sitting on a hedge. Patience wished to include it in a poem, but Pearl had no idea what type of bird it was. Finally, Patience became frustrated and said, "He who knoweth the hedgerows knoweth the yellow-hammer." Pearl and her husband later consulted an old encyclopedia and saw that the yellow-hammer in her vision was not a type seen in America, but only in England.

In spite of the visions, Pearl never went into a trance during the writing sessions. She understood the writing as it came and while calling out the words to the stenographer, she would smoke cigarettes, drink coffee, and eat. She seemed always to be aware of her surroundings, no matter what else might be going on with her.

As time passed, Pearl was not completely satisfied with the literary reputation that was being achieved by Patience Worth. She became determined to take up writing herself, even though she had never written anything before and had never had the urge to do so. Unfortunately, her writings reflected her lack of education and talent. She wound up selling two of her stories to the *Saturday Evening Post*, but likely more for her fame as a conduit for Patience than for her own literary ability.

Patience was tolerant but condescending of her host's abilities, which may have been what prompted the love-hate relationship between them. Patience often scorned Pearl, but never failed to show her kindness. She simply seemed to think that her human counterpart was slightly stupid and that only by perseverance was she able to make herself known, especially when Pearl failed to grasp the spellings and meanings of certain words. But they plodded on together, continuing to amass a great body of work until about 1922. In this year, the connection between the two of them began to deteriorate, possibly due to changes in Pearl's life and the fact that she had become pregnant for the first time at age 39. After her husband and her mother both died, the contact between Patience and Pearl became less and less frequent, and eventually it died away.

By this time too, public interest in the mystery had faded, especially as no solution had ever been posed as to how the St. Louis housewife was accomplishing such remarkable feats. After the publication of several books and hundreds of poems, interest in

Patience Worth vanished and cynicism replaced it. Debunkers accused Pearl of hiding her literary talent in order to exploit it in such a bizarre way and become famous. However, exhaustive studies have shown this to be highly unlikely, if not impossible. Scholars have analyzed Patience's works and have found them too accurate in historical detail and written in such a way that only someone with an intimate knowledge of the time could have created them.

Pearl Curran died in California on December 4, 1937. The *St. Louis Globe-Democrat* headlined her obituary with the words: "Patience Worth is Dead." And whatever the secret of the mysterious ghost writer, it went to the grave with her. So, what really happened in this case and why does it remain today as one of our great unsolved mysteries? Was there actually an entity speaking to Pearl from beyond the grave? Or could the writings have simply come from her unconscious mind?

No verification was ever made that Patience Worth actually lived in the 1600s and yet experts who studied Pearl Curran doubted that she could have produced the works attributed to the ghost on her own. She was a woman of limited education with no knowledge of the language used or the history and subject matter that was written of by the alleged Patience Worth. Pearl simply could not have created the works of literary quality that have become known as the works of her spiritual counterpart.

Was Patience Worth a secondary personality of Pearl Curran? This too seems unlikely because on the rare occasions when secondary (or split) personalities have been documented, they have always been shown to supplant the main personality for a time. This was not true in Pearl's case. Her own personality co-existed with that of Patience Worth and Pearl was well aware of this fact.

So, what was it? Was it a true case of afterlife communication or the greatest hoax ever perpetrated on both the literary and paranormal communities? It's unlikely that we will ever know for sure, but in the absence of any other explanation, this one will have to be filed under unexplained.

Spiritualism's Greatest Mystery?

According to newspaper and Spiritualist accounts of 1874, some very strange things were happening on a small Vermont farm near the town of Chittenden. Allegedly, all manner of bizarre phenomena were said to be taking place in the home of William and Horatio Eddy, two middle-aged, illiterate brothers, and their sister Mary. The Eddys lived in an unkempt, two-story building that was reported to be infested with supernatural beings of such numbers that had never been reported before, or since. The events at the farm were said to be so powerful and so strange that people came from all over the world to witness them. Spiritualists began calling Chittenden the "Spirit Capital of the Universe."

Needless to say, not everyone was convinced of the legitimacy of the reported events on the Eddy farm. Once such man was a successful attorney named Henry Steel Olcott. Prior to hearing of the Eddy brothers, Olcott had no interest whatever in the burgeoning Spiritualist movement. However, one day as he returned to his office from lunch, he picked up a copy of the Spiritualist newspaper, the *Banner of Light*. In the paper, he read a graphic account of the strange happenings that were being reported in Chittenden, Vermont. It's unlikely at that time that Olcott had any idea how a simple newspaper article was going to change his life.

It is important that we establish the fact that Henry Olcott was not connected in any way to the Spiritualist movement, nor was he a proponent of the paranormal. What might have prompted him to pick up a copy of the *Banner of Light* that day is unknown. Olcott was born in New Jersey in 1832 and attended college in New York City, studying agricultural science. While still in his early 20s, he received international recognition for his work on a model farm and for founding a school for agriculture students. During this same time, he published three scientific works. He went on to become the farm editor for Horace Greeley's newspaper, the *New York Tribune*.

When the Civil War broke out, Olcott enlisted in the Union Army. He was appointed as a special investigator to root out corruption and fraud in military arsenals and shipyards. He was soon promoted to the rank of Colonel and, after the war, was part of a three-person panel that investigated the assassination of President Lincoln. After the war, Olcott studied law and became a wealthy and successful attorney.

So how would an agriculturist and military investigator go on to become one of the first American psychic researchers? After buying a copy of the Spiritualist newspaper, Olcott read with interest the reports from the Eddy farm. Although skeptical, he knew that if the stories were true, "this was the most important fact in modern physical science," he later wrote. A short time after first reading the story, Colonel Olcott traveled to Vermont, accompanied by a newspaper artist named Alfred Kappes. Together, they planned to investigate the strange events at the Eddy farm and if the stories were a hoax, they would expose the Eddy brothers in the *Daily Graphic* newspaper as nothing but charlatans. If the Eddys were true mediums, Olcott would announce the validity of Spiritualism to the world. In either event, Olcott was determined to be fair and open-minded in his judgments.

Olcott and Kappes traveled to the secluded town of Chittenden, located within the Green Mountains. The trip out to the farm was uneventful, but the first meeting with the Eddy brothers was anything but ordinary. The two distant and unfriendly farmers were rough-hewn characters with dark hair and eyes, and New England accents so thick the New York attorney and writer could scarcely understand them.

Olcott would later learn that the brothers were descended from a long line of psychics. Mary Bradley, a distant relative, had been convicted of witchcraft at Salem in 1692. She had escaped the village with the help of friends. Their own grandmother had been blessed with the gift of "second sight" and often went into trances, speaking to entities that no one else could see. Their mother, Julia, had been known for frightening her neighbors with predictions and visions although her husband, Zepaniah, condemned her powers as the work of the Devil. Julia quickly learned to hide her gifts from the cruel and abusive man.

However, the supernatural could not be hidden once the couple began having children. Strange poundings began shaking the house, disembodied voices were heard in empty rooms, and occasionally, the children even vanished from their cribs. They were likely to be discovered anywhere in the house and even outside. As William and Horatio got older, their strange powers strengthened. On many occasions, Zepaniah would see the boys playing with unfamiliar children, who would vanish whenever he approached. When these visitors vanished, he would take his boys to the barn and beat them with a rawhide whip as punishment. The strange children returned again and again, earning the young Eddy boys countless beatings. Eventually, they would grow to both fear and hate their father.

The boys soon learned they were unable to attend school. Their initial attempts were marked by inexplicable happenings and disturbances, as invisible hands threw books, levitated desks and caused objects like rulers, inkwells and slates to fly about the room. Zepaniah tried everything he could to stop the disturbances, although this mostly consisted of him beating and abusing the youngsters. But, the strange events continued. When he realized that he couldn't stop the weird antics, he grew furious. Each time the boys fell into a trance, he would berate and verbally abuse them. He would try to rouse them by pinching and slapping them until they were black and blue. Once, on the advice of a sympathetic Christian friend, he doused the boys with boiling water. When this didn't work, he also allowed this friend to drop a red-hot coal into William's hand. He had hoped to "exorcize his devils." The boy never awakened from his trance, but he bore a scar on his palm for the rest of his life.

On occasion, the spirits would attempt to defend the boys, appearing in front of Zepaniah and scaring him from the house.

Needless to say, these eerie and frustrating happenings were more than the man could stand. So, tiring of the boys but realizing their moneymaking potential, he sold the Eddy brothers to a traveling showman, who for the next 14 years took them all over America, Canada and Europe. As part of the performance, he would challenge audience members to try and awaken the boys from their trances. These audiences made their father's abuse look tame. The Eddys were locked into small wooden boxes to see if they could escape and hot wax was poured into their mouths to see if they could produce "spirit voices" when they were unable to talk. The skeptics poked, prodded, and punched the sleeping brothers, leaving them scarred and damaged for the rest of their lives. On several occasions, they were even stoned and shot at by angry mobs. William Eddy bore a number of bullet scars on his body. According to writer John Mason, "They were mobbed in Lynn, Massachusetts and stoned at South Danvers. On a second trip to Danvers they were shot at. They were ridden on a rail out of Cleveland and barely escaped a coat of tar and feathers." Only after their father died were the boys able to return home. They moved onto the family farm with their sister Mary and opened the house as a modest inn called the Green Tavern.

These things were all learned later. On his arrival, Olcott was only able to gain a first impression of the belligerent and unfriendly men. They were certainly not the deceitful con men he had expected. So, what were they?

On Olcott's first day at the farm, he was witness to an outdoor seance. In the bright moonlight of a warm summer evening, a group of ten participants traveled down a path and into a deep ravine. They assembled in front of a natural cave, formed by two large stones that had collapsed atop one another, forming a large arch. Olcott later learned that it was called "Honto's Cave," in honor of the Native American spirit who often appeared there. Olcott suspiciously investigated the cave and saw that no exit could be found at the back of the rocks. He determined there was no way that anyone could slip in or out of the cave without being seen.

Horatio Eddy acted as the medium for the seance. He sat on a camp stool under the arch and then was draped in a makeshift "spirit cabinet" formed by shawls and branches that had been cut from small saplings. As Horatio rested there, a gigantic man, dressed as a Native American, emerged from the darkness of the cave. While the medium addressed this spirit, someone cried out and pointed up toward the top of the cave. Standing there, silhouetted against the moon, was another gigantic Indian. To the right, another spectral female had materialized on a ledge. In all, ten such figures appeared during the seance. The last, the spirit of William White, the late editor of a Spiritualist newspaper, emerged from within Horatio's cabinet. He was dressed in a black suit and white shirt was supposedly recognizable to some who had read the newspaper and recognized his picture from it. He vanished at the same time the others did. Moments later, Horatio appeared from the cabinet and signaled that the seance was at an end. After the bizarre display was over, Olcott and Kappes carefully searched the cave and the surrounding area for footprints in the soft earth. They found no trace that anyone had been there.

Olcott found the seance to be convincing but was sure that he would be able to more easily detect fraud within the controlled setting of the Eddy house. He and Kappes thoroughly examined the large circle room, which was located on the second floor of the farmhouse. He drew maps, charts and diagrams and took numerous measurements, sure that he would find false panels, secret doors or hidden passages. However, he found nothing out of the ordinary. He was determined not to give up though and he convinced the newspaper to hire men to come to Chittenden and examine the place. Using carpenters and engineers as consultants, another thorough search was conducted. The experts also found nothing strange. After this, Olcott and Kappes were finally convinced that the walls and floors were as solid as they seemed. Because of this, what Olcott witnessed during the nights that followed became even stranger.

Each seance was basically the same. On every night of the week, except for Sunday, visitors would assemble on wooden benches in the seance room. A platform, which had been assembled there, was lit only by a kerosene lamp, recessed in a barrel. William Eddy, who acted as the primary medium, mounted the platform and entered a small cabinet. A few moments later, soft voices began to whisper in the distance. Often, it would be singing, accompanied by spectral music. Musical instruments came to life and soared above the heads of the audience members, disembodied hands appeared, waving and touching the spectators and odd lights and unexplained noises filled the air. Then, the first spirit form emerged from the cabinet. They came one at a time, or in groups, numbering as many as 20 or 30 in an evening. Some were completely visible and seemed solid. Others were transparent and ethereal. Regardless, they awed the frightened spectators. The spirits ranged in size from over six feet to very small (it's worth noting here that William Eddy was only five feet, nine inches tall). Most of the ghostly apparitions were elderly Yankees or Native Americans but many other races and nationalities also appeared in costume—Africans, Russians, Asians and more.

Where had they come from? Olcott had examined the spirit cabinet and platform and had found no trap doors, nor hidden passages. In fact, there was no room in the cabinet for anyone other than the medium himself. Olcott was familiar with the workings of stage magicians and fraudulent mediums, but could find none of their tricks present at the Eddy house. The apparitions not only appeared but also performed, sang and chatted with the sitters. They also produced spirit articles like musical instruments, clothing and scarves. In all, nearly every type of supernatural phenomena was reported at the Eddy farmhouse. These included rappings, moving physical objects, spirit paintings, automatic writing, prophecy, speaking in tongues, healings, unseen voices, levitation, remote visions, teleportation and more. And of course, the full-bodied manifestations of which Olcott observed more than 400 during the weeks he visited the house. He concluded that a show like that which he had seen would have required an entire company of actors and several trunks of costumes.

Yet, Olcott's inspection of the premises revealed no place to hide either actors or props. The idea of stage actors was further dispelled by the convincing manner of the spirits. One woman spoke, in Russian, to the alleged spirit of her deceased husband. A number of other dialects were also heard. How was this possible when the Eddys could barely read and write, and were scarcely capable of speaking coherent English? In addition, such an elaborate show would have cost a fortune to produce each night. They would have had to pay actors, invest in costumes and hire someone to create the marvels of the spirits. This would have been impossible given that the brothers were almost penniless. Most of the visitors who came to the farm did not pay and the rest only gave $8 per week for room and board at the inn. No admission was ever charged for the seances. In Olcott's mind, fraud would have been physically and financially impossible.

The investigator's ten-week stay on the Eddy farm was surely a test of endurance. He left disliking the house, the food, the weather, and the Eddy brothers. However, he was also convinced of the fact that the two men could make contact with the dead.

Not only did Colonel Olcott chronicle his visit in the newspaper, but he also wrote a massive book called *People from Other Worlds*. The book, over 500 pages long, is full of precise drawings of the apparitions, the grounds, the house and even detailed plans of its construction, proving that no hidden passages existed. He also recorded over 400 different supernatural beings and collected hundreds of affidavits and scores of eyewitness testimony to the amazing events. He also reproduced dozens of statements from respected tradesmen and carpenters who had examined the house for trickery. A modern reader would have to look very hard to discover anything that Olcott did not investigate.

Eventually, the Eddy brothers and sister Mary went their separate ways. Their bickering and feuding had driven them apart.

Horatio moved out and took a house across the road, where he took up light gardening, occasional seances and doing magic tricks for local children. Mary moved to the nearby village of East Pittsford, where she became a full-time professional medium. William dropped out of public life altogether and became a bitter recluse on the family farm. The first of the Eddys to die was Horatio on September 8, 1922. William lived for another 10 years. He never married and refused to ever participate in Spiritualism again. He died on October 25, 1932 at the age of 99. If either of the men had any secrets about the weird events at their home, they took the secrets with them to the grave.

So, what really happened on the Eddy farm in Chittenden, Vermont? The credentials of Colonel Olcott prohibit us from dismissing the story out of hand. His extensive documentation, along with his investigative skills, suggests that the events were not part of a hoax. Olcott remained skeptical and analytical throughout his ten-week stay at the farm, and yet he came away convinced that the Eddys had the power to contact and communicate with the dead.

Colonel Olcott came away from Chittenden a believer. So whatever you choose to believe, it cannot be denied that something amazing and mysterious occurred in Chittenden in 1874 although what this may have been, we may never know for sure.

A MAGICIAN AMONG THE SPIRITS

Houdini and the Other Side

Harry Houdini is still considered today as one of the greatest illusionists and magicians in history. In addition to his fantastic escapes and stunts, he was also well known in the 1920s for his debunking of fraudulent Spiritualist mediums. In this, modern information about Houdini tends to be skewed. Today, many skeptic organizations have claimed Houdini as one of their own, but this is far from the truth. Unlike these groups, Houdini did not start out attacking fake mediums because he did not believe in the supernatural. In fact, he had gone to them in an attempt to try and contact his dead mother, but found that the mediums he met were often frauds. This was when he turned to exposing them, still searching for the truth. Before his death, Houdini stated that should it be possible to contact the living from the other side, he would do so. The question remains as to whether or not he actually succeeded.

Houdini was born in Budapest, Hungary on March 24, 1874 but grew up as Erich Weiss in the small Wisconsin town of Appleton. Later, his father, Rabbi Meyer Samuel Weiss, moved the family to Milwaukee and he took over a Jewish congregation there. At about this same time, Erich became interested in magic and stage performing. Legend has it that he was apprenticed to a locksmith, where he learned to assemble and take apart locks with his eyes closed. If this part of the story is true, it was a skill that served him well later in life.

Erich was determined to become a professional magician and later began appearing in New York beer halls and theaters, taking the name of Houdini, which was based on the name of Robert Houdin, a famous French magician. He played traveling shows and theaters for several years, meeting his wife, Bess, while performing at Coney Island. He employed a variety of new and strange stunts in his act and devised incredible escapes that had never been attempted before. He became known as the "Handcuff King," due to the ease from which he escaped any restraints. Soon, his escapes became more daring and he allowed police officers and various officials in the cities where he played to design their own challenges for him as a publicity stunt. Houdini never failed.

It was not long before the enigmatic showman became both an American and worldwide sensation, performing to sold-out crowds. He became an expert in the field of magic and even today, magicians and scholars have no idea as to the extent of his secrets of magic, or how many of his stunts were performed. Houdini's many journals and notes remained in the possession of his brother after his death and were destroyed when his brother died.

But Houdini was as troubled as he was famous. He was obsessed with the death of his mother, having been almost unnaturally close to her during her lifetime. After she died, he was observed many times at the cemetery where she was buried, lying face down on her grave and holding long conversations with her. He felt that he had to communicate with her and he turned to Spiritualism.

In a short time, Houdini's visits to the Spiritualists revealed a number of fake mediums who were using poor stage magic and trying to pass the tricks off as the work of the spirits. He claimed that he could duplicate the tricks on stage and it was not long before his efforts to reach his mother became secondary to his need to expose the fraudulent mediums. He quickly became very bitter and willing to believe that all of the mediums were fakes. He began investigating their methods and claims and became a self-appointed crusader against them.

In 1920, during a tour of England, Houdini met Sir Arthur Conan Doyle, the creator of Sherlock Holmes and a spokesperson for Spiritualism. The two of them became good friends, despite their opposing views on the supernatural. Houdini was delighted to learn that there was at least one intelligent person who believed in Spiritualism. Conan Doyle was convinced of the value of the movement to the world and had given up most of his lucrative writing career to lecture about Spiritualism around the world. He also found that Houdini's knowledge of the spirit world was as vast as his own, although their attitudes differed.

Houdini continued to regularly attend seances, in an attempt to communicate with his mother and also to expose the frauds who continued to prey on the public. Sir Arthur Conan Doyle was an occasional guest at these events but their friendship was soon to end amid accusations of mistrust and deceit. The two men met up again in Atlantic City in 1922 and there, Lady Jean Doyle, who was said to be a medium, went into a trance and produced an emotional letter to Houdini from his mother, using her gift of automatic writing. Houdini was originally said to have been amazed by the message but later dismissed it as false, stating that he believed Sir Arthur and Lady Jean were good people, but they had been misled by their contact with the Spiritualist movement. He did not believe they had deliberately tried to deceive him but he thought they were deceiving themselves with their own gullibility.

The rift between the two men, which began with this event, deepened shortly afterward when Conan Doyle and other Spiritualists began stating that Houdini's exposure of mediums was simply to cover the fact that he was a medium himself. They claimed that many of his extraordinary escapes were actually done by Houdini dematerializing from the traps. "This ability," Doyle stated publicly, "to unbolt locked doors is undoubtedly due to Houdini's mediumistic powers and not to any normal operation of the lock. The effort necessary to shoot a bolt from within a lock is drawn from Houdini the medium, but it must not be thought that this is the only means by which he can escape from his prison. For at times, his body can be...dematerialized and withdrawn."

Now, Houdini was placed in the classic magician's "catch" position, meaning that he could only go so far in denying the Spiritualist claims. By going any further than he had, he would have to expose how his escapes were accomplished, which he could never do. His reply was simply that all of his escapes were managed by purely physical means. He stated that his crusade against Spiritualism was simply a way to protect the general public from charlatans but he, however, was able to keep an open mind on the subject and did not assume that all mediums were frauds. Spiritualist leaders declared that Houdini's actions did not agree with his words and so the magician made a pact with a number of friends. The pact promised that whichever of them died first, he should make every attempt to contact the others by way of a secret code.

But Houdini still could not escape the claims being made by Doyle, so he devised a plan to make the author realize that all of his tricks were just that—tricks. He assured Doyle that he would give him proof that magic was accomplished through simple trickery. Three persons were present at the test: Houdini, Doyle and Bernard Ernst, the president of the American Society of Magicians. A slate was hung in the center of the room by Doyle, and he was given five plain cork balls to examine. He chose one of the balls at random and placed it in a container of white paint. Doyle was then given a piece of paper and was told to walk anywhere that he wanted and then write a message on the paper. Doyle left the house, walked three blocks away and then turned a corner. He shielded the paper with his hand and wrote down a short message. Meanwhile, Ernst stayed in the room with Houdini to insure that the other magician remained in the room. When he finished writing, Conan Doyle folded the paper carefully and placed it in his pocket. He then returned to the house. Houdini then told Doyle to pick up the paint-soaked ball and stick it on the suspended slate. The ball then inexplicably began to roll over the surface of the slate and it spelled out the biblical phrase, *Mene Mene Tekel Upharsin*—the exact words that Doyle had written on the paper.

Houdini claimed that it was all done by simple trickery but Doyle was more convinced than ever of his former friend's supernatural powers. Ernst begged Houdini to explain how the trick worked, either to himself or Doyle, in the strictest confidence, but Houdini refused. Strangely, he would never use the trick again in any of his shows and no one has ever been able to reproduce it. At that time, Bernard Ernst admitted that the trick reminded him of a certain mind-reading stunt that Houdini had stopped using because, as it was explained to Ernst, it was "too spooky."

Despite the private death pact that Houdini had made with his friends, he continued to debunk the mediums in his stage shows and through articles and books, showing how so-called "spirit forms" like ectoplasm"could easily be created by the clever stage magician. But not all of the things he witnessed during his psychic investigations was he so sure could be debunked. He kept vast files and records of his investigations and, when he died, these reports came into the possession of Joseph Dunninger, Houdini's friend and fellow conjurer.

In the wealth of material, there was a record of one case that baffled Houdini. His handwritten record of it was contained in the files, dated in Los Angeles on April 11, 1923. The case centered on Mrs. Mary Fairfield McVickers who, before she died, requested that photographs be taken of her body at 5:00 on the afternoon of her funeral. According to reports, she claimed that she would appear in spirit form at that time. Mrs. McVickers made this unusual pronouncement on the occasion of her 73rd birthday in July 1922. She told her friends at the First Spiritualist Temple of Los Angeles, where she was a member, that she had experienced a vision of her approaching death. "I feel that if a picture is taken over my body about 5:00 pm on the day of my funeral," she told those present at the gathering, "I will be able to appear in spirit form." Mrs. McVickers died the following April, and a friend, Albert H. Hetzel, contacted Houdini about the woman's request. Houdini was intrigued and so he got in touch with a friend and movie producer named Larry Semon about borrowing a cameraman.

On the afternoon of the funeral, Nathan B. Moss, who worked for Keystone Press Illustration Service in Hollywood, arrived with his camera and plate holders loaded with 14 negatives. Houdini had not told the man what they would be photographing, and he and Moss went to a place called Howland and Dewey. Houdini wrote that Moss "had no idea what I wanted but was under the impression that I was going to do a stunt and wanted a stunt picture. I told him that I wanted him to reload his plate holder with brand new plates that I would buy. He, not knowing the importance of the test, derided the fact of my not wanting to use his plates, but I told him that I might have to take an oath that I bought the plates and that therefore it was important."

When they arrived at the camera store, they asked for a dozen 5 x 7 plates and the clerk, Frank Hale, pulled out four packages of 12 each. Mat Korn, a customer in the store and a stranger to

Houdini, was standing nearby and was asked to choose one of the packets. He handed it to the magician, but Houdini noticed that one end of the package was not tightly sealed. He asked for five more packages and he asked another customer, identified as a Mr. Wheeler (a photographer for the *Los Angeles Record* newspaper), to choose a perfect one for him. Houdini purchased the package of plates and he and Moss entered the darkroom on the premises and removed the plates that Moss had already placed in the camera. He replaced them with the brand new plates. A few moments later, they left for the church so that they could arrive just before 5:00.

At the church, the body of Mrs. McVickers had been placed in a white open casket, surrounded by flowers, located at the right of the pulpit. Moss then took ten photographs of the scene; each of them was taken under the same time exposure of three minutes. In addition to Houdini and Moss, the witnesses included Albert Hetzel, J.M. Hall, Virgil Vlasck and Stanley Bruce of the *Los Angeles Examiner*. After the photos were taken, the men left and went immediately to the Keystone Press Illustration office. The plates were immediately developed in Houdini's presence and on one of the plates they noticed a peculiar streak. Houdini wrote that "Mr. Moss made a print from this plate which caused a great deal of talk. Not one photographer could explain how this could be tricked. Mr. Moss offered a hundred dollars to anyone who could produce it under the same conditions, whereas no one could duplicate it." Houdini thought enough of this incident to make a note of it in his personal diary as well. "Took pictures at church," he penned. "A peculiar test."

Dunninger published Houdini's notes in his 1928 brochure *Houdini's Spirit Exposes* and stated that Houdini offered a number of magicians $1,000 if they could duplicate the photo. No one accepted the challenge. The photograph with the mysterious light was the second one taken. The streak was a heavy band of light that started a few inches from the floor and then extended up to about two feet above a five-foot high black screen that had been placed between the open casket and the auditorium. At the upper end of the streak, the light became a diffused, glowing mass of a larger shape than the trail that descended from it. Looking closely at the streak, it has an interesting formation, starting as a sharply defined, broad band and then shifting to make two parallel lines. Just before it turned into a glowing mass, a third lines starts to appear. A number of photographic experts studied the plate but stated that because of the nature of the image, it would have been practically impossible for it to have been caused by a defective plate, plate holder or camera.

Needless to say, a hoax was out of the question—for it certainly would have not helped Houdini's campaign against fraudulent Spiritualists for him to admit that a ghost photograph had been achieved in the church. Even so, he did have the integrity to admit that no satisfactory explanation could be found for the photograph. Joseph Dunninger wrote that Houdini made no attempt to debunk or explain the photograph. "He did not see the light. It made itself only evident on the photograph," said Dunninger. "This report shows that Houdini was willing to believe if the proof was brought before him... and was willing to give credit whenever credit was due."

While Houdini may have been willing to believe in the unexplainable, he was still unwilling to suffer those he considered fools and frauds. In 1923, Houdini joined a panel from *Scientific American* magazine that had offered a reward to any medium who could prove their psychic gifts were genuine. The investigative panel had deadlocked over a medium named Mina Crandon, who used the stage name of Margery. In 1924, they stated that they believed Crandon to be genuine and were prepared to give her the $2,500 reward.

Houdini was shocked and traveled to Boston to witness a seance for himself. What happened next remains shrouded in mystery—although it is clear that Crandon did not trust Houdini and the magician himself had said he was determined to expose the medium as a fraud. During the sessions, Houdini claimed to see Margery performing a number of tricks like making noises with her feet and lifting objects that were said to have moved on their own. In spite of this, he did not expose her publicly and asked that more stringent tests be performed. It was rumored that Margery had somehow outwitted Houdini and rumors flew that perhaps her powers were genuine after all.

The following month, Houdini placed the medium in a wooden box with a hole in the top for her head and holes on each side so that her hands could be held during her entire seance. According to reports from the session, Margery's spirit control, which was her dead brother Walter, took such a dislike to Houdini that the top of the box was allegedly ripped off by an invisible force.

The seance continued the next evening and Margery was placed back in the box. Shortly after she went into her trance and her spirit guide came through, the committee asked that she ring the bell that had been placed in the box with her. Immediately, Walter (the spirit guide) exclaimed that Houdini had done something to the bell so that it would not ring. An examination of the bell revealed that a piece of rubber had been wedged against the clapper so that it would not ring. However, there was no proof that Houdini had tampered with it. Then Walter said that Houdini had placed a ruler inside the box so that he could later accuse Margery of cheating. The ruler too was found and later, Houdini's assistant would say that he had been instructed to place it there in case Houdini could not find another way to prove she was a fraud. It certainly appeared that Houdini had been caught cheating and he was widely discredited, leading many to doubt the integrity of some of his earlier investigations. In this case, the committee scheduled further tests of Mrs. Crandon but they were later cancelled. The decision on Margery's abilities was split and because of this, the money was never awarded.

Houdini quickly recovered from the scandal and went on to continue his work against the Spiritualists until his death on Halloween of 1926. At that time, the curtain fell on the great magician for all time—or did it?

On the night of October 11, a chain slipped during Houdini's famous Underwater Torture escape and fractured his ankle. A doctor in the audience advised him to end the show and go to the hospital but he refused. In fact, he finished the entire performance painfully hopping on one foot. Afterwards, he was ordered to stay off his feet for at least one week, but he continued his shows anyway.

It was the afternoon of October 22 when two students, who had heard Houdini give a lecture the week before, stopped by the magician's dressing room before the evening show. Houdini was very courteous to the young men but was also occupied with his mail. He wasn't paying close attention when one of the boys asked if it was true that Houdini could withstand powerful blows to the stomach. He absently replied that he could if he had time to brace himself in anticipation of the punch. The boy, thinking that Houdini had given permission for such a demonstration, suddenly leaned forward and struck him sharply in the abdomen with a clenched fist. When Houdini looked startled, the boy quickly backed away, explaining in a panic that he thought that Houdini had given him permission to hit him. The boy felt terrible seeing the performer so clearly in pain, but the magician soon recovered enough to reassure the young man and then step onto the stage for his show.

Throughout the evening, Houdini was seen wincing in pain and late that night, he admitting to crippling pangs that continued to get worse. His performances over the next two days consisted of hours of agony, save for brief intermissions when he fell into a restless sleep. He was examined by doctors upon his arrival in Detroit and was diagnosed as having acute appendicitis. He had a fever of 102 degrees but refused to stay at the hospital. He was scheduled to perform at a sold-out show that night and was determined to be there.

By the time he took the stage, his fever had gone up to 104. He was tired, feverish and tormented by abdominal pains, plus the broken ankle from a few weeks past. He somehow managed to perform the entire show, but his terrified assistants were constantly forced to complete some motion that Houdini couldn't manage. Spectators reported that he often missed his cues and that he seemed to hurry the show along. Between the first and second acts, he was taken to his dressing room and ice packs were placed on him to try and cool his fever. This was repeated between acts two and three as well. Toward the end of the evening, he began doing what he called "little magic" with silks and coins, card sleights and questions and challenges from the audience. He remained on the stage throughout the evening but just before the third act, he turned to his chief assistant and said "Drop the curtain, Collins, I can't go any further." When the curtain closed, he literally collapsed where he had been standing. Houdini was helped back to his dressing room and he changed his clothes but still refused to go back to the hospital.

He went to his hotel, still convinced that his pain and illness would subside. It was not until the early morning hours, when Bess threw a tantrum, that the hotel physician was summoned. He in turn contacted a surgeon and Houdini was rushed to the hospital, of course, against his will. An operation was performed immediately, but the surgeons agreed that there was little hope for him to pull through. His appendix had ruptured and, despite the efforts of medical experts, it was suggested that Bess contact family members. Despite the seriousness of his condition, Houdini managed to hang on until the early morning hours of October 31. In the darkness, he turned to Bess and his brother, Hardeen, who he affectionately called "Dash," and spoke quietly to them. "Dash, I'm getting tired and I can't fight anymore," he murmured, and then turned away. Houdini then stepped through the curtain from this world to the next.

Strangely, all of the property from the show had been crated up and shipped to New York when Houdini was taken to the hospital but one crate was accidentally left behind. It was opened and it was found to contain a bronze casket that had been used as a prop. To add further to this strange twist of fate, a call to Houdini's attorney confirmed that the magician had asked to be buried in the casket in the event of his death.

His body was placed in the casket and was taken by train to New York. His funeral service was held in the huge Elks Lodge Ballroom on West 43rd Street and over 2,000 people attended. There were tributes from the Society of American Magicians, the Jewish Theatrical Guild, the St. Cecile Masonic Lodge and the Elks; the honorary pallbearers included Edward Albee, Marcus Loew, Charles Dillingham, Adolph S. Ochs, Adolph Zukor and many others. As the coffin was lifted one pallbearer (entertainment magnate Florenz Ziegfield) whispered to another, "Suppose he isn't in it?"

The funeral cortege traveled to Machpelah Cemetery in Ridgewood where Houdini's most trusted assistants lowered his coffin into the ground next to that of his mother. As he had requested, his head rested on a black bag that contained her letters to him. A year later, as Jewish custom requires, a bust of Houdini was set in its appointed place atop the enormous tomb. Beneath it, under a plaque that tells of his presidency of the Society of American Magicians from 1912 to 1926 are large letters that simply read "Houdini".

Many mysteries still surround the death of Houdini, although most have come about due to the fact that there are at least seven different versions of how his death occurred. They include him dying in the arms of Bess in Boston and Chicago, dying while hanging suspended upside-down in a glass tank, dying while performing at the bottom of a river, dying while trapped in a locked casket and others. What actually happened is what you have just read; it is known that Houdini died of a ruptured appendix. It's likely that the appendix did not rupture when the young man punched him in the abdomen in his dressing room. This could have caused the actual rupture, but Houdini was probably suffering from appendicitis before the incident. However, the infamous punch is generally accepted as the cause of death.

And more mysteries came about in the days following his death as reports from clairvoyants who claimed to have predicted Houdini's death and to have witnessed signs and omens of it began coming in. A Mr. Gysel stated that at 10:58 on the evening of October 24, a photograph of Houdini that he had framed and hung on the wall suddenly "fell to the ground, breaking the glass. I now know that Houdini will die," he allegedly said.

Gysel's prediction came as no surprise to Houdini's Spiritualist adversaries, who had been predicting his death for years. Sooner or later, they were bound to be correct. In 1924, Margery's spirit guide, Walter, had given him "a year or less" and then he predicted his demise on December 25, 1925. According to his former friend Conan Doyle, he and others in his "home circle" had recorded an ominous message about the magician several months before his death. The message read, "Houdini is doomed, doomed, doomed!" And on October 13, a medium named Mrs. Wood wrote a letter to the novelist Fulton Oursler that read: "Three years ago, the spirit of Dr. Hyslop said 'the waters are black for Houdini' and he foretold disaster would claim him while performing before an audience in a theatre. Dr. Hyslop now says the injury is more serious than has been reported and that Houdini's days as a magician are over."

According to accounts, Houdini himself had premonitions of the coming events. Among his clippings was one from 1919 recording the collapse, onstage in Detroit, of a comedian named Sidney Drew. The performer had taken ill in St. Louis, but had continued to play, against all advice, until he could simply go no further. Those who discovered this clipping among Houdini's belongings must have found the death of the comedian to be eerily similar to that of Houdini himself.

His friend, fellow magician Joseph Dunninger, also had an eerie story to recall after Houdini's death. He said that on one early morning in October 1926, Houdini called him in New York and asked him to come with his car to West 113th Street, as he was in a hurry and had to move some things. When the car was loaded, he asked Dunninger to drive through the park. Dunninger said that as they got to the exit on Central Park West, around 72nd Street, Houdini grabbed him by the arm and urged him to go back to his house. Puzzled, Dunninger asked him if he had forgotten something. "Don't ask questions, Joe," Houdini replied, "just turn around and go back." Dunninger drove back to the house and when they arrived, Houdini climbed out of the car and stood looking at the house in the rain. He stayed that way, water dripping down his face and soaking his clothing, for a few minutes and then he got back into the auto without saying a word. Dunninger drove off and when the two men again approached the western exit of the park, he glanced over and saw that Houdini's shoulders had started to shake. He was crying. His friend asked him what was wrong and Houdini gave a rather cryptic answer: "I've seen my house for the last time, Joe. I'll never see my house again."

"And as far as I know," Dunninger later wrote, "he never did."

Not long after Houdini's death, the famous Houdini Seances began, and not surprisingly, continue today although the official sanction of the Houdini estate ended years ago. While Bess planned to honor her husband's requests about attempting contact with him after death, this may not have been what prompted her to seek the secret code that he promised to send her from beyond the grave. Like her husband had been at the death of his mother, Bess was at a loss as to what to do with her life with Houdini gone. They had been together since Bess had been a young woman and she had been living inside his closed world and filling the role as his wife. She had been his partner in a very real sense and he always stated that Bess was his "beloved wife, and the only one who had ever helped me in my work." Although their life had not been perfect, it had never been dull and, as huge as Houdini's ego had been, he never made it a secret that he depended on her totally. With him gone, Bess seemed to be drifting and empty. It's no surprise that she wanted desperately to speak with him again.

But her life moved shakily on. While she was not rich, Houdini had left a trust fund for her and substantial amounts of life insurance had been carried on him. She had to pay heavy inheritance taxes but she had more than enough to live comfortably for the rest of her life. She sold their house on West 113th Street to Rose Bonanno, whose father had looked after it when the Houdinis were away. As time passed and as the surrounding neighborhood grew rougher, Rose was able to remain unbothered, thanks to her connections to the famous Bonanno crime family. She lived in the basement, among piles of old photos and did nothing to dispel the legend of Houdini's secret stashes and compartments in the house. She would never open the padlocked attic because "Mrs. Houdini wouldn't like it." She kept the secrets of the house, the mysterious chambers and all, and carried them with her to the grave.

Bess Houdini moved to Payson Avenue in another part of New York City and became lost in alcohol and misery. She tried opening a tea room and thought of taking a vaudeville act on the road, but none of these projects really got off the ground. She soon began to spend her time attempting to contact her husband. Every Sunday at the hour of his death, she would shut herself in a room with his photograph and wait for a sign. She spread the word that she was waiting for a secret message from her husband and word spread far and wide that Bess had offered $10,000 to any medium who could deliver a true message from Houdini.

Almost weekly, a new medium came forward claiming to have broken the code, but none of them did until 1928, when famed medium Arthur Ford announced that he had a message for Bess. He told her that the message had come from Houdini's mother and consisted of a single word: "forgive". With this, Bess had a startling announcement to make, claiming that Ford's message was the first that she had received which "had any appearance of the truth." In November, another message came to Ford, this time from Houdini himself. In a trance, the medium relayed an entire coded message—"Rosabelle, answer, tell, pray, answer, look, tell, answer, answer, tell."

After this information was relayed to Bess, she invited Ford to her home and he asked her if the words were correct. She said they were, and Ford asked her to remove her wedding ring and tell everyone present what "Rosabelle" meant. This was the word that made the message authentic, a secret known only to Bess and Harry. It was the title of a song that had been popular at Coney

Island when they first met. The rest of the message was a series of code words that spelled out the word "believe"—the final clue that Houdini had promised to relay from the next world. But did Houdini actually communicate from the other side?

Not surprisingly, there were soon accusations of fraud leveled against Arthur Ford. Even though Bess claimed the message was correct, many claimed that Ford had learned the code from a book about Houdini published in 1927. The press, the skeptics and Houdini's friends refused to accept that Ford had broken the code, and Bess, on their advice, withdrew her reward offer.

So, did he really break the impossible code? Arthur Ford went to his grave in 1974 with the firm belief that he had actually received a message from Houdini. In 1928, Ford had been the pastor of the First Spiritualist Church of Manhattan and was a respected member of the psychic community. He had also recently distinguished himself by challenging the magician Howard Thurston to a debate at Carnegie Hall, which Ford won. Thurston, who had been carrying on Houdini's tradition of exposing fraudulent mediums, was stymied by being unable to explain some of the effects that Ford produced. After he came forward with the code, jealous colleagues turned on Ford, and newspaper reporters and debunkers charged him with perpetrating a hoax with the help of Bess. Shortly afterwards, Arthur Ford was expelled from the United Spiritualist League of New York but was later reinstated "on the grounds of insufficient evidence."

But was he a fraud? Many people believe so and state that he actually found the secret code on page 105 of a book that was published the year before. Incidentally, the code was not one that was specially prepared by Houdini and Bess. It was very old and had been used in their mind-reading act for years. Despite all of this however, it should be noted that while Ford could have easily found the code somewhere—there has never been an adequate explanation (outside of fraud, which was denied by both parties) as to where he got the message that he gave to Bess. Could it have come from the other side?

Bess Houdini continued to hold seances in hopes of communicating with her late husband but as the years went by she began to lose hope. The last official Houdini seance was held on Halloween night of 1936, ten years after Houdini had died. A group of friends, fellow magicians, occultists, scientists and Bess Houdini herself gathered in Hollywood, on the roof of the Knickerbocker Hotel. The gathering had been arranged by Eddy Saint, a former carnival and vaudeville showman who had also worked as a magician. He had been recommended to Bess a few years before in New York to act as her manager, although concerned friends had actually hired him to watch over her and to protect her from being taken advantage of. A genuine affection developed between then and eventually they began sharing a bungalow together in Hollywood, a place where Bess had enjoyed living during her husband's brief movie career.

Coverage for the Final Houdini Seance was provided by radio, and it was broadcast all over the world. Eddy Saint took charge of the proceedings and started things off with the playing of "Pomp and Circumstance," a tune that had been used by Houdini to start his act in the later years. He noted for radio audiences that "every facility has been provided tonight that might aid in opening the pathway to the spirit world. Here in the inner circle reposes a 'medium's trumpet,' a pair of slates with chalk, a writing tablet and pencil, a small bell and in the center reposes a huge pair of silver handcuffs on a silk cushion."

Saint continued coverage of the event, finally crying out to make contact with the late magician. "Houdini! Are you here? Are you here, Houdini? Please manifest yourself in any way possible... We have waited, Houdini, oh so long! Never have you been able to present the evidence you promised. And now, this, the night of nights, the world is listening, Harry, Levitate the table! Move it! Lift the table! Move it or rap it! Spell out a code, Harry...please! Ring a bell! Let its tinkle be heard around the world!"

Saint and the rest of Bess' inner circle attempted to contact the elusive magician for over an hour before finally giving up. Saint finally turned to Bess. "Mrs. Houdini, the zero hour has passed. The ten years are up. Have you reached a decision?"

The mournful voice of Bess Houdini then echoed through radio receivers around the world. "Yes, Houdini did not come through," she replied. "My last hope is gone. I do not believe that Houdini can come back to me—or to anyone. The Houdini shrine has burned for ten years. I now, reverently, turn out the light. It is finished. Good night, Harry!"

The seance came to an end, but at the moment it did, a tremendously violent thunderstorm broke out, drenching the seance participants and terrifying them with the horrific lightning and thunder. They would later learn that this mysterious storm did not occur anywhere else in Hollywood—only above the Knickerbocker Hotel. Some speculated that perhaps Houdini did come through after all, as the flamboyant performer just might have made his presence known by the spectacular effects of the thunderstorm.

Legends or lies? Who can really say? Houdini was (and remains) a riddle. On one hand, he was an open-minded seeker of truth, but on the other, a heated disbeliever in all things supernatural. If it can be said that a man is gone, but never forgotten, this should be said about Harry Houdini. He is truly an American enigma.

Chapter Four

BLOODY MURDER

America's Mysterious Unsolved Crimes

It is no secret to those who have managed to read this far into the book that I am fascinated with mysteries. There are perhaps no mysteries as great as those that involve the loss of human life. Whether we are reading about it or an unfortunate bystander to it, there is something about this type of mystery that grabs each of us by the throat and refuses to let us go until the mystery is solved.

But what about those mysteries that cannot be solved? What is it about these bloody crimes that captures the imagination of the public and keeps our gruesome interest in them even after many years have gone by? I'll have to let the reader decide this for himself but none of us can deny the grisly fascination that each one of us feels about unsolved crimes from the past.

The Impossible Suicide?

One hot summer evening in July 1872, a body was discovered on a busy street in Bridgeport, Connecticut. The corpse belonged to a man named Captain George M. Colvocoresses and he had been shot to death. Lying next to the body on the street was a revolver and a leather satchel. Police investigators who were summoned to the scene took one look at it and were sure that they were examining a murder. It seemed a clear-cut case, until they began studying the body itself.

Colvocoresses was wearing a three-piece suit but there was no bullet hole in his jacket or his vest. However, the bullet had torn through the man's shirt, leaving a jagged hole. In addition, they found powder burns on the inside of the vest and on the outside of his shirt. This bit of evidence seemed to point to the fact that Colvocoresses was killed by someone who put the gun inside of his jacket and had wedged it between his vest and his shirt.

For several days after the body was discovered, the police and the press speculated that the man may have committed suicide. They began this line of the investigation after the discovery of a $193,000 life insurance policy that had been taken out by Colvocoresses a few months earlier. But this still didn't seem to provide a solution for the strange death. Why would the man have gone to so much trouble to kill himself in such an unusual manner? Did he want to keep from damaging his favorite suit so that he could be buried in it? How could he be sure that he would not die before he could remove his hand and the gun from his vest? In an attempt to duplicate this suicide, police officers were only able to remove their hands from the inside of dummy's clothing, and at a speed needed for a man to remain alive, a fraction of the times they tried it. And none of these queries would provide answers to the biggest mystery of all, which was why Colvocoresses would want to make his suicide appear to be a murder?

While the police delved into the case, the press started an

investigation of their own. What they learned made the mystery even greater. As far as they could tell, Captain Colvocoresses had no enemies, had no great debts, was not reported to be depressed; in his will he bequeathed generous amounts to his friends and relatives and left the rest of his sizable estate to charity. No one seemed to want him dead and he seemed to have no reason to take his own life. So, what happened? The answer remains a mystery.

The Original Locked Room Mystery

Over the years, scores of mystery writers have penned the idea of a man being killed inside a locked room. The idea of such a puzzle may have originally come from the murder of a man named Isodore Fink, the first locked room murder victim.

On the night of March 9, 1929, a woman named Mrs. Locklan Smith reported screams, shots and the sounds of a struggle coming from the Fifth Avenue Laundry in New York. The building was located next to her home and she heard the sounds clearly enough that she immediately reported them to the police. When the police arrived, they found that the back room of the laundry, which was owned by Isodore Fink, was locked. With no other way to get inside of it, they gained entry by boosting a small boy into the room by way of a transom window.

Fink had been shot twice in the chest and once through the left hand, although they could find no powder burns on his skin or clothing. It was obvious that the shots had come from a close range. They also found that Fink's valuables had not been touched and that there was still money in the laundry's cash register. The man was certainly dead and while it was a puzzle as to who had killed him, it was an even greater mystery as to how the killer had escaped from the scene of the crime.

Detectives had been able to determine that Fink always bolted the doors to the laundry whenever he worked at night, making it difficult for anyone to get in. The only possible access to the laundry was through the transom window and it would have required a very small killer to have used it. It was also the only way out. Even if Fink had allowed his murderer inside, the man could not leave and bolt the doors behind him again. Locking the doors had to be accomplished from the inside. So, if the killer had entered through the window, why wouldn't he leave through the front door? Perhaps the fatal shots had been fired at Fink from the window? But the coroner's exam ruled that out. The shots had indeed, as the original officers on the scene determined, been fired from very close range.

Investigators were stumped and no crime historians have ever been able to come up with a logical explanation as to who killed Isodore Fink and why. More than two years after the crime, New York Police Commissioner Edward P. Mulrooney called the murder an "insoluble mystery." It went unsolved in 1929 and remains that way today.

The Pig Woman, the Preacher & Murder!

One of the strangest unsolved American murders took place in 1922 near New Brunswick, New Jersey. It would capture the attention of the curiosity-seekers all over the New York area and would take years to untangle. Unfortunately, it would never be solved.

The events were set into motion on a warm September evening along secluded De Rossey's Lane in New Brunswick. On that night, two young lovers were searching for a quiet spot for a midnight tryst, and they were disappointed to find that another couple had already found their favorite spot under a sprawling apple tree. The young man, Raymond Schneider, 22, wanted to roust the other pair from the spot but his girlfriend, Pearl Bahmer, 15, protested. She didn't want to disturb anyone but didn't try to stop her boyfriend when he began kicking gravel and loudly clearing his throat. Instead of being startled that someone had walked up on their lovemaking, the couple under the tree remained motionless. Schneider noticed that they didn't seem to be engaged in romance either, so he ducked under the tree branches for another look.

The moon overhead was bright enough to illuminate the scene and Raymond saw an older man and a young woman, both well dressed, nestled in one another's arms. This would have been a placid scene if not for the fact that the man had a bullet hole in his head and the woman had been shot in the face three times. Blood was splashed all over the ground and onto their clothing as the woman's throat had been cut from ear to ear. Raymond and Pearl ran from the scene in a panic and went to the nearest house to call the police.

When the authorities arrived, they began piecing together what had happened. Although the man and woman had been killed nearby, they appeared to have been carefully placed under the apple tree. Their clothing had been hurriedly pulled on and buttoned wrong, leading the investigators to believe they had been naked when killed and then dressed by someone else. Scattered about on the grass were a number of love letters that the woman had apparently written to the man and bore her signature. A business card of the man's had been purposely propped up against his shoe so that the officers would have no trouble identifying the victims.

The man was Reverend Edward Wheeler Hall and he was the rector of the St. John the Evangelist Church in New Brunswick. The woman who was dead in his arms was Mrs. Eleanor Mills, the young choir director of the church. From the looks of the letters that she had written to him ("Oh honey, I am fiery today. Burning flaming love, it seems ages since I saw my babykin's body and kissed every bit of you!"), it seemed that the preacher and the choir director had been lovers for some time.

Reverend Hall had taken over the position at the church in 1909. Two years later, he had married a wealthy local woman named France Stevens. She was seven years older than the handsome reverend and was considered a spinster. Rumors had it that Hall married for money but the marriage seemed to be a stable and peaceful one.

Mrs. Hall's family was rather peculiar though. Willie Stevens, her brother, was an unkempt and eccentric man. He wore shabby clothing and grew his hair long and wild. Although quite rich, he was incapable of managing his own fortune and was given an allowance each week. Living in the family mansion with his sister and Reverend Hall, Willie kept himself busy by becoming a self-taught but recognized expert on entomology and botany. He also volunteered as a fireman, and occasionally, when he was bored, he would start a large fire in his backyard and then run into the house, returning in his fireman's uniform to extinguish the flames. Mrs. Steven's other brother, Henry, was quite normal in comparison and lived about 60 miles away in his own home. He was a quiet man who managed his family's investments and pursued his great passions of hunting and target shooting. He also maintained close contact with the family's cousin, Henry Carpender. Henry was an attorney and member of the New York Stock Exchange. He was a frequent visitor to the Stevens estate and acted as a troubleshooter for the family.

The murdered woman, Eleanor Mills, was married to James Mills, who was employed as a sexton and handyman at Reverend Hall's church. He knew that his wife had some sort of relationship with Hall but assumed that it was one based on religion and a love of music. He knew that they often had dinner together but never suspected an affair. And neither did Mrs. Hall. She had befriended Eleanor to the extent that the older woman was almost a mother figure to her. She often took her out shopping for new clothing and always made sure she was invited to the finest social affairs. Shortly before Eleanor's death, Mrs. Hall had even paid for the young woman's appendectomy.

Not long after the bodies were discovered, news of the murders began to spread. Mrs. Hall learned of her husband's death when a reporter called and asked for details. She hung up on him without comment. As crowds began to gather at the murder site, the authorities began a battle over jurisdiction for the case—no one wanted responsibility for it. While the bodies were found just inside the

Somerset County line, both victims resided in Middlesex County. Each county prosecutor insisted that the case belonged to the other one. It would be years before the matter was entirely settled.

While the bickering and investigation were taking place, Henry Carpender arrived at the crime scene with a family attorney to view the bodies and leave almost unnoticed. The officers present recovered several . 32 caliber shells but managed to find little else that was not carried away by the crowds of curiosity-seekers who arrived. The spectators began taking away souvenirs, ripping bark from the apple tree, pulling up large chunks of grass and stripping the tree of its leaves. Onlookers dipped handkerchiefs in the bloody grass, hoping for a gruesome remembrance. Finally, the police decided to take the bodies to the Somerset County morgue before they were carried away as well.

Soon after, the police began digging deeper into the case and interviewing everyone involved in any way. According to Mrs. Hall, she last saw her husband at 7:30 on the night of the murders when he left the house on business. She was disturbed when he did not return that night and went to the church looking for him the next day. She found Mr. Mills there and soon realized that neither of their spouses had come home during the previous night.

In Mills' statement, he too said that his wife had left the house around 7:30 in the evening. She did not tell him where she was going, and later that night he went to bed. Around 2:30 am, he awoke and realized that his wife was not home. He dressed himself and their two small children and went to the church to search for Eleanor. Not finding her there, he returned home to sleep fitfully the rest of the night.

The investigation continued and more information came in. Several witnesses stated that they had seen Mrs. Hall leave the mansion around 2:30 am on the night in question with her brother Willie. When confronted with this, she did admit that yes, she did go out that night looking for her husband, but when she arrived at the church, she saw that the lights were out. She assumed that

Reverend Hall was visiting a sick parishioner, and so she drove to the Mills house. When she saw that the lights were out there too, she and Willie returned home.

Detectives were suspicious of both stories told by Mrs. Hall and Mr. Mills, but each of them had an alibi that could not be broken. There was nothing to suggest that they were lying but investigators felt certain that someone was. But with nowhere else to turn, they began taking a closer look at Raymond Schneider and Pearl Bahmer, the young couple who had found the bodies under the tree.

Schneider told the police that he believed a man named Clifford Hayes had killed the couple, believing that they were he and Pearl. Hayes had dated Pearl several times and was very jealous. He killed the couple but after they were dead, realized his mistake. In a matter of hours, detectives discovered that Schneider made up the whole thing and when confronted, he quickly confessed to fabricating the accusation. He refused to admit why he had done so, but the detectives didn't care. They had already taken a strong dislike to Schneider and to Pearl as well. Schneider had a minor police record and had recently walked out on his pregnant wife. Pearl, even at the age of 15, was a pool hall hustler and had a reputation for dabbling in prostitution. In short time, Schneider was arrested, indicted and convicted to serve time on perjury charges.

After weeks of dead ends, a new lead was discovered. The clues came from the account of a woman named Mrs. Jane Gibson. She was a hog farmer who had been given the colorful nickname of the "Pig Woman." She came forward and told the police that she had witnessed members of the Stevens family kill Reverend Hall and Eleanor Mills near the apple tree. During the grand jury investigation though, her story changed a little. She could not say under oath that it had been Mrs. Hall, Willie Stevens, Henry Stevens and Henry Carpender who committed the murders but she had seen the crime. The night had been too dark for her to see their faces, but she felt sure that it was them. Based on this, the grand jury was unable to return an indictment and the case went into limbo.

Four years passed before the case began making headlines again. Phillip Payne, the managing editor of the *New York Daily Mirror*, received information that allowed him to push the case into the active files again. One of the newspaper's reporters was covering a routine divorce case and realized that the defendant had been employed as a maid for Reverend Hall at the time of the murders. The maid's husband was suing for divorce on the grounds that she had committed adultery, and one of the men she was accused of sleeping with was Reverend Hall. It was further alleged that Mrs. Hall gave the maid $6,000 to keep quiet about the affair and to confirm an alibi that she was home at the time of the murders. The reporter informed Payne, and he put pressure on the New Jersey governor and the state's attorney to re-open the investigation.

The police moved quickly and made simultaneous arrests of Mrs. Hall and her two brothers. Henry Carpender was not implicated again in the crime. The clan was indicted and went to trial for murder. Crowds filled the courtroom during the trail and the newspapers loved the strangeness of the affair. The Stevens family, thanks to their numerous eccentricities, made great copy. The key witness in the case was the Pig Woman, who was now dying of cancer. Unable to move, she was forced to testify from her hospital bed, which was wheeled into the courtroom each day. Mrs. Hall's mother also came to the courtroom each day and sat behind her daughter. During testimony, she would repeatedly mutter the word "liar" whenever anyone said something that she didn't like. Another addition to the unusual cast of characters was Charlotte Mills, the daughter of murder victim Eleanor Mills. She had become a reporter after her mother's death and thanks to her familiarity with the case, she was assigned to cover the trial by her editor. Her reporting was far from unbiased and almost every article had a reference to Mrs. Hall's dowdy wardrobe and frumpy appearance.

There were a number of witnesses called by the state, but they chose to hinge the prosecution on the testimony of the Pig Woman, Jane Gibson. She managed to moan her testimony from her death bed with Mrs. Hall and her brothers glaring at her and Mrs. Hall's mother loudly protesting each statement with "liar, liar, liar, liar." It would have been humorous if not for the tragic nature of the case.

Mrs. Gibson testified that she had been riding her mule on the night of the murders, chasing corn thieves from her property. A short distance away, she saw the defendants get out of a car and walk quietly into the apple orchard. Gibson dismounted and began following them to see where they were going. She saw five figures near the tree and heard a voice exclaim, "Explain these letters!". She heard more shouts, cursing and the sounds of fighting and then saw two men, Reverend Hall and Henry Stevens, on the ground. A shot was fired and then a woman began screaming "My God! My God!". Three more shots were fired and the woman was silent. Gibson decided to get back to her mule but as she started to leave, she looked back and saw Mrs. Hall bending over what appeared to be a body. She saw something silver flash in the woman's hand and then Mrs. Hall make slashing motions toward the figure on the ground. The Pig Woman then fled to her mule and left the scene.

While her story was compelling, Gibson's memory proved to be faulty under cross-examination. The defense was unable to break her account of what happened that night but they were able to show that she did not remember her three husband's names, nor when she divorced any of them. Her memory of anything, outside of the murders, was hazy at best. The dying woman's efforts to recall the normal aspects of her life created enough reasonable doubt in the minds of the jury that they simply could not bring back a guilty verdict. Mrs. Hall and her brothers were released.

Jane Gibson lived until 1930, and to the day that she died, she insisted that her story of the events on that night was true. Mrs. Hall and her brothers sued the *New York Daily Mirror* and received an undisclosed settlement. After that, they faded away into his history and were never heard of again. And if the killer was anyone outside of the Stevens family, he disappeared too. The murders of the reverend and the choir director have never been solved.

FAREWELL TO THE GRIMES SISTERS

Who Killed the Chicago Sisters?

It was December 28, 1956, and Patricia Grimes, 13, and Barbara Grimes, 15, left their home at 3624 South Damon Avenue and headed for the Brighton Theater, only a mile away. The girls were both avid fans of Elvis Presley and had gone to see his film *Love Me Tender* for the eleventh and final time. The girls were recognized in the popcorn line at 9:30 PM and then seen on an eastbound Archer Avenue bus at 11:00 PM. After that, things are less certain but this may have been the last time they were ever seen alive. The two sisters were missing for the next twenty-five days, before their naked and frozen bodies were found along the banks of Devil's Creek in the southwest part of Cook County.

The girl's mother, Loretta Grimes, didn't expect the girls to come home until 11:45 but was already growing uneasy. At midnight, she sent her daughter Theresa, 17, and her son Joey, 14, to the bus stop at 35th and Hoyne to watch for them. After three buses had stopped and had failed to discharge their sisters, Theresa and Joey returned home without them. They never saw the girls again, but strangely, others claimed to.

The last reported sightings of the two girls came from classmates who spotted them at Angelo's Restaurant at 3551 South Archer Avenue, more than twenty-four hours after their reported disappearance. How accurate this sighting was is unknown, as a railroad conductor also reported them on a train near the Great Lakes Naval Training Center in north suburban Glenview. A security guard on the northwest side offered directions to two girls he believed were the Grimes sisters on the morning after they disappeared. On January 1, both girls were allegedly identified as passengers aboard a CTA bus on Damen Avenue. And the following week, they were reported in Englewood by George Pope, a night clerk at the Unity Hotel on West 61st Street, who refused them a room because of their ages. Three employees at Kresge believed they saw the girls listening to Elvis Presley songs at the record counter on January 3.

The police theorized that the girls had run away but Loretta Grimes refused to believe it. She was sure the girls were not missing voluntarily. Regardless, it became the greatest missing persons hunt in Chicago police history. Even Elvis Presley, in a statement issued from Memphis, asked the girls to come home and ease their mother's worries. The plea went unanswered.

More strangeness would be reported before the bodies of the girls were found. A series of ransom letters, that were later discovered to have come from a mental patient, took Mrs. Grimes to Milwaukee on January 12. She was escorted by FBI agents and instructed to sit in a downtown Catholic Church with $1,000 on the bench beside her. The letter promised that Barbara Grimes would walk in to retrieve the money and then leave to deliver it to the kidnapper. She and her sister would then be released. Needless to say, no one ever came and Mrs. Grimes was left sitting there for hours to contemplate her daughters' fate. By that time, it's likely that the bodies of the two girls were already lying along German Church Road, covered with snow.

But if that's true, then how can we explain the two telephone calls that were received by Wallace and Ann Tollstan on January 14? Their daughter, Sandra, was a classmate of Patricia Grimes at the St. Maurice School and they received the two calls around midnight. The first call jolted Mr. Tollstan out of his sleep but when he picked up the receiver, the person on the other end of the line did not speak. He waited a few moments and then hung up. About 15 minutes later, the phone rang again and this time, Ann Tollstan answered it. The voice on the other end of the line asked, "Is that you, Sandra? Is Sandra there?" But before Mrs. Tollstan could bring her daughter to the phone, the caller had clicked off the line. Ann Tollstan was convinced that the frightened voice on the telephone had belonged to Patricia Grimes.

And that wasn't the only strange happening. On January 15, a police switchboard operator received a call from a man who refused to identify himself but who insisted that the girl's bodies would be found in a park at 81st and Wolf. He said this revelation had come to him in a dream and he hung up. The call was then traced to Green's Liquor Market on South Halsted and the caller was discovered to be Walter Kranz, a 53-year-old steamfitter. According to a *Chicago Sun-Times* article, he was taken into custody after the bodies were found on January 22—less than a mile from the park that Kranz said he dreamed of. He became one of the numerous people who were questioned by the police and then released.

Finally, the vigil for the Grimes Sisters ended on January 22, 1957 when construction worker Leonard Prescott was driving south on German Church Road near Willow Springs. He spotted what appeared to be two discarded clothing store mannequins lying next to a guardrail, about five feet from the road. A few feet away, the ground dropped off to Devil's Creek below. Unsure of what he had seen, Prescott nervously brought his wife to the spot, and then they drove to the local police station. His wife, Marie Prescott, was so upset by the sight of the bodies that she had to be carried back to their car.

Once investigators realized the mannequins were actually bodies, they soon discovered they were the Grimes Sisters. Barbara Grimes lay on her left side with her legs slightly drawn up toward her body. Her head was covered by the body of her sister, who had been thrown onto her back with her head turned sharply to the right. It looked as if they had been discarded there by someone so cold and heartless that he saw the girls as nothing more than refuse to be tossed away on a lonely roadside.

The officials in charge, Cook County Sheriff Joseph D. Lohman and Harry Glos, an investigator for Coroner Walter E. McCarron, surmised that the bodies had been lying there for several days, perhaps as far back as January 9. This had been the date of the last heavy snowfall and the frigid temperatures that followed the storm had preserved the bodies to a state that resembled how they looked at the moment of death. As the newspapers broke the story on the morning of January 23, both the press and the investigators in the case began to draw connections between the murders of the Grimes sisters and the killings of three young boys who had been found under similar circumstances in October 1955.

One of the most shocking and terrifying events in the history of Chicago took place in that month, when the bodies of three boys were discovered in a virtually crime-free community on the northwest side of the city. With what was called the Schuessler-Peterson murders, the city would be stunned by the horror of violence against children.

The terrifying events began on a cool Sunday afternoon in the fall of 1955 when three boys from the northwest side of the city headed downtown to catch a matinee performance of a movie at a Loop Theater. The boys made the trip with their parent's consent. The boys had always proven dependable in the past and this time should have been no exception. With $4 between them, John and Anton Schuessler and Bobby Peterson ventured into the Chicago Loop to see a movie that Bobby's mother had chosen for them. Around 6:00 pm that night, long after the matinee had ended, the boys were reported in the lobby of the Garland Building at 111 North Wabash. There was no explanation for what they might have been doing there, other than that Peterson's eye doctor was located in the building. It seems unlikely that Bobby would be visiting the optometrist on a Sunday afternoon.

Around 7:45 pm, the three entered the Monte Cristo Bowling Alley on West Montrose. The alley was a neighborhood eating place and the proprietor later recalled to the police that a "fifty-ish" looking man was showing an "abnormal interest" in several younger boys who were bowling. He was unable to say if the man made contact with the trio. The boys left and walked down Montrose to another bowling alley, then thumbed a ride at the intersection of Lawrence and Milwaukee Avenue. They were out of money by this time, but not quite ready to go home. It was now 9:05 in the evening and their parents were beginning to get worried. They had reason to be, for the boys were never seen alive again.

Two days later, the boys' naked and bound bodies were discovered in a shallow ditch about 100 feet east of the Des Plaines River. A salesman, who had stopped to eat his lunch at the Robinson Wood's Indian Burial Grounds nearby, spotted them and called the police. Coroner Walter McCarron stated that the cause of death was "asphyxiation by suffocation." The three boys had been dead about 36 hours when they were discovered. Bobby Peterson had been struck repeatedly and had been strangled with a rope or a necktie. The killer had used adhesive tape to cover the eyes of all three victims. They had then been thrown from a vehicle. Their clothing was never discovered.

The city of Chicago was thrown into a panic. Police officials reported that they had never seen such a horrible crime. The fears of parents all over the city were summed up by the grief-stricken Anton Schuessler Sr. who said, "When you get to the point that children cannot go to the movies in the afternoon and get home safely, something is wrong with this country."

Police officers combed the area, conducting door-to-door searches and neighborhood interrogations. Search teams combed Robinson's Woods, looking for clues or items of clothing. The killer (or killers) had gone to great length to get rid of any signs of fingerprints or traces of evidence. By this time, various city and suburban police departments had descended on the scene, running into each other and further hampering the search for clues. There was little or no cooperation between the separate agencies and if anything had been discovered, it would have most likely been lost in the confusion.

While investigators were coming up empty, an honor guard of Boy Scouts carried the coffins of the three boys from the St. Tarcissus Roman Catholic Church to a hearse that would take them to St. Joseph Cemetery. The church was filled to capacity with an estimated 1,200 mourners. This marked the end of innocence in Chicago. The horror felt by parents in Chicagoland was only compounded by the disappearance of the Grimes sisters and the subsequent discovery of their bodies. Like the Schuessler boys and Bobby Peterson, the girls had been found naked and dumped in a secluded, wooded area. And strangely, the bodies had looked to be mannequins by those who discovered them.

The bodies along German Church Road sent the various police departments into action. A short time after the Grimes discovery, more than 162 officers from Chicago, Cook County, the Forest Preserves and five south suburban police departments began combing the woods—and tramping all over whatever evidence may have been there. Between the officers, the reporters, the medical examiners and everyone else, the investigation was already botched. Despite the claims of Lt. Joseph Morris, the head of a special police unit investigating the Schuessler-Peterson murders, who said, "We're not going to repeat some of the mistakes that we made the last time," things were already off to a bad start.

And the investigation became even more confusing in the days to come. The bodies were removed from the scene and were taken to the Cook County Morgue, where they would be stored until they thawed out and an autopsy became possible. Before they were removed, both police investigators and reporters commented on the condition of the corpses, noting bruises and marks that have still not been adequately explained to this day. According to a newspaper article, there were three ugly wounds in Patricia's abdomen and the left side of her face had been battered, resulting in a possibly broken nose. Barbara's face and head had also been bruised and there were punctures from an ice pick in her chest. Once the bodies were moved, investigators stayed on the scene searching for clothing and clues but neither was found.

Once the autopsies were performed, all hopes that the examinations would provide new evidence or leads were quickly dashed. Despite the efforts of three experienced pathologists, they could not reach agreement on a time or cause of death. They stated that the girls had died from shock and exposure but were only able to reach this conclusion by eliminating other causes. And by also concluding that the girls had died on December 28, the night they had disappeared, they created more puzzles than they had managed to solve. If the girls had died on the night they had gone missing, then how could the sightings that took place after that date be explained? And if the bodies had been exposed to the elements since that time, then why hadn't anyone else seen them?

Barbara and Patricia were buried on January 28, one month after they disappeared, but their mystery was no closer to being solved than it had been in December. The case of the murdered girls became an obsession. The local community organized searches for clues and passed out flyers looking for information. Money was raised to assist the destitute Grimes family and eventually the funds paid off their Damen Avenue home. The *Chicago Tribune* invited readers to send in theories about the case and paid $50 for any they published. The clergy and the parishioners from St. Maurice offered a $1,000 reward. Even photographs were taken of friends of the girls that duplicated the clothing they wore on December 28 in hopes that it might jog the memory of someone who saw them. The clothing, like the girl's killer, was never found.

Investigators questioned an unbelievable 300,000 persons, searching for information about the girls, and 2,000 of these people were seriously interrogated, which in those days could be brutal. A number of suspects were seriously considered and among the first was the dreamer Walter Kranz, who called police with his mysterious tip on January 15. He was held at the Englewood police station for some time and was repeatedly interrogated and given lie detector tests about his involvement in the murders. No solid evidence was ever found against him though.

The police also named a 17-year-old named Max Fleig as a suspect but the law at that time did not allow juveniles to be tested with a polygraph. Police Captain Ralph Petaque persuaded the boy to take the test anyway and in the midst of it, he confessed to kidnapping the girls. Because the test was illegal and inadmissible, the police were forced to let Fleig go free. However, Fleig was sent to prison a few years later for the brutal murder of a young woman.

In the midst of all of this, the police still had to deal with nuts and cranks, more so-called psychic visions and a number of false confessions, making their work even harder. Eager to crack the floundering case, Cook County Sheriff Joseph Lohman then arrested a Tennessee drifter named Edward L. "Benny" Bedwell. The drifter, who sported Elvis-style sideburns and a ducktail haircut, had reportedly been seen with the Grimes sisters in a restaurant where he sometimes washed dishes in exchange for food. When he was initially questioned, Bedwell admitted that he had been in the D&L Restaurant on West Madison with two girls and an unnamed friend but he insisted that the owners of the place were mistaken about the girls being the Grimes sisters.

According to the owners, John and Minnie Duros, the group had entered the diner around 5:30 on the morning of December 30. They described the taller girl as being either so drunk or so sick that she was staggering as she walked. The couples sat in a booth for a while and listened to Elvis songs on the jukebox and then went outside. According to Minnie Duros, "The taller girl returned to the booth and put her head on the table. They wanted her to get into the car, but she didn't want to. The other girl and the two men came back later and I told them to leave the girl alone—she's sick. But they all left anyway and on their way out, the shorter girl said they were sisters."

Lohman found the story plausible, thanks to the unshakable identification of the girls by Minnie Duros, their respective heights, the fact that one of them said they were sisters and finally, Bedwell's resemblance to Elvis. Lohman believed this might have been enough to get the girls to go along with him. And then of course, there was Bedwell's confession, which related a lurid and sexually explicit tale of drunken debauchery with the two young teenagers. He made and recanted three confessions and even re-enacted the crime for Lohman on January 27. Everyone doubted the story but Lohman. He booked Bedwell on murder charges, but the drifter's testimony was both vague and contradictory and (most likely) his confession had been beaten out of him. On January 31, he testified that he had confessed out of fear of Lohman's men, who had struck and threatened him while he was being questioned.

Another of the chief investigators in the case, Harry Glos, believed that Bedwell might have been implicated in the murders in some way but that he was a dubious suspect. State's Attorney Benjamin Adamowski agreed and ordered the drifter released. All charges against Bedwell were dismissed on March 4 and, upon leaving the courtroom, he was re-arrested on a fugitive warrant from Florida for the rape of a 13-year-old girl. The crime he was charged with in Florida closely resembled the one that took the lives of the Grimes sisters but he managed to avoid conviction for it, thanks to the passage of time while he was a fugitive. According to reports, Bedwell's accuser had been held captive for three days before escaping and notifying the police of her abduction and rape. Bedwell later spend time in prison on a weapons charge and died at some point after his release in 1986.

The dismissal of charges against Bedwell in the Grimes case set off another round of bickering between police departments and various jurisdictions. It got even worse when coroner's investigator Glos publicly criticized the autopsy findings concerning the time and cause of death. He shocked the public by announcing that Barbara and Patricia could not have died on the night they disappeared. He said that an ice layer around the bodies proved that they were warm when they were left along German Church Road and that only after January 7 would there have been enough snow to create the ice and to hide the bodies. Glos also raised the issues of the puncture wounds and bruises on the bodies, which had never been explained or explored. He was sure that they girls had been violently treated prior to death and also asserted that the older sister, Barbara, had been sexually molested before she was killed. The pathologists denied this but the Chicago Police crime lab reluctantly confirmed it. However, they were angry with Glos for releasing the information because they wanted to keep it secret so that they could use it when questioning suspects.

Coroner McCarron promptly had Glos fired, and many of the other investigators accused him of being reckless political grandstanding. Only Sheriff Lohman, who later deputized Glos to work on the case without pay, remained on his side. He agreed that the girls had likely been beaten and tortured by a sexual predator who lured them away. Lohman remained convinced until his death in 1969 that the predator who had killed the girls had been Benny Bedwell.

Other theories maintain that the girls may have indeed encountered Bedwell or another older man, and rumors circulated that the image of the two girls had been polished to cover up some very questionable behavior on their parts. It was said that they sometimes hung around a bar on Archer Avenue where men would buy them drinks. One of the men may have been Benny Bedwell. Harry Glos, who died in 1994, released information that one of the girls had been sexually active but later reports from those who have seen the autopsy slides say there is evidence that both of them may have been. It is believed that Coroner McCarron may not have released this for religious reasons or to spare additional grief for the family.

Today, veteran detectives believe that there was much more to the story than met the eye. According to Richard Lindberg's book, *Return to the Scene of the Crime*, they are convinced that Barbara and Patricia were abducted by a front man for a white slavery ring and taken to a remote location in the woods surrounding Willow Springs. They are convinced that the girls were strangled after refusing to become prostitutes. It's also possible that the girls may have been lured into the prostitution ring by someone they knew, not realizing what would be required of them, and then they were killed to keep them silent.

Others refused to even consider this and were angered by the negative gossip about the two girls. Old friends maintained that Barbara and Patricia were nice girls. They didn't hang around in bars; they were simply innocent teenage girls, just like everyone else at that time. As for myself, I'd like to think these old acquaintances are right. There are few stories as tragic as the demise of the Grimes sisters and perhaps it can provide us comfort knowing that the girls were simply in the wrong place at the wrong time and that such a thing could have happened to anyone. But does believing this make us feel better or worse?

Years passed. As there is no statute of limitations for murder, the case officially remained open but there was little chance that it would ever be solved. The Grimes family saw their hopes for closure in the case slowly fading away. Loretta Grimes passed away in December 1989 and by all accounts was a tragic and broken woman.

For the next several years, the investigation continued and more suspects were interviewed. A $100,000 reward was posted but the trail went cold. Then, decades later, hope was raised for the Grimes case when a solution was finally discovered to the Schuessler-Peterson murders from 1955. In a bizarre turn of events, a government informant named William Wemette accused one Kenneth Hansen of the murders during a police investigation into the 1977 disappearance of candy heiress Helen Vorhees Brach.

In 1955, Hansen, then 22-years-old, worked as a stable hand for Silas Jayne, a millionaire from Kane County. Jayne himself was wild and reckless and had been suspected of many violent and devious dealings during his rise to power in the horse-breeding world. He went to prison in 1973 for the murder of his half brother, George. Hansen himself was no prize either, and soon investigators were able to build a case against him. The case resulted in the deviant's arrest in August 1994.

Cook County prosecutors showed jurors how Hansen had lured the Schuessler brothers and Bobby Peterson into his car under false pretenses. They retraced the path of the killer in what author Richard Lindberg called "chilling detail." Hansen wanted to show the boys some prize horses belonging to Silas Jayne. According to the testimony of several men that Hansen had bragged to, he molested and then killed the Schuesslers and Peterson. When Jayne discovered his crime, the horse breeder burned the stables in order to obliterate any evidence that Hansen had left behind. Hansen's brother had then dumped the boys' bodies at Robinson's Woods and Jayne had filed a bogus insurance claim for the lost building.

This case came to trial in 1995 and breaking a 40-year silence, many of Hansen's other victims came forward, recalling promises of jobs made to young men in return for sexual favors. He forced their silence with threats that included warnings that they might end up "like the Peterson boy." Even without evidence and eyewitnesses to corroborate the prosecution's allegations against him, a Cook County jury convicted Kenneth Hansen of the murders in September 1995. They deliberated for less than two hours, and Hansen was sentenced for 200 to 300 years in prison.

Bobby Peterson and the Schuessler brothers could finally rest in peace—but the same could not be said for Barbara and Patricia Grimes. Despite the new public awareness and police interest, the case became cold once again. The investigators' theories about a connection between their murders and those of the Schuessler and Peterson boys were not correct after all. Those who still have an interest in the case will sometimes travel down German Church Road, in the southern suburb of Willow Springs, and wind up at a low point in this "haunted highway" where the bodies of the two girls were discovered. The impact of tragedy is still being felt today, as is the impression of what may have been a depraved killer's most desperate moments.

Today, the tree-lined roadway is heavily shadowed and quiet. There is almost a silence in the air that a traveler only seems to notice if he knows the reason why this is a haunted place. Away from the road, those who listen closely can hear the rippling of Devil's Creek below and one has to wonder if the whispering of the water could actually speak—what dark secrets would it have to reveal?

The bodies of the Grimes sisters were tossed without ceremony at the edge of a ravine, only a few feet from the shoulder of the road. A short distance away from this site, its entrance now blocked with a chain, was a narrow drive that once led to a house that was nestled in the trees. Mysteriously, the house was abandoned by the young family who lived there soon after the girls' bodies were discovered. Many of the belongings were left behind in the house and toys and furniture lay scattered about the yard for years. Even a 1955 Buick sat rusting in the driveway but it was eventually taken away. At some point, vandals set fire to the house and the owner had to demolish what was left. And while the owner never lived there again, people would occasionally see a tall, gaunt man roaming about the property in the spring and fall, when the trees and brush were thin. It was assumed that he had once occupied the place, but those who saw him were afraid to ask.

Why the family abandoned the home remains almost as great a mystery as who killed Barbara and Patricia Grimes. Nobody knows for sure, but people do have theories. Some believe the owner had been questioned about the crime and simply felt too embarrassed to stay. It has also been suggested that the family had seen something on the night the bodies were dumped near their house and became too frightened to remain behind. Others claim that the house, located so near the place where the bodies were found, became haunted.

For years, the police have received reports from those who had heard a car pulling up to the location; then a door opening, followed by the sound of something being dumped alongside the road. The door slams shut and the car drives away. They have heard these things—and yet there is no car in sight. According to author Tamara Shaffer, there was a young woman who took a number of her friends on a tour of the old house and the murder site one evening. They circled the ruins of the house, and saw a car approaching up the gravel drive from the road. It was a dark vehicle with no lights and it sped past them and around the house, then disappeared. The woman and her friends decided to leave and as they did, they encountered the police, who had been called to chase off the tour group. The chain that had been used to close off the driveway was still hanging in place and the police officers had seen no other car. Another woman claimed that, in addition to the sounds, she saw what appeared to be the naked bodies of two young girls lying on the edge of the roadway. When police investigated, there was no sign of the bodies.

Many researchers believe in residual hauntings, which means that an event may cause an impression to be left behind on the atmosphere of a place. It seems possible that the traumatic final moments of the Grimes sisters may have left such an impression on this small stretch of German Church Road. It may have also been an impression caused by the anxiety and madness of the killer as he left the bodies of the young women behind. But whether you believe in hauntings or not, should you ever travel along German Church Road, I defy you to stop along the roadway where the bodies of Barbara and Patricia were found and to say that you are not moved by the tragedy that came to an end here.

NEVERMORE

The Unsolved Puzzle of Edgar Allan Poe

Perhaps it is fitting that the man who is regarded as the "father of the American mystery," Edgar Allan Poe, has a number of unsolved puzzles connected to both his life and death. There is the mystery of what actually happened to Poe in the days before his death, when he vanished without a trace and then re-appeared in an incoherent state a few days later, wearing another man's clothes and carrying a stranger's walking stick. Where did he vanish to and who was the mysterious "Reynolds" that Poe whispered of in his dying breath? And who is the stranger who appears at Poe's grave each year on the anniversary of his birth, leaving roses and cryptic messages behind? And perhaps strangest of all, did the man who spent his life writing of gruesome death and horror actually commit the brutal murder of a young woman and create a crime that has never been solved?

Edgar Allan Poe was a man of many paradoxes. He wanted to be remembered as a poet and yet his macabre tales still stand today as his greatest contribution to literature. He was an American but not accepted in this country until after his death, even though he was seen as a genius in Europe. His works were straightforward on the surface and yet provide for numerous interpretations. They are complex yet simple; autobiographical yet pure fiction. In his stories, he gives the appearance of great learning and yet his schooling was not extensive. He wrote for money, aiming his work to the general reader of the day, but at the same time, he included other levels of meaning to impress more astute readers and the critics.

And then there was the man himself. He was always broke but played the part of the Southern gentleman. He also had a drinking problem but was enormously defensive about his background and talent and often rewrote his life history to suit the moment or his mood at the time. He married his 13-year-old cousin and lived with her and her mother while he carried on romances with several other women. After a period of insane grief, he asked three other women to marry him within a month of his wife's death from tuberculosis. And of course, his final five days of life are a blank slate. Even after more than a century and half of detective work, no one knows for sure what happened to Poe before he was found delirious on the streets of Boston.

By his own request, the executor and editor of his final writings was a man that he disliked and who returned the sentiments by distorting and fabricating Poe's biography to the extent that much of the writer's life remains a puzzle. Some believe that Poe knew this would happen and that he had the last laugh. By allowing his name to be slandered as it was, he created a controversy that has kept his name and his writings alive to this day. Even long after his death, we still don't have the answers to the mystery that was Edgar Allan Poe.

Poe was born on January 19, 1809 in Boston. He was the son of a talented actress named Elizabeth Arnold and her second husband, David Poe, Jr. , who was also an actor. Poe's father later deserted his wife and she died in December 1811. Her son was taken into the home of a wealthy merchant, John Allan, who became the boy's godfather, but did not adopt him. Regardless, Poe took the man's last name as his middle name and from that point on was Edgar Allan Poe.

In 1815, Allan moved his family to England to set up a European branch of his business. While there, Poe attended an academy at Stoke Newington but moved to Richmond, Virginia with the Allans in 1820 when business interests took a downturn in England. Poe later attended the University of Virginia and while there became secretly engaged to a young woman named Elmira Royster in February 1826. Her family, from southern aristocracy, did not approve of Poe and, after intercepting one of his letters to her and discovering the engagement, quickly married her off to another man. Although Poe did well at the university, his depression over the severed romance kept him at school for only a single term. It was during this period that stories began to circulate about Poe's drinking problem. There were numerous reports of his wild binges and of his being found in a drunken stupor in taverns and in ditches. It didn't seem to be that Poe drank too much, but that he had a bizarre reaction to even a small amount of liquor. He became a drifter after leaving school, and, since his godfather refused to give him any spending money, Poe took to gambling to sustain his living. He was unsuccessful at it though and, after piling up a large number of debts, Allan bailed him out.

Things began to go badly between Poe and Allan. When Poe returned to Richmond, he and Allan quarreled, and Poe left for

Boston. He took to writing and in 1827, he managed to have a small volume of poems (*Tamerlane*) privately printed. But the book sold poorly and, unable to find work, he joined the Army under the name Edgar A. Perry. He was sent to Fort Moultrie in Charleston but soon found that life as a common soldier was not to his liking. He begged Allan to get him out of the military but his godfather refused until his wife, on her deathbed, pleaded with him to reconcile with Poe. Allan sent for his godson, and the two agreed to forget about their differences—but only on the condition that Poe enter the Military Academy at West Point.

In 1829, Poe published another collection of poetry and resigned himself to entering West Point. Not surprisingly, he didn't like life as a military officer either and in 1830 he posted a bitter letter to a friend about how much he hated the Army and blamed Allan for his predicament. Allan learned of the letter and Poe was disowned and left with no financial support. Without it, he soon set about getting himself expelled from West Point. He succeeded and made his next stop New York.

In 1831, he published another book of poems and then moved to Baltimore, where he began writing short tales. He submitted several to a contest sponsored by the *Philadelphia Saturday Courier* in 1832 and although he did not win, the stories were published anonymously. The following year, the *Baltimore Saturday Visitor* awarded Poe $50 for his story "MS. Found in a Bottle." More stories followed. Under the auspices of his friend novelist John P. Kennedy, Poe began to write for the *Southern Literary Messenger*, becoming its editor in 1835. During his time at the helm, readership increased from 500 to 3,500, a remarkable achievement for the time. But even then, Poe began to sabotage his success. In his editorials, he began to launch a series of attacks on other literary figures of the day. This petty bickering, which began in the early 1830s, would plague him for the remainder of his life.

Poe was now living in Baltimore with his aunt, Marie Poe Clemm, and she arranged a marriage for him with her daughter,

Virginia, who was only 13. The marriage was an odd one by anyone's standards, although the age difference and the fact that the two were cousins was not as unusual in those times as we might consider it today. Still, Virginia read little of Poe's work and he never wrote a poem about her until after she died. He was obviously devoted to her however and, despite his often odd behavior, probably loved her very much.

Poe continued writing and produced a series of tales and poems and his only complete novel, *The Narrative of Arthur Gordon Pym*. In January 1837, he resigned from the *Messenger* and moved to New York with his wife. Over the course of the next two years, he assisted Professor Thomas Wyatt with two books on natural history and in 1839 became the editor for *Burton's Gentleman's Magazine*. He remained on staff with the magazine until June 1840, when he and Burton had a falling out. However, six months later, George R. Graham bought out *Burton's* changed the name of the magazine, and rehired Poe as a reviewer. As with his past endeavors, readership increased greatly during his time with the publication, and Poe was able to keep his drinking in check.

Poe published his first volume of tales in 1840, but it did not sell well. He kept on writing though, despite the failure, and managed to create one of the greatest detective stories of all time, "The Murders in the Rue Morgue." And it was also at this time that Poe became embroiled in a mystery that continues to haunt researchers and biographers to this day.

On a hot summer day in 1841, the body of a young woman was found floating in the Hudson River near Weehawken, New Jersey. Investigators learned that the corpse belonged to 21-year-old Mary Cecilia Rogers, a pretty young woman who was well known to the writers, actors and other celebrities who stopped in to see her at John Anderson's tobacco shop on Liberty Street, just across the river from lower Manhattan. The newspapers eagerly exploited the tragedy, publishing daily updates on the police investigation and wildly speculating on the identity of the girl's killer. There was little doubt that the girl had met with foul play, even though she had left a note behind at the time of her disappearance stating that she was going to kill herself.

The first suspect was John Anderson, Mary's employer, who had often accompanied her home in the evenings. Even though he could offer no alibi for the day of her disappearance, he was released when attention began to focus on Mary's fiancée, David Payne, a resident of her mother's boarding house in Hoboken, New Jersey. Payne admitted to seeing Mary on the morning that she vanished, three days before her body was found in the river.

The first evidence in the case turned up in a wooded area near the river. Police discovered a slip, a shawl, a parasol and a handkerchief with the initials "M. R." The ground around the site appeared to have been trampled down and gouges in the earth seemed to indicate that a struggle had taken place there. A short time later, David Payne committed suicide at this site by taking an overdose of the opiate laudanum. "This is the place," he wrote in his suicide note. "May God forgive me for my misspent life!" Many believed that this meant that he had killed Mary, but the police insisted that he had not. He had an ironclad alibi for the time of her murder. The case remained open and unsolved.

Among the readers of the newspaper reports about Mary Roger's murder was Edgar Allan Poe. He was then supporting his tubercular wife on his $800 annual salary at *Graham's Gentleman's Magazine* and working hard to come up with new ideas for his tales. His stories had not sold well, but he refused to quit writing He was especially interested in creating a sequel to his detective story "The Murders in the Rue Morgue" and saw the story of Mary Rogers as the perfect crime for his fictional Inspector Dupin to solve. In Poe's tale, the dead young woman was re-named Marie Roget, New York became Paris and the Hudson River became the Seine.

"Under the pretense of showing how Dupin unraveled the mystery of Marie's assassination, I, in fact, enter into a very rigorous analysis of the real tragedy in New York," Poe wrote to a friend in June 1842. "No point is omitted. I examine, each by each, the opinions of our press on the subject, and show (I think satisfactorily) that this subject has never yet been approached. The press has been entirely on a wrong scent. In fact, I really believe, not only that I have demonstrated the falsity of the idea that the girl was the victim of a gang of ruffians, but have indicated the assassin in a manner that will give renewed impetus to the investigation."

Poe's story, "The Mystery of Marie Roget," was serialized over three issues of *Snowden's Ladies' Companion* in November 1842 through February 1843. The story's conclusion was delayed a month due to revisions that Poe made to the tale (which will soon be explained). The most drastic revisions to the story came with a break-through in the actual investigation: the deathbed confession of a woman named Frederica Loss, who owned a roadhouse near Weehawken. After being accidentally shot, she told police that on Sunday, July 25, 1841, she had procured an abortionist for a young woman who subsequently died during the operation. The body was then dumped into the river and was believed to have been that of Mary Rogers. Poe went to work on his story and tied in the new evidence between the December and February installments of the story, explaining the delay in the last section of the tale.

With his usual utter logic, Inspector Dupin proves that there could be only one murderer of the girl, the "man of dark complexion," a naval officer with whom Marie was last seen and with whom she had disappeared some three weeks earlier. At this point, Poe ended his tale, declining to give the name of the killer, as he had done in his earlier crime story. An editor's note explained: "For reasons which we shall not specify, but to which many readers will appear obvious, we have taken the liberty of her omitting, from the manuscript placed in our hands, such portion as details following up of the apparently slight clew obtained by Dupin. We feel it is advisable to state, in brief, that the result desired was brought to pass."

It was not long after the story was published that people began to speculate that perhaps Poe knew more about the real Mary

Rogers case than he was willing to disclose. There are some who have claimed that the owner of the tobacco shop where Mary worked, John Anderson, hired Poe to write "The Mystery of Marie Roget" in order to draw suspicion away from himself. No evidence exists either way but it is true that he and Poe were friends and that Anderson later bought space in Poe's magazine *The Broadway Journal*, the only tobacconist to do so. But Felix McCloskey, Anderson's business partner, testified in an unrelated trial that Anderson had told him that Mary had received an abortion "the year before her murder took place, and that he got into some trouble about it. Outside of that, there were no grounds on earth for anybody to suppose he had anything to do with the murder."

So, if not Anderson, then who could Poe have gained his intimate knowledge of the crime from? Was he covering up for someone else? Or worse yet, could the writer have actually been involved in the crime? There are those who feel that Poe did indicate the murderer in his story, although he did not name him, and that the murderer was Poe himself.

Theorists have suggested that Poe met Mary while visiting the shop of his friend, John Anderson. There is no question that Mary occasionally became involved with assorted men, as evidenced by the abortion that she had. Did Anderson encourage her to become involved with some of the well-known and wealthy clients of the store? Did Poe have a relationship Mary? It has long been known that Poe engaged in affairs outside of his marriage and by 1841, his young wife was so ill with tuberculosis that she could not have provided him with much in the way of sexual gratification.

But was he capable of murder? At this period in his life, Poe was oppressed by poverty and a lack of literary recognition. He was continuing to fight his battles with alcohol and his wife was dying. To his family and friends, he appeared physically, if not mentally, ill. Poe's state of mind was mirrored by many of the characters in his crime and horror stories. He gave his literary creations the opportunity to indulge in crime, murder and bloodshed. They

committed the deeds that he would never dare to act on himself—
or would he?

Could Poe, in a moment of mental or alcohol-induced frenzy, have surrendered to the dark instincts that he kept trapped inside? Could he have killed Mary Rogers? Most would say no, but behavioral psychologists have demonstrated that criminals often give tips to reveal their identities to the police, especially those consumed with guilt and with a subconscious desire to be caught. Was this what Poe was doing when he gave his decisive hint about the identity of Marie Roget's murderer? The writer was, as the killer in the story was described, dark-skinned, with a full head of black hair falling over his large forehead.

I have to admit that while all of this does seem unlikely, it is not completely outside of the range of possibility. It should be noted however that no hard evidence exists that can link him to Mary Rogers or her murder, other than that he knew her and frequented the shop where she worked. There are many that feel Poe's knowledge of the case was just too detailed for a man merely writing it into fictional form, but we do know that Poe did adjust the facts in his story to fit the actual case. He made several changes between the release of the first two installments and the final one and it's likely that his "man with a dark complexion" was written to be the abortionist that Mary was taken to by the naval officer. It is also likely that she died from the result of a botched operation in 1841 and not in any fit of murderous passion. Poe would go on to make more changes before the story was published in 1845. When it appeared in book form, he had made fifteen minor changes to support the possibility that Marie Roget died following a bungled abortion. He then added footnotes to the story to make it appear that he had been right about the real-life case after all. Were the changes in the story merely to go along with the official version of events? Or did Poe know something that no one else possibly could? Did he know what really went through the mind of the killer?

In 1842, disaster struck in Poe's life when his wife Virginia broke a blood vessel while singing and her health began to rapidly decline. Poe worked harder than ever to support his ailing wife and her mother. He wrote for several publications and then finally achieved some amount of fame in 1845 with the publishing of his now classic poem "The Raven." He soon became the editor of the *Broadway Journal* and while he was still not making any money, he had found fame.

He began to give lectures on poetry and literature and at this point, met and fell in love with Mrs. Frances Sargent Osgood, apparently with Virginia's knowledge and acceptance. It's likely that she was so sick by this time that she could not carry on as the wife she thought she should be. Although Poe did nothing to curb his attraction to other woman, he was reportedly riddled with guilt over it, and took to heavy drinking again. Financial pressures continued to plague him as well. At a lecture in Boston, it became too much. He read his poem "Al Aaraaf" while drunk and first baffled, then outraged, the audience.

Poe took what money he had and bought out the owners of the *Broadway Journal*, but, as Poe's luck always seemed to go, the paper folded in January 1846. Poe then began to write a series of articles called the "Literati of New York" which sealed his fate for good. The profiles of 38 authors were caustic and one of them, written about Thomas Dunn English, was so harsh that the subject replied scathingly in print. Poe sued English for libel and won but the publicity from the trial, which included stories of Poe's drunkenness, ruined his reputation. Publicly, Poe became seen as unstable, irresponsible and possibly insane.

Then, in early 1847, Virginia died, sending Poe over the edge. He was seriously ill throughout most of the year that followed and was eventually nursed back to health by Mrs. Clemm. In 1848, he moved to Providence and was engaged for a brief time to Sarah Helen Whitman but the romance cooled after another of Poe's drunken lectures. That same year, he fell in love with Mrs. Annie Richmond, but nothing ever came of it.

Poe was again desperately broke and began writing for a cheap paper called the *Boston Flag of Our Union*. In June 1849, he went to Philadelphia, where he reportedly went on a drunken binge and was rescued by two friends. This seemed to sober Poe up for awhile and he joined the Sons of Temperance in an effort to stay away from alcohol for good. Poe ended up moving back to Richmond and, according to some biographers, began to revive in his former boyhood home. Revisiting his youth, he became acquainted again with the now widowed Elmira Royster Shelton. The two seemed to be very much in love and Poe at last seemed to have everything to live for. Success and true love were now in his grasp, he believed, but soon everything was going to come to an end.

Poe's intentions had been to leave Richmond and to travel to New York to bring the beloved Mrs. Clemm to Virginia for the wedding of him and his Elmira. On September 26, Poe visited a young doctor in Richmond named Dr. John Carter, complaining of a fever and distress. When he left, he took with him Dr. Carter's walking stick and left his own behind. Poe departed in the early morning hours of September 27, bound for New York. He set out by steamer with a trunk containing clothing, some books and some manuscripts. Somehow though, his trip came to a tragic conclusion on October 3 when he was discovered at Gunner's Hall, a Baltimore tavern, by a printer named Joseph Walker. Poe was strangely dressed and unconscious at the time. It was Election Day for Congress and the tavern was a local polling place. Poe seemed to Walker "rather the worse for the wear" and "in great distress." He believed that Poe was drunk and was now ill from exposure to the winds and soaking rains that had recently plagued the city. Poe managed to tell Winter that he knew Joseph Evans Snodgrass, the Baltimore publisher, and Walker sent his friend a message that told him Poe was in dire need of immediate assistance.

Snodgrass arrived to find Poe in a stupor. He wore neither vest nor tie, his dirty trousers fit badly and his shirt was crumpled and stained. He assumed that Poe was wearing castoff clothing and that he had been robbed of his own. Snodgrass arranged for a room at the tavern for Poe but this was changed by the arrival of Henry Herring, Poe's uncle by marriage. He realized that his nephew was quite sick and called for a carriage to the hospital instead.

Poe was taken to the Washington Medical College and given a private room, reportedly in a section of the hospital reserved for cases of drunkenness. According to doctors, he was delirious when he arrived and often cried and trembled. He was repeatedly questioned, but his answers were mostly incoherent. He thrashed violently about for an entire day, moaning and weeping and he once screamed the name "Reynolds"—although who this could have been also remains a mystery. He died on October 7, 1849.

Some said Poe's death was caused by alcohol, others say that he was in a psychotic state or had rabies. Other writers believe that he may have been drugged and murdered as the clothes that he wore were not his own and the walking stick he carried belonged to another man. There have been literally dozens of theories posed as to what caused Poe's death but no one will ever know for sure. Perhaps the fact that his death remains unexplained is the reason why Poe's ghost remains in the Old Western Burial Ground.

Located in Baltimore, the Old Western Burial Ground holds the remains of a number of famous politicians, generals, and one writer, Edgar Allan Poe. Legend has it that Poe's ghost has been seen near his grave and in the catacombs of the church. But Poe's restless spirit is not the only enduring mystery of this unusual cemetery. But Poe's restless spirit is not the only enduring mystery of this unusual cemetery. For more than fifty years, another strange figure has haunted Poe's grave. Dressed completely in black, including a black fedora and a black scarf to hide his face, he carries a walking stick and strolls into the cemetery every year on January 19, the birth date of Edgar Allan Poe. On every occasion, he has left behind a bottle of cognac and three red roses on the gravesite of the late author. After placing these items with care, he then stands, tips his hat and walks away. The offerings always remain on the grave, although one year, they were accompanied by a note, bearing no signature, which read: "Edgar, I haven't forgotten you."

The identity of the man in black has been an intriguing mystery for years. Many people, including Jeff Jerome, the curator of the nearby Edgar Allan Poe house, believe that there may be more than one person leaving the tributes. Jerome himself has seen a white-haired man while other observers have reported a man with black hair. Regardless, Jerome has been quoted as saying that if he has his way, the man's identity will never be known.

WAS JACK THE RIPPER AN AMERICAN?

The Whitechapel Killer and Doctor Tumblety

In the year 1888, the city of London, England was terrorized by a killer who called himself "Jack the Ripper." The mysterious madman prowled the streets of the Whitechapel District in East London and slaughtered a number of prostitutes, carving his way into the historical record as the first modern serial killer. As the years have passed, the Ripper has held the morbid curiosity of professional and amateur sleuths, alike. Having eluded capture in the 1880s, his identity has been debated ever since. Not surprisingly, many suspects have been named as the Ripper over the years with the vast majority of them being British. Many readers, may be surprised to learn that there are those who believe Jack the Ripper may have actually been an American.

One of these infamous suspects lived and died in the city of St. Louis. His name was Dr. Francis J. Tumblety, and suspicion about him being the Ripper came about in 1913, a number of years after the murders took place. In a letter dated September 23, Inspector John Littlechild, head of the Special Branch in England, wrote to George Sims, a journalist, about a medical man who may have been the killer. He was apparently replying to Sims about other possible suspects when he wrote:

I never heard of a Dr. D in connection with the Whitechapel murders, but amongst the suspects, and to my mind a very likely one, was a Dr. T (which sounds much like a D). He was an American quack named Tumblety and at one time was a frequent visitor to London and on these occasions constantly brought under the notice of police, there being a large dossier concerning him at Scotland Yard. Although a "Sycopathis Sexualis" [sic] subject, he was not known as a sadist (which the murdered unquestionably was) but his feelings toward women were remarkable and bitter in the extreme, a fact on record. Tumblety was arrested at the time of the murders in connection with unnatural offenses and charged at Marlborough Street, remanded on bail, jumped his bail and got away to Boulogne. He shortly left Boulogne and was never heard of afterwards. It is believed that he committed suicide but certain it is that from the time the "Ripper" murders came to an end.

And while not all of Inspector Littlechild's facts were correct, he did make an interesting case toward the American doctor being the fiendish killer. In fact, the idea was so compelling that when the letter resurfaced years later, the theory was later turned into a flawed but fascinating book by two British police officers, Stewart P. Evans and Paul Gainey, called *Jack the Ripper: First American Serial Killer*. But was the medical man the real Whitechapel killer?

Francis J. Tumblety was born in Canada in 1833 and moved with his family to Rochester, New York at a very young age. Although uneducated, he was a clever man and became wealthy and successful as a homeopath and mixer of patent medicines. There is no record as to whether or not these snake oil cures worked or not, but it is certain that Tumblety held no medical degree. He did claim to possess Indian and Oriental secrets of healing and good health, and he was described as charming and handsome, so it's not surprising that he made quite a bit of money in this questionable field. When not charming customers, Tumblety was said to have been disliked by many for his self-aggrandizing and constant boasting. He had a penchant for staying in fine hotels, wearing expensive clothes and making false claims. Often these tall tales got him into trouble, and he left town on more than one occasion just a step ahead of the law.

In the late 1850s and early 1860s, Tumblety was living in Washington and from this period, the first stories of his deep-seated hatred for women began to surface. During a dinner party one night in 1861, Tumblety was asked by some guests why he did not invite any single women to the gathering. Tumblety replied that women were nothing more than cattle and that he would rather give a friend poison than see him with a woman. He then began to speak about the evils of women, especially prostitutes. A man in attendance that evening, an attorney named C. A. Dunham, later remarked that it was believed that Tumblety had been tricked into marriage by a woman who was later revealed to be a prostitute. This was thought to have sparked his hatred of woman, but none of the guests had any idea just how far the feelings of animosity went until Tumblety offered to show them his collection. He led his guests into a back study of the house, where he kept his anatomical museum. Here, they were shown row after row of jars containing women's uteruses.

In 1863, Tumblety came to St. Louis for the first time and took rooms at the Lindell Hotel. As he recounted in letters, his flamboyant ways did not appeal to those in St. Louis, and he claimed to have been arrested there and in Carondelet, an independent city nearby, for "putting on airs" and "being caught in quasi-military" dress. Regardless of his claims, Tumblety most likely caused trouble during these highly charged times because of his apparent Southern sympathies. In 1865, he was arrested on the serious charge of what amounted to an early case of biological terrorism. Federal officers had him arrested after he was allegedly involved in a plot to infect blankets, which were to be shipped to Union troops, with yellow fever. The whole thing did turn out to be a case of mistaken identity (an alias of Tumblety's was remarkably close to a real doctor involved) but it's likely that he would not have been suspected if not for some actions on his part. Tumblety was taken to Washington and imprisoned until the confusion over the plot could be cleared up and was later released. According to British records, Tumblety was then arrested again after the death of President Abraham Lincoln, this time as a conspirator in the assassination. He was again released, but this time, his reputation was destroyed in Washington so he fled to New York. After that, he began traveling frequently to London during the 1870s and 1880s.

Although there has been much debate as to how many victims Jack the Ripper claimed and just when the murders began, it is generally believed that the first killing occurred on August 31, 1888. The victim was a prostitute named Mary Ann Nichols. Her death was followed by those of Annie Chapman and Elizabeth Stride on September 8. On September 30, the Ripper claimed Catherine Eddowes. Organs had been removed from the bodies of both Chapman and Eddowes, including the latter woman's uterus.

Just prior to the start of the murders, Dr. Tumblety had come to London and had taken lodgings in Batty Street, the heart of Whitechapel and within easy distance of the murder scenes. It is known that he was watched closely by the police, especially after an incident involving a pathological museum. During the Annie Chapman inquest, police investigators heard information that has created the most pervasive and enduring myth of the Whitechapel murders, that of the Ripper as a surgeon. Only one medical examiner, arguing against all other expert testimony, believed that the killer had expert anatomical knowledge. He based his theory on a witness that claimed the killer was hunting for women's uteruses to sell to an unknown American. This bizarre bit of testimony came about because Tumblety did indeed visit a pathological museum in London and had inquired about any uteruses that might be for sale. He apparently wanted to add them to his collection.

On November 7, Tumblety was arrested, not for murder, but for "unnatural offences," which was usually a reference to homosexuality, but could also include procuring young girls. He was later released on bail, although when exactly has been a matter of debate. According to some records, he was released on November 16, but according to others, he was actually let go on November 8. The entire theory of whether or not he was Jack the Ripper hinges on the date that he was released from jail. The reason for this is that on November 9, the Ripper claimed his last victim. Her name was Mary Kelly, and she was mutilated in her own bed in ways that cannot be imagined. She was butchered beyond recognition, and a number of her organs were removed, including her heart and uterus.

If Tumblety was actually released on November 8, then he could have killed Mary Kelly. One account of the days following the murder states that he was arrested on suspicion of her murder on November 12, was released without being charged and then vanished from Whitechapel. On November 24, it is alleged that he took a steamer to France and then sailed from France to New York. Scotland Yard detectives were said to have pursued him to New York, and though they kept an eye on him, had no evidence to arrest him and were unable to extradite him for the still outstanding indecency charges. They eventually gave up and went home.

Those who do not believe that Tumblety could have been the Ripper give a different accounting of the days after Mary Kelly was killed. According to them, Tumblety was not released on bail until November 16. As Inspector Littlechild wrote, he was then believed to jump bail and escape to Boulogne with the police pursuing him. From there, he booked passage to New York, where police staked out his lodgings. He eluded them, however, and vanished. He was not, as far as recorded, further pursued for his part in the killings. With that said, it would have been impossible for Tumblety to be the Ripper. If he were the killer, then someone would have had to copy and exceed his previous work on Mary Kelly while the doctor was still in jail. Most would agree that this seems highly unlikely.

But our story is not quite over. Regardless of what is written about the last days of Tumblety in London, all will agree that after his escape he did end up in St. Louis. He also traveled for a time, avoiding Washington but frequently visiting Baltimore, New Orleans and St. Louis continuing to live in hotels. In April 1903, Tumblety checked himself into St. John's Hospital and Dispensary at 23rd and Locust Streets in St. Louis. The hospital, which was then located in the old Catlin-Beach-Barney Mansion, provided care for indigents, which is how Tumblety was presenting himself at this time.

According to accounts, Tumblety was suffering from a long and painful illness, although what it may have been has never been specifically identified. Some have suggested that it may have been a debilitating case of syphilis, the contraction of which might have been cause for his hatred of women and especially prostitutes. Whatever it was though, Tumblety remained at St. John's until his death on May 28, 1903. However, he was far from indigent when he died. Court records showed that Tumblety left an estate of more than $135,000 when he died, some of which St. John's managed to recover. The hospital asked for about $450 to cover the room expenses and medical tests for a man who was clearly not poor. The rest of the estate, except for costs to a St. Louis undertaker, went to Tumblety's niece, Mary Fitzsimmons of Rochester, New York.

Aside from the hospital, there was one other claim to Tumblety's estate. However, this claim was quite strange, especially in light of Tumblety's clear prejudices on the subject. A will written by Tumblety shortly before his death was challenged by a Baltimore attorney named Joseph Kemp. He claimed that Tumblety had written an earlier will in October 1901 that left $1,000 to the Baltimore Home for Fallen Women, in other words, a halfway house for prostitutes. The claim was thrown out of court but it does provide an interesting final note to the life of a man who has been suspected of being the most famous killer of prostitutes in history.

The Serial Murders of Dr. Thomas Neill Cream

Tumblety was unquestionably odd and quite possibly deranged, but his insanity and deviousness never reached the bounds of another American Jack the Ripper suspect, Dr. Thomas Neill Cream. Cream thought of himself as a master criminal and his ego knew no bounds. He seemed to love to do evil and he was said to have revolutionized the concept of murder in the late 1800s. His motives would later provide much in the way of study to crime psychologists and just what he may have done (and when) continues to baffle crime historians to this day. He specialized in the murder of women and perhaps for this reason, and the fact that he was so adept at covering his trail, Cream emerged in John Cashman's 1973 book *The Gentleman from Chicago* as a Ripper suspect. And while many have disputed these charges, Cream is worthy of mention as an American connection to the most heinous murders of the Victorian era.

Cream was born in Scotland in 1850 and immigrated with his parents to Canada four years later. Though little is known about his early life, his parents were hardworking decent folks, and Cream lacked for nothing when it came to education and comfort. Somewhere along the way though, some twist in his makeup caused him to develop an overwhelming hatred of women. Perhaps it developed in childhood or later, when he attended McGill University in Montreal to study to be a doctor. He qualified as a physician but years later, the college would remove his name from the graduate rolls to avoid being connected to his crimes.

During his senior year of college, Cream met and seduced a young woman named Flora Eliza Brooks. When it was discovered that the girl was pregnant, Cream performed a crude abortion on her, leaving Flora permanently scarred and weak for the rest of her life. Her parents, when they discovered what had occurred, forced Cream to marry the girl, but he vanished soon after the nuptials and sailed for England in 1876.

In London, Cream enrolled in a post-graduate course at St. Thomas' Hospital, which was located in the Waterloo-Lambeth section of the city, an area teeming with diseased prostitutes. It is believed that it is here where Cream first came into contact with the whores of London and where he also contracted syphilis. The effects of the disease on his brain have been blamed for his constant thoughts of murder and his psychopathic rages. Although it's likely that he was mad previous to the disease.

Cream returned to Canada a few years later and set up practice in Ontario. He learned that his wife had passed away and while she is listed as having died of consumption, the horrific abortion at Cream's hands undoubtedly contributed to her early demise. His medical practice was anything but savory, and he soon earned a reputation for insurance fraud and performing illegal operations on women, especially abortions. He began a prosperous practice among local prostitutes and young women in trouble until the body of a young hotel chambermaid was discovered in his apartment one night with a bottle of chloroform beside her body. Cream had performed a savage abortion on her and it had failed, claiming her life. He was arrested and, despite the evidence against him, the girl's death was ruled a suicide and Cream was freed.

This would be the first of a series of miraculous escapes for Cream. He now took his operation to the teeming red-light districts of Chicago. His career as an abortionist found him plenty of new patients among the dirty and sickly prostitutes of Chicago's Levee districts. He seemed to enjoy inflicting pain on these women, but his deviant desires were truly inflamed by the opportunities to work on proper young ladies who had been compromised. One such woman was Julia Faulkner, who died on Cream's operating table in August 1880. He was charged with murder but the Chicago authorities lacked proof, and Cream was released once again. Detectives suspected that Cream had given Miss Faulkner a poison called strychnine in the guise of a painkiller.

In 1881, Cream struck again. After one of his abortions, a Miss

Stack perished after taking strychnine-laced medicine prescribed by Cream. He attempted to blackmail the chemist that provided the medicine (some medicines contained a small amount of the poison in those days), asking to be paid off to keep silent about the bad mixture. The chemist, knowing that he was not at fault, turned the blackmail letter over to the police and Cream was arrested. Again he was tried, and again he was turned loose for lack of evidence.

Cream then began marketing a special elixir that he had created and which he claimed would cure epilepsy. Amazingly, he acquired a considerable following of patients who swore by the medicine. Then, into his office one day walked Julia Stott, an attractive young woman who was looking for Cream's epilepsy cure. Her husband, Daniel Stott, was a station agent on the Northeastern Railway and suffered from epilepsy. Cream began making advances toward Julia and found the woman receptive. She said that her husband's illness and advanced age had ruined her sex life.

It's hard to imagine what could have attracted the beautiful woman to Cream. The doctor was a slight and scrawny man with thinning hair and gold-rimmed glasses through which he constantly squinted. He often gave off an appearance of being from the upper crust though, with upscale dress and a bushy mustache that he kept waxed and turned up at the ends. Likely though, Julia's attraction to him went beyond just looks as she spoke of the doctor as being insatiable and stated later that he ravished her several times during their first meeting.

Daniel Stott began to grow suspicious of his wife's frequent trips to Cream's office and suspected that he was giving Julia more than medicine on these visits. Not surprisingly, Cream repaid the man's suspicions by adding strychnine to his medicine, and Stott died on June 14, 1881. Originally, Stott's death was attributed to epilepsy, but Cream wanted to collect on Stott's life insurance for he and Julia. Cream wrote to the district attorney and stated that a pharmacist was responsible, having given Stott some bad medicine. He suggested that Stott's body be exhumed. The prosecutor decided to check into the letter and had the body exhumed. An exam discovered that there was poison in Stott's stomach, something that would have never been found if not for Cream's letter.

Cream may have realized his blunder once the letter was sent and he soon fled the city with the widow Stott. They were quickly apprehended by the police. Cream insisted at his trial that Stott's death had been the pharmacist's fault, but Julia turned state's evidence against him and testified that she had seen Cream "put some white powder" into her husband's medicine bottle. This time, Cream's luck didn't hold and he was sentenced to life imprisonment at Joliet Prison. He was admitted in 1881 and was regarded as a model prisoner. Over the years, the only complaints ever filed about him came from other prisoners who claimed to be awakened in the middle of the night to the sound of low, hissing laughter coming from his cell. At such times, he could be found sitting on his bunk, speaking to phantom women that appeared in his cell and promising them slow and agonizing deaths. He created detailed plans of revenge and sexual savagery he would wreak should be ever be released.

And then fate reared its ugly head in Thomas Neill Cream's life again. In 1887, his father died and left his son a sizable sum of money. His accountant and bookkeeper, Thomas Davidson, wrote to Illinois authorities and requested the complete records of Cream's trial. After studying the case, he became convinced that Cream was innocent of the charges that had sent him to Joliet. He began petitioning for Cream's release and a number of family friends in Canada took up the cause, perhaps never realizing what sort of man their friend's son had become. The petitions and letters arrived in Illinois by the bagful and finally, Governor Joseph W. Fifer relented and he commuted Cream's sentence. He was released from Joliet on July 31, 1891.

Cream immediately went to Quebec and collected his inheritance. It's likely that the accountant finally realized his mistake. He later wrote: "In my first interview with him, I concluded that he was unmistakably insane." Of course by that time, it was too late for the victims that still lay ahead.

Wealthy and free to do what he wished, Cream returned to England. He arrived in October 1891 and took rooms in a boarding house on Lambeth Palace Road, back in the slums that he had once reveled in. He told his landlady that he was at work on his postgraduate studies at St. Thomas' Hospital but when he failed to see any patients or to keep any sort of office hours, he had to tell her that he had been ill and was recovering from a strange disease. His eyes bothered him constantly, he explained, forcing him to take large doses of morphine and cocaine. His landlady replied that she hoped his health would improve.

A short time after his arrival, Cream went to work. He began visiting the local prostitutes and killing them. He met one such woman, Matilda Clover, just two days after he arrived and she later died from nux vomica poisoning, a liquid that caused vomiting and which was often prescribed by doctors as a tonic. The same fate also befell a woman named Ellen Donworth but as in the past, Cream was not charged with anything.

After a short break from murder, and an even shorter attempt at a love affair with a woman named Laura Sabbatini, Cream poisoned two other women, Alice Marsh and Emma Shrivell. He would have escaped detection in these crimes too, but, as he did in Chicago, he inexplicably tried to place blame for the crimes on someone else. This time, he accused his neighbor of the murders and tried to blackmail him. He told Walter J. Harper, a medical student who lived in the same boarding house, that he had incriminating evidence against him, but that for a large sum of money, he would not notify the police. He also wrote a letter to Harper's father and told him that his son was a murderer. The elder Harper did not respond, but he held onto the letter. Cream then wrote to the coroner and told him that Harper had committed the murders and that he had proof. He also wrote to John Haynes, a photographer who lived in his building, and told him the same thing. He constantly talked of the two dead women, often shocking his land-lady with his vile descriptions of Harper's alleged crimes.

It was finally John Haynes (after Cream took him on a guided tour of the murder sites) who went to detectives at Scotland Yard and told them of his suspicions about Cream being the killer. At that point, his attempts to blackmail Harper were also revealed and Cream was finally arrested. He went to trial in October 1892, pro-claiming his innocence and capturing newspaper headlines across the nation. A number of people testified against him and only a sobbing Laura Sabbatini testified on his behalf. Cream's tin box that contained vials of poison was placed on display in the courtroom and was later added to Scotland Yard's infamous Black Museum.

There was a strange incident that jarred the proceedings of the trial. A letter was received and was read aloud in court by coroner Braxton Hicks. It read:

> Dear Sir, The man that you have in your power, Dr. Neill, is as innocent as you are. Knowing him by sight, I disguised myself like him, and made the acquaintance of the girls that have been poisoned. I gave them pills to cure them of all their earthly mis-eries, and they died. . . If I were you, I would release Dr. T. Neill, or you might get into trouble. His innocence will be declared sooner or later, and when he is free he might sue you for dam-ages. Beware all. I warn but once.
>
> Yours Respectfully,
> Juan Pollen,
> alias Jack the Ripper

The mere utterance of the name attached to the letter caused the entire assemblage to gasp, except for Cream, who smiled widely. The letter later turned out to be the work of a crank, as Cream could not have sent it himself from his cell, but it stayed in Cream's mind until the end of his life. It only took the jury ten minutes to find Cream guilty; Judge Sir Henry Hawkins lived up to his reputation as the hanging judge by ordering Cream to be executed on the gallows on November 15, 1892.

While awaiting execution, Cream talked incessantly to his jailers, mostly insisting that he was a great man and that the world had refused to recognize it. He also claimed to have killed many more women in order to end their misery and aid society, hinting at even darker things than those he had been found guilty of. On the night before his execution, Cream could be heard moaning in his cell, no longer bragging of his crimes but now protesting his innocence. At dawn on the 15th though, he went calmly to the gallows. He was bound hand and foot and placed on the trap as the black hood was slipped over his head. Cream saved his most dramatic and strange proclamation for last. The lever was pushed to release and the trap, and moments before he plunged to his doom, Cream shouted out: "I am Jack the. . ." The rope cut him off before he could finish and in that split second, Cream created an enigma that has inspired many to believe that he was confessing to having been the killer Jack the Ripper. And in death, Cream became as mysterious as he was in life.

Cream's last words have plagued both crime historians and Ripperologists for years. There have been a number of theorists who have concocted some convincing (and some not so convincing) cases that Cream may have been the Whitechapel killer. Sir Edward Marshall Hall, who had once defended Cream on a charge of bigamy, later wrote that he believed Cream sometimes employed a double who used his name and that both men "used each other's terms of imprisonment as alibis for each other." Cream had earlier told Hall that he refused to plead guilty to charges against him because he was in prison at the time of the offenses. A check with officials did reveal that a man matching Cream's description had been in prison at the same time, and Cream was released.

Ripper expert Donald Rumbelow has stated that this has led to the suggestion that even though Cream was serving time in Joliet Prison when the Whitechapel murders were taking place, he may have actually been in England. His double could have been imprisoned, or vice versa. As the double had given Cream an alibi for the bigamy charges, Cream then tried to repay the debt by shouting those last words from the scaffold. Others have suggested that the letter that was read at Cream's trial could have been from Cream's double, the real Jack the Ripper, attempting to save the doctor's life.

Unfortunately for those who feel they have solved the Whitechapel murders by pinning them on Cream, the idea of the *doppelganger* is not very convincing and neither is the other theory as to how the good doctor could have committed the crimes from behind the walls of Joliet prison. In some accounts, Cream was able to bribe his way out of the corrupt prison in the middle 1880s, journey to London, commit the murders and then return to his cell in order to be released in 1891. Author and crime historian Jay Robert Nash personally checked the records at Joliet prison in the late 1970s and found that the ledger from the era was still intact, although Cream's personal files had long ago been destroyed in a fire. The ledger states that Thomas Neill Cream, prisoner no. 4374, was imprisoned at Joliet on November 1, 1881 and not released until July 31, 1891. There are also records attached about the commuting of Cream's sentence by the governor but nothing to indicate that he was ever released. The idea that he bribed his way out of the prison is merely a theory, with no real evidence existing to support it.

And perhaps the biggest problem with the idea of Cream being the Ripper is his method of murder. Although he was a brutish and bloody abortionist, his method of dispatching young women was by poison, not the knife. It seems unlikely that he would poison his victims prior to 1888 and then suddenly go on a wild mutilating spree, only to go back to poisoning them again a few years later.

So it seems that we have to look beyond Dr. Cream when seeking the identity of Jack the Ripper. Admittedly the two killers did have some similarities in that both enjoyed killing prostitutes and then writing letters about their deeds to the authorities, but beyond that, the comparisons end, continuing a mystery that will not be solved anytime soon.

A Butcher's Dozen

The Cleveland Torso Murders

The American equivalent of the terrifying crime spree of Jack the Ripper was undoubtedly the "Cleveland Torso Murders" that took place in an area called Kingsbury Run in the middle 1930s. Like the Ripper case, the murders left a number of mutilated victims behind and they remain unsolved to this day. It was a series of killings that had tragic results, terrifying the city of Cleveland, ending human lives and destroying the career of a law enforcement icon, "Untouchable" Eliot Ness.

Kingsbury Run was a barren wasteland on the east side of Cleveland in 1935. It tore through the rugged area, sometimes plunging to depths of 60 feet, and was scattered with overgrown weeds, patches of wild grass, tumbling pieces of old paper, piles of garbage and even the occasional skeletal remains of an abandoned car. Along the edges of the ravine were ramshackle frame houses, built close together and of such shabby construction that they seemed to almost be teetering on the brink of collapse. As the ravine angled toward downtown, it emptied out into the muddy waters of the Cuyahoga River, where concrete and steel bridges, tanks and old factory buildings dotted the banks. It was a forbidding and shunned place in those days and yet among the refuse and decay were small cities of homeless men, forced into the ravine by the blight of the Great Depression. They squatted there in cardboard boxes and in shacks made from scavenged wood, huddling near small campfires and trying to ignore the lonesome cries of the freight trains that passed nearby.

It was through this desolate region that two young boys walked home from school on a warm afternoon in September 1935. As they ambled along a weed-covered slope known as Jackass Hill, one challenged the other to a race and they plunged down the steep incline to the bottom. The older of the two, James Wagner, reached the bottom first and, as he stopped running, he noticed something white in the bushes a short distance away. He peered a little closer and was stunned to see that the something was a pale, naked body from which the head had been severed.

The police arrived soon after and started their investigation. The body was that of a young, white male, clad only in a pair of black socks. The man's head and his genitals had been removed. The body had been positioned on its back with the legs stretched out and the arms placed directly at its sides. And as they began searching the area, they discovered another shocking surprise. Just 30 feet away from the first body was another corpse, this time of an older man. This body was placed in the same position and the head and genitals had also been removed.

The area was cordoned off and soon a clump of hair was seen protruding from the ground. Officers carefully dug around it and discovered one of the missing heads. The other was also found a short distance away, as were the severed genitals. It looked as though the killer had merely tossed them away like garbage. One thing the search did not reveal however was the murder site. It appeared as though the men had been killed somewhere else, as no blood was found on the ground or on the bodies. The corpses had obviously been cleaned after bleeding from the fatal wounds had ceased.

The forensic examination that followed revealed even more puzzling evidence. The body of the older man turned out to be badly decomposed and the skin discolored from some sort of solution that the pathologists believed had been used to try and preserve it. The man had been dead for about two weeks and yet someone had kept the body, only dumping it when it had become too decayed to keep any longer. The younger man had been dead for about three days and his fingerprints enabled the police to identify him as Edward Andrassy, 28, who had a minor police record for carrying a con-

cealed weapon. He lived near Kingsbury Run and had a reputation
for being a drunk and for frequently getting into fights. The most
chilling discovery came when pathologists realized that Andrassy
had actually died from the decapitation. He had been alive at the
time and bound hand and foot by ropes, against which he had
struggled violently. The operation was done very skillfully and the
investigators suspected that the killer might be a butcher, a surgeon, or at least someone familiar with killing animals.

The older man turned out to be impossible to identify. But the
police hoped that it would be easy to find Andrassy's killer by following the dead man's trail through the sleazy bars and gambling
parlors that Andrassy frequented. He was known to be a procurer
of young girls for prostitution and also admitted to having male
lovers. Detectives followed lead after lead from dangerous characters who bore Andrassy a grudge, including a husband who had
vowed to kill the man for sleeping with his wife. The investigations
and interrogations led nowhere and lead after lead came to a dead
end. Every clue seemed to fall apart in both murders, and the press
soon began calling the killer the "Mad Butcher of Kingsbury Run".

Four months after the first bodies were found, on a cold
Sunday afternoon in January, the howling of a dog led a woman
who lived on East Twentieth Street (not far from Kingsbury Run)
to make another gruesome discovery. She found the chained animal trying to tear open a basket that was standing near the wall of
a factory. Minutes later, after a brief glance inside, she told a passing neighbor that the basket contained hams. The neighbor recognized the hams as being a human arm. A burlap bag was pulled
from the basket and they discovered a female torso, from which
the head, the left arm and lower legs were missing. The police were
able to trace the fingerprints to a 41-year-old prostitute named
Florence "Flo" Polillo, an overweight and unattractive woman who
was well known in the local dives and gin joints. Once again, there
were plenty of leads to follow in the investigation but once again,
they all led nowhere. Two weeks later, Polillo's left arm and the

remainder of her legs were found discarded in an empty lot but her head was never recovered.

The discovery of the woman's body had dire repercussions for detectives assigned to the earlier murders. They had been convinced that they were dealing with a homosexual killer and the investigation had been slanted in that direction. Now, with the latest victim being a woman, it appeared that the killer had no real motives in mind. To make matters worse, a cold case from 1934 was recalled when the torso of an unknown woman was found along the shore of Lake Erie. The newspapers began calling her "victim zero." It began to look as though the so-called Mad Butcher was really mad after all.

The biggest advantage in the new case, was that a new director of public safety had been appointed to oversee the police department. His name was Eliot Ness and he had achieved fame just a few years before for cleaning up the city of Chicago with the assistance of his Untouchables. He had come to Cleveland to fight the gangsters, gambling and corruption in the city and soon found himself embroiled in the hunt for the sadistic killer. The newspapers and the people on the street were confident that Ness would make the city safe again. Ness was not so confident. It soon became clear to him that hunting down a lone killer was not like battling organized crime. The Butcher struck at random, leaving no clues behind, and despite well-organized searches and investigations, the killer managed to stay several steps ahead of the police department and Cleveland's famous public safety director.

The killing began again that summer when the head of a young man was found wrapped in a pair of trousers beneath a bridge in Kingsbury Run. Two boys discovered the head on June 22 and summoned the police. The body was found a quarter mile away, and this time, it was obvious from the blood at the scene that the man had been killed at the site. He had also been killed by being beheaded but it was unclear to investigators how the murderer had restrained him while the deed was being committed. No identification could be found for the man, although it was estimated that he was about 25-years-old and was described as "heavily tattooed."

Three weeks later, a hiker discovered another decapitated male body in the ravine. The head was found nearby but again, the man could not be identified. The body was so decomposed that examiners realized that he had been killed before the previously discovered victim.

The Butcher struck again in 1936. The body of a man was found in Kingsbury Run. His genitals had been severed and his body was sliced completely in two. A hat that was lying nearby did manage to give detectives one lead. It was identified by a housewife who lived nearby as being one that she had given to a homeless man. Not far from the site where the body was found was a hobo camp, where those who rode the rails and drifted would sometimes sleep or look for something to eat. Apparently, this was where the Butcher had found this latest victim.

Months passed, and while the Butcher was silent, the newspapers were anything but quiet. Attention was being paid to the murders by press all over the country. Just recently, Cleveland had been the scene of a Republican convention and a Great Exposition and this led to even more police activity and harsh criticism from the press. The weight of this fell on the shoulders of the police department and most specifically Eliot Ness. As no leads in the case panned out, the investigators could do little more than wait for the Butcher to strike again—and hope that he made a mistake.

They only had to wait until February 1937. Unfortunately, the Butcher was just as efficient as he had been before, leaving the body of a butchered young woman along the frozen shore of Lake Erie. She was never identified, but the same cannot be said for the eighth victim. She was identified by her teeth as Mrs. Rose Wallace. Like the body discovered by the hiker, it appeared that Wallace had been killed in 1936 and just now discovered.

Victim number nine was a male and was likely another of the legion of homeless people who had been set adrift by bad economic times. His body was discovered in the river and his head was never found. The corpse had also been badly mutilated. The detectives were sent into action by what seemed to be a promising lead when a witness spoke of seeing two men in a boat the night before, just near where the body was found. The sighting never panned out though, and the investigation continued to go nowhere.

The Butcher was not heard from again until later that year. Several months later, a leg was pulled out of the river and three weeks after that, two burlap bags were found that contained more body parts. The coroner was able to determine that the body had belonged to a woman, about 25 years of age. This would mark another period of inactivity for the killer, lasting more than a year. But he would return to strike two more times, at least, in Cleveland. In August 1938, the dismembered torso of a woman was found in a dump along the lakefront and a search of the area revealed the body of a man. The remains of the twelfth victim were found wrapped in a quilt that had been given to a junkman, but neither body was ever identified.

Finally certain that the Butcher was selecting his victims from the homeless and down and outs of Kingsbury Run, Ness took a drastic step. Two days after the police found the last two bodies, officers raided the shantytown that was located in the ravine. They arrested hundreds of vagrants and burned down the shelters, shacks and shanties. Whether it was a coincidence or a brilliant move on the part of Eliot Ness, the murders stopped.

The Cleveland Torso Murders were never officially solved, but that has not stopped scores of crime historians and curious readers from speculating as to who the Mad Butcher actually was. Detectives in the case believed that they were close to catching the killer several times. They spent many hours searching for the killer's laboratory, believing that the Butcher was slaughtering his victims in a convenient location and then dumping the bodies somewhere else. At one point, they believed they had found it. They found a photographic negative that had been left behind by one of the early victims,

Edward Andrassy, and when it was developed, it showed Andrassy reclining on a bed in an unknown room. The photo was published in newspapers and was identified as being the bedroom of a middle-aged homosexual man who lived with his two sisters. Detectives searched the house and found blood on the floor of the room and a large butcher's knife hidden in a trunk. Unfortunately though, the blood turned out to be the suspect's (he was prone to nosebleeds) and the knife showed no traces of blood on it. To further prove the man's innocence, another Butcher victim turned up while the man was in jail for sodomy and it became obvious he was not the killer.

In January 1939, the Cleveland Press newspaper reprinted a letter that had been sent from Los Angeles, allegedly from the Butcher himself. It read:

> *Chief of Police Matowitz* ——
>
> *You can rest easy now, as I have come to sunny California for the winter. I felt bad operating on those people, but science must advance. I shall astound the medical profession, a man with only a D. C.*
>
> *What did their lives mean in comparison to hundreds of sick and disease-twisted bodies? Just laboratory guinea pigs found on any public street. No one missed them when I failed. My last case was successful. I now know the feeling of Pasteur, Thoreau and other pioneers.*
>
> *Right now I have a volunteer who will absolutely prove my theory. They call me mad and a butcher, but the truth will out.*
>
> *I have failed but once here. The body has not been found and never will be, but the head, minus the features, is buried on Century Boulevard, between Western and Crenshaw. I feel it is my duty to dispose of the bodies as I do. It is God's will not to let them suffer.*
>
> *X*

No buried heads were found in Los Angeles and the manhunt

shifted back to Cleveland. Investigators found another suspect while backtracking through the last days of Flo Polillo and Rose Wallace. They discovered that the two of them frequented the same saloon and that Andrassy had also been a regular there. Another connection was a man named Frank Dolezal, who carried knives and often threatened people with them when drunk. He was not only a regular at the same saloon, but he also lived with Flo Polillo for a time. He was quickly arrested and a search of his home found a brown substance that resembled dried blood in the cracks of his bathroom floor. They also discovered several knives with old bloodstains on them that further incriminated the man. Finally, after hours of intense questioning, Dolezal confessed to killing Flo Polillo and the newspapers hurriedly announced the capture of the Butcher.

Then, the case against Dolezal began to fall apart. Forensic tests showed that the dried blood on the bathroom floor was not blood at all and Dolezal's so-called confession was riddled with holes and full of errors as to where and how the body was found. In August 1939, Dolezal hanged himself in jail and an autopsy revealed that he had four cracked ribs, which suggested that perhaps his voluntary confession had been obtained the old-fashioned way—by force.

The two August 1938 victims turned out to be the last Butcher killings in Cleveland. In December 1939, three decapitated bodies were found in railroad boxcars in Pittsburgh and although Ness sent three investigators to look into it, there was no solid evidence to connect these murders to the Butcher's earlier handiwork. It should be noted however that no real clues were ever found in these murders and they remain unsolved to this day. Incidentally, the Butcher was also blamed (by some theorists) for the 1947 murder of Elizabeth Short, the Black Dahlia, in California. Her body was also cut in two parts, just like the Butcher's seventh victim.

But who was this depraved killer? Eliot Ness believed that he knew, but sadly, the Kingsbury Run murders really began the downturn of Ness's earlier illustrious career. He never really got over the taint that the unsolved murders left on his reputation. The last decade of his life was full of poverty and frequent disappointment and he passed away in 1957 at the age of 54. Ironically, considering his destruction of the Prohibition bootlegging gangs, Ness became a heavy drinker and suffered from poor health. He resigned from the position of Cleveland's public safety director in 1941, after a scandal involving a hit-and-run accident, and in 1947 was badly defeated in a run for the Cleveland mayor's office. A year later, he was even turned down for a $60 a week job. In 1953, after five years of poverty and obscurity, he became involved with a papermaking company and, through a friend at the company, he had a chance meeting with a journalist named Oscar Fraley. The two men would later collaborate on a book entitled *The Untouchables*. It came out in 1957 and was an immense success, becoming a bestseller and inspiring two television series and a popular film. Tragically, Ness would never learn of this success as he died of a heart attack on May 16, 1957, six months before *The Untouchables* was published.

Ness would tell Oscar Fraley of more than just his glory days in Chicago and told the writer that he was reasonably certain that he knew the identity of the Mad Butcher and that he had managed to bring him to at least some semblance of justice.

Ness explained that he had deduced that the killer must have a house of his own in which he could dismember the bodies and a car in which he could transport them to the dump sites in. He also reasoned that the skill of the mutilations would have required some amount of medical knowledge and that the killer had to have been a big and strong man. This was evidenced by his easy movement of bodies and by a size 12 footprint found at one crime scene.

Using this information, Ness had three of his best agents, Virginia Allen, Barney Davis and Jim Manski, make discreet inquiries among members of Cleveland high society. Virginia Allen was able to discover a man who seemed to fit the profile of Ness's ideal suspect. The man, who Ness called "Gaylord Sundheim," was a large man, who had studied medicine and came from a wealthy family with a history of psychiatric problems. When Ness' agents called at his home, he shut the door in their faces, so Ness pressured him into having lunch with him. Sundheim reluctantly met with Ness and refused to either admit or deny having committed the murders. Finally, Ness forced him to take a polygraph test, and Sundheim badly failed it. When Ness told him that he believed he was the Butcher, perhaps hoping to trigger a confession, Sundheim merely laughed and told him to "prove it."

Soon after he was confronted by Ness, Sundheim (or whatever his real name was) had himself committed to a mental hospital. After that, Ness knew that he could never get the man prosecuted for the crimes, for even if charged, he could plead that he was insane at the time of the murders. Sundheim died in the mental institution around 1940 or 1941 but during the last months of his life, he continually plagued Ness with a barrage of obscene and menacing notes. Ness preserved the cards and letters and they have been saved in the Cleveland archives.

But if Sundheim was the killer, who killed the three victims found in the Pittsburgh boxcar in December 1939 when Sundheim was in the hospital? And if Ness already knew the identity of the Butcher, then why did he allow detectives to beat a confession out of Frank Dolezal in 1939? And why did one of the chief detectives in the case, Peter Merylo, pursue the Butcher into retirement, blaming the killer for more than 50 murders by 1947? Could Ness have been wrong about whom the killer really was? It seems likely that he was.

On July 23, 1950, the body of a man, with his head and genitals removed, was found in a Cleveland lumberyard, just a few miles from Kingsbury Run. The missing head turned up four days later. The victim was identified as Robert Robertson. Coroner Samuel Gerber, who did the autopsies of most of the Butcher's victims, reported that the "work resembles exactly that of the torso murderer." Thanks to this final killing, and the confusing run of dead ends and worthless clues that plagued the case, the identity of the killer—like the whereabouts of most of the victim's missing heads—remains unknown.

The Mystery of the Black Dahlia

Hollywood's Most Notorious Murder

The lobby of Hollywood's Biltmore Hotel is crowded on a warm and sunny afternoon in early spring. A man crosses the room and taps on the call key for an elevator. As the door opens, he steps inside and presses the number 8 button for his floor. He glances down as he does so and he sees that the number 6 is already illuminated. With a quick glance to his left, he realizes that he is not in the elevator alone. A dark-haired young woman stands in the corner and as he looks at her, she offers a faint smile.

The man smiles back and then looks up as the numerals above the door light up with the passage of each floor. He glances at the reflection of the woman in the polished steel of the doors. Even in this blurred view, she is stunning. Her dark, nearly black hair is swept back and up in the style of the 1940s. Her skin is pale, perhaps looking even more so against the jet black of her dress. The shiny material clings to her every curve and the man can almost hear it shimmer in the close confines of the elevator. Other than the soft rustle of her dress though, she makes no sound.

Finally, the elevator reaches the sixth floor and with a soft chime, the doors slide open. The man steps aside to let her pass and notices that she is not moving. She continues to stand in the corner, seemingly unaware that the lift has reached her floor. "This is the sixth floor," the man finally speaks up and seems to startle the girl into awareness. She steps forward and moves past him off the elevator. As she does, the man trembles unconsciously. A wave of chilled, ice cold air seems to brush past him as the girl departs. Gooseflesh appears on his arms as he watches the shapely young woman walk past the doors.

Then, just as she steps out onto the sixth floor, she turns back to look at the man inside the elevator. She does not speak, but there is no mistaking the look of urgency in her eyes. She is begging him for help, the man realizes, but it's almost too late. The elevator doors have started to close, cutting off the young woman as she tries to re-enter the elevator. The man frantically pushes the button that will open the door again and, just before they close completely, they slowly start to slide open again. But the girl in black is gone.

"What the...?" the man mumbles and he leans out into the lobby of the sixth floor. He looks quickly in both directions, but the small lobby and the hallways in either direction are empty and deserted. Where could she have gone so quickly? He calls out, but his voice echoes in the stillness of the corridor. The young woman had vanished, as if she had never existed at all.

Two days later, the man is browsing in a local bookshop and happens to pick up a book about true, unsolved mysteries. As he flips through it, he is startled by a face that he recognizes—it's the girl from the elevator. He looks at the photograph and is convinced that it is the same young woman in black. Then, he realizes such a thing is impossible. Scanning through the text, he sees that the woman died years before. How could she have been at the Biltmore Hotel just two days ago? Could this young woman still be lingering at the last place that she was seen alive? Is she still looking for help, from the other side?

The face he, and many others just like him, recognized once belonged to a beautiful, young woman named Elizabeth Short. In death, she would come to be known by a more colorful nickname, the "Black Dahlia". Her tragic murder would forever leave a mark on Tinseltown. She came here in a search for stardom and only found it in death, becoming lost in the netherworld that is the dark side of Hollywood.

On January 15, 1947 a housewife named Betty Bersinger left her home on Norton Avenue in the Leimert Park section of Los

Angeles, bound for a shoe repair shop. She took her three-year-old daughter with her and as they walked along the street, coming up on the corner of Norton and 39th, they passed several vacant lots that were overgrown with weeds. She couldn't help but feel a little depressed as she looked out over the deserted area. Development had been halted here, thanks to the war, and the open lots looked abandoned and eerie. Betty felt slightly disconcerted and then shrugged it off, blaming her emotional state on the gray skies and the cold, dreary morning.

As she walked a little further, she caught a glimpse of something white over in the weeds. She was not surprised. It wasn't uncommon for people to toss their garbage out into the vacant lot and this time, it looked as though someone had left a broken department store mannequin here. The dummy had been shattered and the two halves lay separated from one another, with the bottom half lying twisted into what was admittedly a macabre pose. Who would throw such a thing into an empty lot? Betty shook her head and walked on, but then found her glance pulled back to the ghostly, white mannequin. She looked again and then realize that this was no department store dummy at all—it was the severed body of a woman. With a sharp intake of breath and a stifled scream, she took her daughter away from the gruesome site and ran to a nearby house where she telephoned the police.

The dead woman, it was noted, seemed to have been posed. She was lying on her back with her arms raised over her shoulders and her legs spread in an obscene imitation of seductiveness. Cuts and abrasions covered her body and her mouth had been slashed so that her smile extended from ear to ear. There were rope marks on her wrists, ankles and neck and investigators later surmised that she had been tied down and tortured for several days. Worst of all was the fact that she had been sliced cleanly in two, just above the waist. It was clear that she had been killed somewhere else and then dumped in the vacant lot overnight. There was no blood on her body and none on the ground where she had been left. The killer had washed her off before bringing her to the dumpsite.

The horrible nature of the case made it a top priority for the LAPD. Captain John Donahoe assigned his senior detectives to the case, Detective Sergeant Harry Hansen and his partner, Finis Brown. He also added Herman Willis, a bright young cop from the Metro Division, to help follow up on the leads that were sure to come in. By the time the detectives were contacted and could get to the scene, it was swarming with reporters, photographers and a crowd of curiosity seekers. Hansen was furious that bystanders and even careless police personnel were trampling the crime scene. Evidence was being destroyed, he knew, and he immediately cleared the scene. Then, while he and his partners examined the scene, the body of the woman was taken to the Los Angeles County Morgue. Her fingerprints were lifted and, with the help of the assistant managing editor of the Los Angeles Examiner (in exchange for information), the prints were sent to the FBI in Washington using the newspaper's Soundphoto equipment.

Meanwhile, an examination of the body was started by the coroner's office. It began to detail an incredible and horrifying variety of wounds to the young woman's body, although the official cause of death was "hemorrhage and shock due to concussion of the brain and lacerations of the face."

An autopsy revealed multiple lacerations to the face and head, along with the severing of the victim's body. It also appeared that the woman had been sodomized and her sexual organs abused but not penetrated. There was no sperm present on the body and most of the damage appeared to have been done after she was dead. The coroner also noted that her stomach contents contained human feces. Even the hardened doctors and detectives were shocked at the state of the woman's corpse.

The coroner also gave the Detectives an important piece of evidence and one that would have a huge bearing on the case as more of the victim's past was later revealed. "It is impossible to tell you if she was raped," he told the detectives, "because traces of spermatozoa are negative, and she did not have fully developed genitals....The area is shallow indicating that she did not have a completed vaginal canal." According to the coroner, the young woman's vagina was child-like, and normal sex for her would have been impossible.

This information would have an important impact on what they would learn about the victim, and Hansen immediately decided not to make this information public. In fact, only a few detectives working the case would know about it. It is a common police practice to hold back some pieces of information when investigating a case. That way, they can tell real confessions from false ones, especially with a highly publicized crime. Hansen's decision was the right one and he must have known how much newspaper coverage such a bizarre murder would get. Soon, tips, calls and false confessions would come pouring into police headquarters. More than 50 people would eventually confess to the killing.

Shortly after receiving the fingerprints, the FBI had a match for the L.A. detectives. The victim of the brutal murder was Elizabeth Short, a 22-year-old woman who originally came from Massachusetts. During World War II, she had been a clerk at Camp Cooke in California, which explained why her fingerprints were on file. Once the detectives had this information, they went to work finding out who knew Elizabeth Short, believing that this would lead them to her killer. What they discovered was a complex maze that led them into the shadowy side of the city—in search of a woman called the Black Dahlia.

Elizabeth Short was an aspiring actress who usually dressed entirely in black. Thanks to her nice figure and attractive face, men easily noticed her. Her hair was black and her skin pale, providing a striking contrast and a look that got her noticed, even in Hollywood, where good-looking dames were a dime a dozen. Like all of the other pretty girls before and since, Elizabeth (who preferred the name Beth) came to Hollywood hoping to make it big in the movie business. She was smart enough to know that looks weren't everything and that to break into films, she had to know the right people. So, she spent most of her time trying to make new acquaintances and to make sure that she was in the right nightspots and clubs. Here, she was convinced, she would come to the attention of the important people in the business. Beth's pretty face got her noticed. She had done some modeling before coming to Hollywood, and men couldn't keep their eyes off of her.

In Hollywood, Beth roomed with a hopeful dancer who introduced her to Barbara Lee, a well-connected actress for Paramount. She took Beth to all of the right places, including the famous Hollywood Canteen, where she met a wealthy socialite her own age named Georgette Bauerdorf. Beth loved to socialize, loved the Hollywood nightlife and loved to meet men. Despite the rumors, Beth was never promiscuous and she did not work as a prostitute. Beautiful, lively and seductive, Beth was sometimes referred to as a tease as her boyfriends never had any idea that romance could only go so far.

She never seemed to appreciate the hospitality given to her by others either, rarely contributing to where she was living and staying out most of the night and sleeping all day. She became known as a beautiful freeloader. Also around this same time, the film *The Blue Dahlia*, starring Veronica Lake and Alan Ladd was released. Some friends of Beth's starting calling her the Black Dahlia, thanks to her dark hair and black lacy clothing. The name stuck and Beth began to immerse herself into the glamorous persona that she had created and that may have led to her death.

Although she is remembered today as the Black Dahlia, Elizabeth Short did not start out as a sexy vamp that haunted the nightclubs of Hollywood. She was born on July 29, 1924 in Hyde Park, Massachusetts. Her parents, Cleo and Phoebe Short, moved the family to Medford, a few miles outside Boston, shortly after Elizabeth was born. Cleo Short was a man ahead of his time, making a prosperous living designing and building miniature golf courses. Unfortunately though, the Depression caught up with him in 1929, and he fell on hard times. Without a second thought, he abandoned his wife and five daughters and faked his suicide. His empty car was discovered near a bridge and the authorities believed that he had jumped into the river below. Phoebe was left to deal with the bankruptcy and to raise the girls by herself. She worked several jobs, including as a bookkeeper and a clerk in a bakery shop, but most of the money came from public assistance. One day, she received a letter from Cleo, who was now living in California. He apologized for running out on his family and asked to come home. Phoebe refused his apology and would not allow him to come back.

Beth (known as Betty to her family and friends) grew up to be a very pretty girl, always looking older and acting more sophisticated then she really was. Everyone who knew her liked her, and she was considered very bright and lively. She was also fascinated by the movies, her family's main source of affordable entertainment. She found an escape at the theater that she couldn't find in the day-to-day drudgery of ordinary life.

While she was growing up, Betty remained in touch with her father (once she learned that he was actually alive). They wrote letters back and forth and, when she was older, he offered to have her come out to California and stay with him until she was able to find a job. Betty had worked in restaurants and movie houses in the past but she knew that if she went to California, she wanted to be a star. She packed up and headed out west to her father. At that time, Cleo was living in Vallejo and working at the Mare Island Naval Base. Betty hadn't been in town for long before the relationship between her and her father became strained. He began to launch into tirades about her laziness, poor housekeeping, and dating habits. Eventually, he threw her out and Betty (now Beth) was left to fend for herself.

Undaunted, she went to Camp Cooke and applied for a job as a cashier at the Post Exchange. It didn't take long for the servicemen to notice the new cashier and she won the title of "Camp Cutie of Camp Cooke" in a beauty contest. They didn't realize that the sweet romantic girl was emotionally vulnerable though and desperate to marry a handsome serviceman, preferably a pilot. She made no secret of wanting a permanent relationship with one of the men with whom she constantly flirted. The word soon got around that Beth was not an easy girl and pressure for more than just handholding kept Beth at home most nights. Several encounters made her uncomfortable at Camp Cooke, and she left to stay with a girlfriend who lived near Santa Barbara.

During this time, Beth had her only run-in with the law. A group of friends that she was out with got rowdy in a restaurant and the owners called the police. Since Beth was underage, she was booked and fingerprinted, but never charged. A kind policewoman felt sorry for her and arranged for a trip back to Massachusetts. After spending some time at home, she came back to California, this time to Hollywood.

At the Hollywood Canteen, Beth met a pilot named Lieutenant Gordon Fickling and fell in love. He was exactly what she was looking for, and she began making plans to ensnare him in matrimony. Unfortunately though, her plans were cut short when Fickling was shipped out to Europe. Beth then took a few modeling jobs but, discouraged, she went back east. She spent the holidays in Medford and then went to Miami, where she had relatives off whom she could live for a while. Beth began dating servicemen, always with marriage as her goal, but fell in love again on New Year's Eve 1945 with another pilot, Major Matt Gordon. A commitment was apparently made between them after he was sent to India.

Beth wrote to him constantly and Gordon remained in touch with her. As a pre-engagement gift, he gave Beth a gold and diamond wristwatch and spoke about her (and their engagement) to family and friends. Best of all, as far as Beth was concerned, he respected her wishes about waiting until their honeymoon to consummate their love. They would get married and have a proper honeymoon, he promised her, after he returned from overseas.

Beth went back home to Massachusetts and got a job, dreaming of her October wedding. Her friends often commented on how happy she was and after the war ended in Europe, she became ecstatic about Gordon returning home. Then came the dreaded telegram from Gordon's mother. As soon as it arrived, Beth tore the message open, believing that it was about plans for the upcoming wedding. Instead, Mrs. Gordon had written: "Received word War Department. Matt killed in plane crash on way home from India. Our deepest sympathy is with you. Pray it isn't true. "Sadly, it was true and we are only left to imagine what Beth's life might have been like if Matt Gordon had returned home alive.

Gordon's death left Beth a little unbalanced. After a period of mourning that she spent telling people that she and Matt had been married and that their baby had died in childbirth; she began to pick up the pieces of her old life and started contacting her Hollywood friends. One of those was former boyfriend Gordon Fickling, who Beth saw as a possible replacement for her dead fiancée. They began to write back and forth to one another and then got together briefly in Chicago when he was in town for a couple of days. Soon, Beth was in love with him again. She agreed to come to Long Beach and be with him, happy and excited once again. Her excitement over the new relationship didn't last long. She had to stay in a hotel that was miles from the base where Fickling was stationed, and he constantly pressured Beth for sex. She had no intention of giving herself to a man except in marriage, she told a friend, and Fickling had no intention of making such a commitment. She began dating other men and when Fickling found out, he ended their relationship. A short time later, Beth was back in California.

In December 1946, Beth took up temporary residence in San Diego with a young woman named Dorothy French. She was a counter girl at the Aztec Theater, which stayed open all night, and after an evening show, found Beth sleeping in one of the seats. Beth told her that she had left Hollywood because work was hard to find due to the actor's strikes that were going on. Dorothy felt sorry for her and offered her a place to stay at her mother's home. She meant that Beth could stay for a few days, but she ended up sleeping on the French's couch for more than a month.

As usual, she did nothing to contribute to the household and she continued her late-night partying and dating. One of the men she dated was Robert "Red" Manley, a salesman from L. A. with a pregnant young wife at home. He admitted being attracted to Beth, but claimed to never have slept with her. They saw each other on an off for a few weeks and then Beth asked him for a ride back to Hollywood. He agreed and on January 8 picked her up from the French house and paid for a hotel room for her that night. They went out together to a couple of different nightspots and returned back to the motel. He slept on the bed, while Beth, complaining that she didn't feel well, slept in a chair.

Red had a morning appointment but came back to pick her up around noon. She told him that she was going back home to Boston but first she was going to meet her married sister at the Biltmore Hotel in Hollywood. Manley drove her back to Los Angeles. He had an appointment at the home of his employer that evening at 6:30, so he didn't wait around for Beth's sister to arrive. She was making phone calls in the hotel lobby when he saw her last— becoming, along with the Biltmore employees, the last person to see Beth Short alive. As far as the police could discover, only the killer ever saw her after that. She vanished for six days before her body was found in the empty lot.

The investigation into the Black Dahlia's murder was the highest profile crime in Hollywood of the 1940s. The police were constantly harassed by the newspapers and the public for results. Hundreds of suspects were questioned. Because it was considered a sex crime, the usual suspects and perverts were rounded up and interrogated. Beth's friends and acquaintances were questioned as the detectives tried to reconstruct her final days and hours. Every hopeful lead ended up leading nowhere and the cops were further hampered by the lunatics and crazed confessions that were pouring in.

As the investigators traced Beth's activities, they discovered their strongest suspect, Red Manley. He became the chief target of the investigation. The LAPD put him through grueling interrogations and even administered two different polygraph tests, both of which he passed. He was released a couple of days later but the strain on him was so great that he later suffered a nervous breakdown.

While the police worked frantically, Beth's mother made the trip to Los Angeles to claim her daughter's body. Her father, who had not seen her since 1943, refused to identify her. Sadly, Phoebe Short had learned of her daughter's death from a newspaper reporter who had called her, using the pretext that Beth had won a beauty contest and the paper wanted some background information about her. Once he had gleaned as much information as he could, he informed her that Beth had actually been murdered

A few days after Beth's body was found, a mysterious package appeared at the offices of the Los Angeles Examiner. A note that had been cut and pasted from newspaper lettering said, "Here is the Dahlia's Belongings Letter to Follow." Inside of the small package was Beth's social security card, birth certificate, photographs with various servicemen, business cards and claim checks for suitcases she had left at the bus depot. Another item was an address book that belonged to club owner Mark Hansen. The address book had several pages torn out. The police attempted to lift fingerprints off the items but found that all of it had been washed in gasoline to remove any trace of evidence. The detectives then began the overwhelming task of tracking down everyone in the address book and while Mark Hansen and a few others were singled out for interrogation, nothing ever came of it. In addition, the promised "letter to follow" never arrived.

The investigation stalled once again, although Aggie Underwood, a crime reporter for the *Herald-Express*, urged the detectives to follow-up on the murder of a young socialite named Georgette Bauerdorf, which had occurred a few years before. Aggie believed the murder was connected to that of Beth Short. The two women had known one another from the Hollywood Canteen and Georgette had been strangled and raped before being dumped into a bathtub facedown. Investigators surmised that Beth had also been killed, severed and then washed in a bathtub.

The Bauerdorf case had never been solved and was under the jurisdiction of the sheriff's department. The investigation had died when deputies were unable to locate a "tall soldier" who had dated Georgette. She had reportedly been frightened by him and had stopped seeing him. Investigators suspected that he was involved in her death but the links were never made between the two murders. Jurisdictional problems kept the two departments from working together and Aggie Underwood was ordered off the story by William Randolph Hearst himself, the publisher of the newspaper. As a friend of the wealthy Bauerdorf family, he didn't want the sordid details of the girl's murder stirred up again.

Not surprisingly, the leads in the Black Dahlia case came to dead ends and the investigation fizzled, and then came to a halt. A possible killer first came to the attention of John St. John, a respected investigator for the LAPD who eventually took over the Dahlia case. St. John had worked many of the city's most notorious murders and was the basis of the book and television series *Jigsaw John*. He had been in charge of the Dahlia case for about a year when a confidential informant came to him with a tape recording that implicated the suspect in the murder. The suspect had also shown the informant some photos and personal items that he claimed had belonged to the Black Dahlia. The suspect turned out to be a tall, thin man with a pronounced limp who went by the name of Arnold Smith. On the recording, Smith claimed that a character named "Al Morrison" was the violent sexual deviant who had killed and mutilated Beth Short. St. John suspected that Arnold Smith and Al Morrison were actually the same person.

The tape was a chilling and detailed account of how Beth had come to Al Morrison's Hollywood hotel room because she didn't have anywhere else to stay. According to Smith, Beth refused both liquor and sex with Morrison and became upset when he drove her to a house on East 31st Street near San Pedro and Trinity Streets.

Here, he assaulted her and prevented her from escaping by beating her into submission. Even though Beth fought back, he was able to overwhelm her with his strength. While she was on the floor, Morrison said he planned to sodomize her and Beth began struggling once again. This time, he hit her so hard that she passed out.

The tape then went on the describe how Morrison got a paring knife, a large butcher knife and some rope and returned to the room to find Beth conscious again. She tried to scream, but he stuffed her underpants into her mouth and tied her up. While she was naked and bound, he began jabbing her over and over again with the knives, cutting and slashing her. One of the lacerations even extended both sides of her mouth and across her face. By this time, the girl was dead. Morrison then laid boards across the bathtub and cut Beth in half with the butcher knife, letting the blood drain into the tub. He wrapped the two pieces of the body in a tablecloth and a shower curtain and put it into the trunk of his car. From there, he drove to the vacant lot and left the body to be found later that morning.

St. John discovered that this same suspect, Al Morrison, had also come to the attention of Detective Joel Lesnick of the Sheriff's Department for the murder of Georgette Bauerdorf. He was thought to be the "tall soldier" that she had been dating. Lesnick had learned that both Al Morrison and Arnold Smith were aliases for a man named Jack Anderson Wilson, a tall and lanky alcoholic with a crippled leg and a record for sex offenses and robbery. Lesnick guessed that "as the years went on, Smith's ego drew him closer, not to confessing, but wanting to tell someone in a roundabout way what he got away with primarily through luck."

After hearing the record of events on the tape recordings, St. John became determined to track down "Arnold Smith." He checked into the story of "Al Morrison," the alleged violent pervert and could find no proof that he existed, thus confirming the idea that Smith (Jack Wilson) was actually the killer. St. John began to leave no stone unturned in his pursuit to link Jack Wilson to

Elizabeth Short.

In the midst of the investigation, word came that the press had learned that a new suspect had emerged in the Dahlia case. Even after all these years (it was the mid-1980s now), interest in the case was still strong. At this point, St. John realized that it was imperative that he move quickly before Wilson/Smith became spooked. The informant did not know where Smith lived, but left a message for him in a cafe. Several messages were left but Smith never returned them, possibly because he got wind of police surveillance of the restaurant. Finally, the informant received a reply and a meeting was set between him and Smith. It was set for a few days later. Unfortunately, just before the meeting took place, Smith passed out while smoking in his bed at the Holland Hotel, where he was staying. He was burned to death in the flames, destroying the photos and belongings that supposedly belonged to Beth Short and all hope that her murder would ever be solved.

A short time after Wilson's body was released to the county for cremation, the Los Angeles District Attorney's office was presented with a file on the matter. The prosecutor's office summed up the case by saying: "The case cannot be officially closed due to the death of the individual considered a suspect. While the documentation appears to link this individual with the homicide of Elizabeth Short, his death, however, precludes the opportunity of an interview to obtain from him the corroboration. . . Therefore, any conclusion as to his criminal involvement is circumstantial, and unfortunately, the suspect cannot be charged or tried, due to his demise. However, despite this inconclusiveness, the circumstantial evidence is of such a nature that were this suspect alive, an intensive inquiry would be recommended. And depending upon the outcome of such an inquiry...it is conceivable that Jack Wilson might have been charged as a suspect in the murder of Elizabeth Short— also known as the Black Dahlia."

But the truth is, no one was ever charged for the murder of Elizabeth Short. Perhaps this is why her ghost still walks at the

Biltmore Hotel. Even today, an occasional guest encounters the spectral image of a woman in a black dress, sometimes in the lobby, waiting in the corridors or even riding to the sixth floor on the elevator. Is she trying to tell us something? Or does the Black Dahlia simply wish to continue the mystery that was created more that a half-century ago? For tragically, she had found the fame in death that she never achieved in life.

THE AXEMAN'S JAZZ

New Orleans' Ghoulish Murderer

One of the most mysterious, and still unsolved, frenzies to grip the city of New Orleans, Louisiana came in the early 1900s with the arrival of the enigmatic "Axeman." Who was this strange and terrifying creature? Ghost, ghoul or something worse? The period of death and bloodshed that was reigned over by this allegedly supernatural creature is still remembered as one of the darkest times in city's history. The boogeyman had come to New Orleans.

In May 1918, the Axeman, as he came to be known, arrived in the city. His coming would begin a period of terror in the city that would last for the next year and a half. With the fall of darkness, the residents of New Orleans would spend each night listening to every sound, looking at every shadow and would open their newspapers with trembling hands each morning. The Axeman had come to the city—and no one was safe. To this day, the identity of the Axeman remains a mystery. Many believe that he was not a man at all, but a supernatural creature that was able to appear and disappear at will. There are others who believe that he was merely a demented serial killer who hacked off the heads of his victims while they slept. Needless to say, the riddle remains unsolved.

On May 23, 1918, an Italian grocer named Joseph Maggio and his wife were butchered while sleeping in their apartment above the Maggio grocery store. Upon investigation, the police discovered that a panel in the rear door had been chiseled out, providing a way in for the killer. The murder weapon, an axe, was found in the apartment, still coated with the Maggio's blood. Nothing in the house was stolen, including jewelry and money that were in plain sight. Detectives quickly went to work on the case and while several suspects were picked up and questioned, all were released for lack of evidence. The only clue that was discovered was a message that had been written in chalk near the victim's home. It read: "Mrs. Joseph Maggio will sit up tonight. Just write Mrs. Toney"

Investigators began digging into old files, looking for possible cases that matched the Maggio murders, and to their surprise, discovered that three murders and a number of attacks against Italian grocers had already taken place in 1911. The murders bore a striking resemblance to the Maggio crime in that an axe was used and access to each home had been gained through a panel in the rear door. These earlier crimes had been thought to be a vendetta of terror organized by the Mafia, which had come to America through New Orleans in the late 1800s. The police and the Italian residents of the French Quarter braced themselves for the worst.

Almost exactly a month after the Maggio murder came a second crime. Louis Bossumer, a grocer who lived behind his store with his common law wife, Annie Harriet Lowe, was discovered by neighbors one morning, lying in a pool of blood. Although badly injured, he was not dead. Beside him was Annie, also injured but, amazingly, also not dead. Both of them had been hacked with an axe. The weapon was lying next to Bossumer and was covered with blood. A panel of the kitchen door had been removed, a chisel was lying on the back steps, but nothing had been stolen. After she regained consciousness in Charity Hospital, Annie first claimed her attacker had been young and very dark, but later, she changed her story and said that Bossumer attacked her. The police were skeptical however, never being able to ascertain how Bossumer could have attacked Annie and then fractured his own skull with the axe. After he recovered from his injuries, he was released.

Later that year, in August, a woman named Mrs. Edward Schneider awakend in the night to see a tall, phantom-like form standing over her bed. She screamed just as the axe fell. A few minutes later, her neighbors found her unconscious with her head gashed and bloody and several of her teeth knocked out. But, she recovered from her injuries. A few nights later, an Italian grocer named Joseph Romano was also attacked. This attack was just like the others but Romano did not survive.

By this time, hysteria was sweeping through the city. Families divided into watches and stood guard over their relatives as they slept. People went about with loaded shotguns and waited for news of the latest Axeman sightings. On August 11, the killer was seen in the neighborhood of Tulane and Broad, masquerading as a woman, the rumors said. A manhunt was organized but without success. On August 21, a man was seen leaping a back fence but despite a quickly organized search party, the fiend escaped. Were these sightings real or merely fright-fueled imaginations at work?

While most of the so-called sightings can be attributed to panic among local residents, the Axeman did leave tangible evidence behind as well. On August 11, a man named Al Durand discovered an axe and a chisel lying outside his rear door in the early morning hours. His back door had been damaged but had apparently proved too thick for the killer to cut through. Then in late August, the rear door of Paul Lobella's grocery and residence was chiseled through, but no one was home at the time. The same day, another grocer named Joseph Le Bouef reported an attempt had been made to chisel through his rear door in the night. Awakened by the noise, he frightened the intruder away. An axe was discovered dropped on his steps. The following day, another axe was found in the yard of A. Recknagle, also a grocer. Chisel marks were also found on his back door. On September 15, a grocer named Paul Durel found that someone had attempted to cut through his rear door. A case of tomatoes that had been resting against the inside panel had foiled the attack.

Then, as mysteriously as he had come, the Axeman vanished—at least for a while. But in the early morning hours of March 10, 1919 the Axeman struck again. It was perhaps his most terrible crime yet. Mrs. Charles Cortimiglia, wife of a grocer in Gretna, just across the river from New Orleans, awakened to find her husband struggling with a large man in dark clothing who was armed with an axe. As her husband fell in a bloody heap to the floor, Mrs. Cortimiglia held her two-year-old daughter in her arms and begged her attacker for mercy, at least for the child. But the axe came down anyway, killing the little girl and fracturing the skull of her mother.

The police were once again stumped and rumblings began to suggest that perhaps the Axeman really wasn't a man at all. Some claimed that he might be a woman, or a midget, enabling him to slip through the small space that he cut in the doors. But others maintained that he was a creature from the world beyond. How else, they questioned, could all of the witnesses describe the killer as being a large man when only a small person could have slipped through the chiseled panels in the rear doors? The killer had to enter through supernatural means as each door was still locked when the attacks were discovered.

Following the Cortimiglia murders, New Orleans was again filled with terror. The police stated that they believed all of the crimes to have been committed by the same man, "a bloodthirsty maniac, filled with a passion for human slaughter." And perhaps they were right. On Friday, March 14, 1919, the editor of the *New Orleans Times-Picayune* newspaper received a letter from a man who claimed to be the Axeman. The letter appeared as follows:

Hell, March 13, 1919

Esteemed Mortal:
They have never caught me and they never will. They have never seen me, for I am invisible, even as the ether that

*surrounds your earth. I am not a human being, but a spirit and
a demon from the hottest hell. I am what you Orleanians and
your foolish police call the Axeman.*

*When I see fit, I shall come and claim other victims. I alone
know whom they shall be. I shall leave no clue except my bloody
axe, besmeared with blood and brains of he whom I have sent
below to keep me company.*

*If you wish you may tell the police to be careful not to rile
me. Of course, I am a reasonable spirit. I take no offense at the
way they have conducted their investigations in the past. In fact,
they have been so utterly stupid as to not only amuse me, but
His Satanic Majesty, Francis Josef, etc. But tell them to beware.
Let them not try to discover what I am, for it were better that
they were never born than to incur the wrath of the Axeman. I
don't think there is any need of such a warning, for I feel sure
the police will always dodge me, as they have in the past. They
are wise and know how to keep away from all harm.*

*Undoubtedly, you Orleanians think of me as a most horrible
murderer, which I am, but I could be much worse if I wanted to.
If I wished, I could pay a visit to your city every night. At will I
could slay thousands of your best citizens, for I am in close relationship with the Angel of Death.*

*Now, to be exact, at 12:15 (earthly time) on next Tuesday
night, I am going to pass over New Orleans. In my infinite
mercy, I am going to make a little proposition to you people.
Here it is:*

*I am very fond of jazz music, and I swear by all the devils
in the nether regions that every person shall be spared in whose
home a jazz band is in full swing at the time I have just mentioned. If everyone has a jazz band going, well, then, so much
the better for you people. One thing is certain and that is that
some of your people who do not jazz it on Tuesday night (if
there be any) will get the axe.*

Well, as I am cold and crave the warmth of my native

Tartarus, and it is about time I leave your earthly home, I will cease my discourse. Hoping that thou wilt publish this, that it may go well with thee, I have been, am and will be the worst spirit that ever existed either in fact or realm of fancy.

The Axeman

The people of New Orleans did their best to follow the Axeman's instructions to the letter. Restaurants and clubs all over town were jammed with revelers. Friends and neighbors gathered in their homes to "jazz it up" and midnight found the city alive with activity. Banjos, guitars and mandolins strummed into the night while Joseph Davilla, a well-known local composer, created the theme song for the night. He titled his composition "The Mysterious Axeman's Jazz" and in typical New Orleans fashion, it became a huge hit. When the sun rose the next morning, it was learned that not a single attack had occurred that night. Even though it's doubtful that every home was filled with the sounds of jazz, the Axeman passed the city by, perhaps well satisfied by the celebration that was held in his honor.

All was quiet for some time, until the night of August 3, 1919. In the darkest hours, a young girl named Sarah Laumann was attacked with an axe while she slept in her locked and shuttered home. She received a brain concussion but recovered. The new attack pushed hysteria in the city to new heights. Miss Laumann was not the owner of a grocery store, she was not Italian, and her attacker had not entered through a door panel, but a window. In other words, if he could attack Sarah Laumann, then no one was safe. Was it really the Axeman, or an imitator?

On August 10, a man named Steve Boca stumbled from his home on Elysian Fields Avenue with axe wounds in his skull. Dripping blood, he managed to make it to his friend's home about a half block away and called for help. The police who searched Boca's house found the classic signs of the Axeman, including the chiseled door panel and the bloody axe left lying on the floor. On September 2, a local druggist named William Carson fired several shots at an intruder who had broken into his home. The intruder left a broken door and an axe behind, but managed to escape.

Then in October, the Axeman appeared for a final slaughter. A grocer named Mike Pepitone was butchered in his bed during the night. His wife and six children, asleep in the next room, were not touched. The usual clues had been left behind but the authorities were no closer to learning his identity than they had been in the beginning. But the horror had come to an end. The Pepitone killing was the last murder attributed to the Axeman. He was never seen or heard from in New Orleans again. No one would ever learn the true identity of the Axemanor—would they?

More than a year after the Axeman's final appearance, a former New Orleans man named Joseph Mumfre was shot to death on the Pacific Coast. He had been killed by a woman named Esther Albano, who was later discovered to be the widow of the Axeman's last victim, Mike Pepitone. The police began working to try and untangle the mystery that might linked Mumfre's murder to the Axeman case. Some curious coincidences were revealed during the investigation. Mumfre had once been the leader of a band of black-mailers in New Orleans who had preyed on Italians. He had also been sent (for a separate matter) to prison just after the first axe murders in 1911. In the summer of 1918, he was paroled—at the same time the Axeman appeared again. Immediately after the Pepitone murder, Mumfre had left New Orleans for the coast and the Axeman had vanished as well. In spite of this, there was no actual evidence to link him to any of the crimes.

Was Joseph Mumfre the Axeman? Or were there several killers working together to terrorize the Italian community? Or was the maniac actually what he claimed to be all along, "the worst demon that ever existed either in fact or in the realm of fantasy"?

Chapter Five

BEYOND THE KNOWN

America's Strangest Tales of the Unexplained

As stated earlier, everyone loves a mystery. We even love those mysteries that cannot be explained away as mere coincidence or misdirection. Throughout the book, I have tried to entertain and intrigue the reader with ghostly enigmas, unsolved murders and other ghastly puzzles, which brings us to a category of riddles for which I have no explanation whatsoever. They are mysteries that have baffled us for generations and likely, may never be solved. They go far beyond just being unusual and mysterious and enter into a realm that can only be described as beyond the known.

In the introduction to the book, I mentioned an unsolved (and possibly paranormal) mystery for which no solution has ever been found and that has been often referred to as the "Moving Coffins of Barbados." This was a story that intrigued me growing up and, while there were many others, one that I have always remembered has been the story of the Thunderbird that was shot and killed near Tombstone, Arizona many years ago. I recall hearing of this story when I was a child and being amazed by it. How, I asked myself, could what seemed to be a prehistoric creature like a pterodactyl be shot by cowboys in the 1800s? Such a thing seemed impossible but evidence existed in the form of many stories and references to the event and of course, existed in the form of a photograph. That was the really exciting part—that photograph! I still remember what it looked like today, or do I?

You see, in more recent years, an even greater mystery has developed than whether or not a group of cowpokes shot down a "flying monster" in the Arizona desert. That mystery surrounds the elusive photograph that was taken of the incident and which many of us (myself included) believe that we saw. But if we did, where is the photo and what has become of it over the years?

One of the first accounts that was written of the Thunderbird that was allegedly killed in Tombstone was in the book *On the Old West Coast* by Major Horace Bell. I was able to track down a copy of this long out of print title and found it to be a very readable and entertaining book about Bell's adventures in California in the late 1800s. *On the Old West Coast* was published in 1930 and edited from Bell's writings by Lanier Bartlett.

Horace Bell had previously written a book called *Reminiscences of a Ranger* about his life in and journeys throughout California, Texas, Mexico and Central America. Bell had been a miner, a ranger who pursued Joaquin Murrietta, a soldier of fortune in the forces of Benito Juarez in Mexico, an aide to General William Walker in Nicaragua, a Union officer in the Civil War and on the Texas border and finally, a newspaper editor in Los Angeles. He was considered a history writer and while he admitted to often writing stories that were tongue in cheek, he declared that he was a truthful history writer, chronicling events as they happened. This is why the events that he wrote about in the Lake Elizabeth area—and by extension,

Tombstone—are so strange to read about today.

The account in Bell's book, in a chapter entitled "Spit in the Mouth of Hell," does not start out to be about the creature that was killed in Tombstone. Bell believed that this same creature had its origins in California instead. In October 1886, a Los Angeles newspaper reported on some strange events that had been occurring for years around nearby Lake Elizabeth. According to early stories from the days of the Spanish occupation of the region, the lake had long been considered a haunted place, plagued by frightening voices, shrieks, screams and groans that apparently emanated from the lake itself. After the Spanish, the Mexican settlers refused to live near the lake. They called it *La Laguna del Diablo* (The Devil's Lake).

In the middle 1830s, Don Pedro Carrillo purchased the land around *La Laguna del Diablo* and built a hacienda, barn and corral by the water. He disregarded the superstitions about the place, but just three months after construction on his ranch was completed, he abandoned the place. He stated that there were supernatural beings nearby and refused to live there. The land remained idle for the next two decades and even after the Americans came to the region, the lake was shunned as a cursed spot.

Some years later, Don Chico Lopez settled on the property and what occurred next was told in a manuscript by Don Guillermo Embustero y Mentiroso, who was a guest at the Lopez ranch. According to Don Guillermo, a great agitation took place during his visit. Around noon one day, Lopez's foreman, Chico Vasquez, rode up to the hacienda very upset. He told of strange happenings at the lake and everyone saddled their horses and rode out to the shore. They arrived to find the water calm and quiet and Lopez began berating his foreman for bothering them with foolishness but then stopped, as a terrifying scream came from some brush at the edge of the lake. The plants whipped back and forth and the account stated that they were so close to whatever was lurking in the brush that they could smell its foul breath. The men were startled when their horses reared up and began running in fright.

As they brought their horses back under control, the men turned and looked back to the lake. Silhouetted against the sky was a large creature with enormous wings. The creature flapped them over and over again as it tried to rise from the mud. It roared and screamed and churned up the water around it. The horses and men fled in a panic. The next morning, all of the vaqueros on the ranch were mustered, armed and sent down to the lake to investigate. There was no sign of the winged monster but it was said that the smell of it still lingered in the air.

In 1883, the Lopez horses and cattle began to vanish. At first, bears or wolves were thought to be responsible but then one night, there was a terrible uproar in the corral. When the vaqueros came running, they found that ten mares and foals had been slaughtered. They said that, outlined against the sky, they saw the huge flying creature as it flapped away into the darkness. Don Chico Lopez promptly sold out and moved away from the area.

Then in 1886, the newspaper reported more strange happenings at Lake Elizabeth. The reports stated that a creature had been feeding on cattle, horses, sheep and chickens and had caused terror and excitement among the local inhabitants. On one occasion, the beast had tried to devour a large steer but, as the animal bellowed and kicked, the sound attracted the attention of its owner, Don Felipe Rivera. The steer put up a fierce fight and managed to free itself. The angry creature then retreated, but not before Rivera got a good look at it. He said that it was at least 45 feet long and had wings that laid flat on its back when not expanded. He pursued the monster as it started towards the lake and fired at it with his Colt revolver. Rivera said that when the bullets struck the monster's side, it sounded as if they were hitting a "great iron kettle."

But Don Felipe was nothing if not enterprising and he made immediate plans to try and capture the creature and sell it to the circus. He even signed a contract with Sells Brothers, who agreed to pay him $20,000 to deliver the beast to him alive. Don Felipe never managed to capture the creature, although it was reportedly seen several times in 1886. The creature was last seen, according to Horace Bell, winging away to the east.

"Since then," he wrote, "it has never been seen in its native valley because it was found and killed 800 miles from Lake Elizabeth, as is proved by the article that appeared in the Epitaph, Tombstone, Arizona." Bell then goes on to quote from the article, which he apparently saw, and provides details to the story. However, he does not say that the event occurred in 1886, as many believe. He provides a follow-up story, which is about the Tombstone article, which appeared in a Los Angeles newspaper in 1890. For this reason, it's safe to assume that the Thunderbird (if it really existed) was killed at some point between 1886 and 1890.

The article states that two ranchers sighted an enormous flying creature in the Arizona desert between Whetstone and the Huachuca Mountains. The beast resembled a huge alligator with an extremely elongated tail and an immense pair of wings. According to their story, the creature was greatly exhausted and was only able to fly a short distance at a time. The men, who were on horseback and armed with Winchester rifles, pursued the creature for several miles before getting close enough to open fire on it and wound it. The creature then turned on the cowboys but due to its exhaustion, they were able to keep far enough away from it until a few more shots could kill it.

An examination of the creature showed that it measured 92 feet in length and that its greatest diameter was about 50 inches. It had only two feet, situated a short distance in front of where the wings joined the body. The beak, as near as they could judge, was about eight feet long and its jaws were set with strong, sharp teeth. They experienced some difficulty trying to measure the wings, as they had folded up underneath the body as the monster had fallen, but eventually unrolled one of them. It was an incredible 78 feet in length, giving the beast a wingspan of about 160 feet. The wings were of a thick, nearly transparent membrane that had no feathers or hair on it. Its flesh was relatively smooth though and had been easily penetrated by their bullets.

The ranchers cut off a portion of the wing and took it with them, perhaps as proof of what they had seen. After arriving in Tombstone, they spread the word of the creature and made plans to return to the site where it had fallen and to skin it. They planned, the article stated, to offer the hide to eminent scientists for examination. They returned to the site to bring the creature back to town and here, the article ends. There are no details of the body being brought to town and no mention whatsoever of any photograph being taken.

The story of the Thunderbird was relegated to the ranks of creatures like the "jackalope" until 1963, when the story was revived. In the May 1963 issue of *Saga*, a men's magazine of the day, writer Jack Pearl recounted the story of the Tombstone Thunderbird, along with some large bird sightings of the early 1960s. Not only did he tell the story though, he went one step further and claimed that the *Tombstone Epitaph* had, in 1886, "published a photograph of a huge bird nailed to a wall. The newspaper said that it had been shot by two prospectors and hauled into town by wagon. Lined up in front of the bird were six grown men with their arms outstretched, fingertip-to-fingertip. The creature measured about 36 feet from wingtip to wingtip."

While this is a different variation of the story (and size of the creature), it seems to be referring to the same incident. Was this nothing more than a mythic legend of the West, or was there something to the story after all?

In the September 1963 issue of *Fate* magazine, a correspondent to the magazine named H.M Cranmer would state that not only was the story true, but the photo was published and had appeared in newspapers all over America. And Cranmer would not be the only one who remembered the photo. Eminent researcher Ivan T. Sanderson also remembered seeing the photo and in fact, even claimed to have once had a photocopy of it that he loaned to two associates, who lost it. The editors of *Fate* even came to believe that they may have published the photo in an earlier issue of the magazine, but a search through back issues failed to reveal it. Meanwhile, the original Epitaph story, which again mentions no photograph, was revived in a 1969 issue of *Old West*, further confusing the issue as to whether the photo was real or not.

The *Epitaph* however stated that it did not exist, or if it did, it had not been in their newspaper. Responding to numerous inquiries, employees of the paper started a thorough search of back issues and files. They could find no such photo and even an extended search of other Arizona and California newspapers of the period produced no results. A number of articles that appeared in *Pursuit, the journal for the Society for the Investigation of the Unexplained* prompted a memory from W. Ritchie Benedict, who recalled seeing Ivan T. Sanderson himself display a copy of the photo on a Canadian television show "The Pierre Benton Show." Unfortunately though, no copies of the show have ever been found.

So, is the photo real? And if not, then why do so many of us with an interest in the unusual claim to remember seeing it? Who knows? In the late 1990s, author John Keel insisted that "I know I saw it! And not only that—I compared notes with a lot of other people who saw it." Like many of us, Keel believes that he saw it in one of the men's magazines (like Saga or True) that were so popular in the 1960s. Most of these magazines dealt with amazing subject matter like Bigfoot, ghosts and more. Keel also remembers the photo in the same way that most of us do: with men wearing cowboy clothing and the bird looking like a pterodactyl or some prehistoric, winged creature.

Interestingly, a reprint of the original article that appeared in *Old West* magazine caused a reader to remember another strange incident. He wrote to the magazine in the summer of 1970 and gave a firsthand account of a separate flying monster incident that also occurred near Tombstone. The writer had met two cowboys who told about seeing a similar creature around 1890, although they had shot at and chased the creature until their horses refused to go any further. This giant bird was not killed, brought to town or photographed. In fact, except for the fact that it was not shot down, their account sounds much closer to Bell's original report.

During the 1990s, the search for the Thunderbird photo reached a point of obsession for those interested in the subject. A discussion of the matter stretched over several issues of Mark Chorvinsky's *Strange* magazine and readers who believed they had seen the photo cited sources that ranged from old books, to Western photograph collections, men's magazines, National Geographic and beyond. As for myself, I combed through literally hundreds of issues of dusty copies of *True* and *Saga* but could find nothing more than the previously mentioned article by Jack Pearl. If the photo exists, I certainly don't have it in my own collection.

So, how do we explain this weird phenomenon of a photograph that so many remember seeing and yet no one can seem to find? Author Mark Hall believes that the description of the photo creates such a vivid image in the mind that many people who have a knowledge and an interest in curious and eclectic things begin to think the photo is familiar. It creates a shared memory of something that does not exist. We think we have seen it, but we actually have not.

To be honest, I can't say for sure if I agree with this or not. I can certainly see the possibility of a memory like this that we have created from inside of our own overcrowded minds, but then again, what if the photo does exist and it's out there, just waiting to be discovered in some dusty garage, overflowing file cabinet or musty basement. I, for one, haven't given up quite yet—and I have a feeling that I am not the only one who is still out there looking.

But are thunderbirds and mysterious flying creatures actually real? Do they fill the skies of anything other than our imaginations? If not, then what have so many people seen over the years? At this point, such creatures remain a mystery but one thing is sure, the sightings have continued over the years and occasionally an unusual report still trickles in from somewhere across America. So keep that in mind the next time that you are standing in an open field and a large, dark shadow suddenly fills the sky overhead. Was that just a cloud passing in front of the sun, or something else?

IT'S RAINING CATS, DOGS—AND FROGS?

High Strangeness from the Sky

Throughout the haunted history of America, there have been many bizarre instances recorded when things have fallen from the skies that simply do not belong there. There have been showers of frogs and toads, along with fish, snakes and worms. Blood has been said to fall from the heavens, as well as meat, muscle and flesh. Reports of these things and others have plagued those who search for a log ical meaning in the world for centuries. The stories of such things range in believability from the logically possible to the downright incredible.

And for those who believe such things only date back to recent times, it should be noted that the earliest reports of strange falls from the sky actually appear in the Bible: the Book of Joshua in the Old Testament, to be exact. According to one story, the Israelites, led by Joshua, have routed the Amorite army and are in hot pursuit of the survivors when a shower of stones fell from the sky and killed more of the enemy than died by the Israelite sword. The Bible goes on to mention other strange happenings in regards to falls from the sky, with the frogs that plagued Egypt not being the least of them.

The earliest reports that I could find of such happenings in America dated back to 1828. It was said that after 10 to 12 days of rain, a partially dug ditch that belonged to a Joseph Muse of Cambridge, Maryland was found to contain hundreds of fish. The creatures ranged in size from four to seven inches long and were apparently jack perch and sun perch. There had been no water in the ditch before the rainfall and the nearest river was over a mile away.

There was no explanation as to how they could have gotten there.

In 1833, something more unusual than fish fell from the sky over the town of Rahway, New Jersey. On November 13, locals saw what they described as "fiery rain" falling to the ground. When the glowing masses struck the ground, they turned into "lumps of jelly." The lumps were said to be transparent and became round, flattened masses when they landed. Within hours, the jelly disintegrated and became a pile of small white particles that crumbled into dust when touched. The strange masses were reported at the same time that a meteor shower was taking place over the eastern United States and may have been connected to it in some way.

Troops stationed at an army post near San Francisco had their own encounters with strange objects from the sky on July 24, 1851. On that afternoon, soldiers who were on the drill field reported being pelted with spatters of blood and pieces of meat, that were apparently beef. The blood and meat fell from a cloudless sky and ranged in size from "a pigeon's egg to that of an orange." Several pieces of meat were given to the post surgeon and he described some of the slices as being slightly spoiled, as if they had been left out in the sun too long.

A similar event was said to have taken place in Simpson County, North Carolina on February 15 of the same year. Witnesses reported that pieces of flesh, liver, brains and blood rained down from the sky over an area that was roughly 30 feet wide and about 250 yards long.

On June 15, 1857 a farmer who lived in Ottawa, Illinois reported that he heard a hissing sound in the sky and he looked up to see a shower of cinders falling to the earth. They landed on the ground in a V-shaped pattern about 50 feet from where he was standing and caused the ground to steam and the grass to catch fire. The larger cinders buried themselves into the earth and even the smallest pieces were inserted into the ground at least partially. The farmer, whose name was Bradley, noticed a small, dense and dark cloud "hanging over the garden" at the time of the fall. The weather that day had been damp and a little rainy but no thunder or lightning had been reported.

The children of Lake County, California must have been happy on the nights of September 2 and 11, 1857. According to the *History of Napa and Lake Counties* by Lyman L. Palmer, a shower of candy apparently fell on some portions of the county on those evenings. The report states: "It is said that on both of these nights there fell a shower of candy or sugar. The crystals were from one-eighth to one-fourth of an inch in length and the size of a goose quill. Syrup was made of it by some of the lady residents of the section."

Another shower of flesh and blood was reported in California on August 1, 1869. The shower occurred for three minutes and covered about two acres of J. Hudson's farm near Los Nietos. The day was clear and windless and the bloody flesh fell in strips that were from one to six inches long. Many of them were reportedly covered with fine hairs, as if stripped from the body of an animal.

In August 1870, a deluge of water lizards hit Sacramento, California. The small animals were from two to eight inches long and alive when they hit the ground. The initial shower rained the lizards down so that they nearly covered the roof of the opera house. They slid down the building and into the rain spouts so that they covered the pavement around the building. The *Sacramento Reporter* stated that hundreds of them survived for several days in rainwater that flooded a partially dug cellar that was located nearby.

One of the strangest stories of this sort took place on March 3, 1876 when flakes of meat fell over an area 100 yards long and 50 yards wide near the Bath, Kentucky home of Mr. and Mrs. Allen Crouch. The sky was clear at the time of the fall and the flakes of meat were described as being one to three or four inches square and appeared to be fresh beef. However, according to two gentlemen who, for some reason, decided to taste the meat, it was neither mutton nor venison.

Or perhaps it wasn't meat at all, wrote Mr. Leopold Brandeis, whose article appeared on the strange fall in a July issue of the *Sanitarian*. He explained that the so-called meat was really nothing more than "nostic…a low form of vegetable substance." He did not however, explain how this substance managed to fall from the sky. His opinion on the matter did not last for long for he was soon contacted by Dr. A. Mead Edwards, president of the Newark Scientific Association, who asked for a sample of the material that had been collected from Bath County. Brandeis was kind enough to give him the entire specimen, along with the information that he had obtained it from a doctor in Brooklyn, who had in turn been given it by a Professor Chandler.

Shortly after this, a letter from Dr. Allan McLane Hamilton was posted to the Medical Record, saying that he and Dr. J.W.S. Arnold had examined the material from the Kentucky meat shower under a microscope. The material, which had been given to them by Professor Chandler, was identified as being lung tissue from a human infant or a horse. According to the letter, "the structure of the organ in these two cases" was apparently "very similar."

After reading the letter, Dr. Edwards called on Dr. Hamilton and was given a sample of the material that he had been studying. He was told that the samples had been sent from Kentucky to the editor of the *Agriculturist*, who had given them to Professor Chandler. And while the trail of where the samples had come from seemed to be growing longer and longer, Edwards noted that they seemed to be similar in character and age, although the sample given to him by Brandeis was less well preserved. Soon after, Edwards was shown a microscopic slide of a third sample of the Kentucky meat, which had been given to Professor J. Phin of the *American Journal of Microscopy* by a Mr. Walmsley of Philadelphia, who had in turn received it from Kentucky. The slide contained something that was "undoubtedly straited muscular fibre."

Phin also showed Edwards a fourth sample that had been collected by A.T. Parker of Lexington, Kentucky. This sample also turned out to be muscle tissue but Edwards wanted to see more. He wrote to Parker and was sent three more samples, two of which turned out to be cartilage and the third, more muscle tissue.

Edwards also passed along an explanation for the bizarre event that was currently making the rounds in Kentucky.

Locals believed that the meat had been disgorged by buzzards, "who, as is their custom, seeing one of their companions disgorge himself, immediately followed suit." Parker did not explain just how many buzzards would be required to vomit that much meat, how much they would have had to have eaten, or just how high they had been flying as to render themselves invisible to those on the ground.

Perhaps almost as strange was the rain of living snakes that fell over the southern part of Memphis, Tennessee in 1877. These creatures reportedly ranged from about a foot to 18 inches in length and were presumed by the people of Memphis to have been swept into the air by a hurricane. Although even Scientific American asked where so many snakes would exist "in such abundance" (they fell by the thousands) "is yet a mystery."

Scientific American also reported another strange occurrence in late October 1881 when Milwaukee, Green Bay and other towns in that part of Wisconsin saw falls of strong, very white spider webs. They were in sizes from a few inches to strands of more than 60 feet long. The webs all seemed to float inland from above Lake Michigan in thick sheets, fading upward into the sky for as high as the eye could see. There was no mention of any spiders being seen or in the presence of the webs and where the substance could have come from was a mystery.

On September 4, 1886, a shower of warm stones purportedly fell on the offices of the *News and Courier* in Charleston, South Carolina. The first shower occurred around 2:30 in the morning and then was repeated at 7:30 and then again at 1:30 in the afternoon. As far as any observers could see, the stones fell only over a small area directly above the newspaper offices. They came down with great force and even broke apart on the pavement. The rocks were described as polished pebbles of flint with the smallest being about the size of a grape and the largest as big as a hen's egg. Many of the stones were gathered up and saved but I was unable to learn what may have become of them.

Scientific American from February 1891 had another tale of strangeness from the skies concerning the Valley Bend District of Randolph County, West Virginia. It seems that over the course of that winter, they were several occasions when ground was thickly covered with worms. Since the snow had been two feet deep at the times when the worms were discovered, and there was a hard crust on the top of it, they seemingly fell from the sky along with the fresh snow. They were said to be a species of ordinary "cut worms" and were abundant enough that a "square foot of snow can scarcely be found on some days without a dozen of these worms on it."

During the early morning hours of a day in November 1896, a deluge of dead birds fell from a clear sky above Baton Rouge, Louisiana. They fell in such numbers that contemporary accounts say that they "cluttered the streets of the city." The birds included wild ducks, catbirds, woodpeckers and many birds of strange plumage, some of them "resembling canaries." The birds were all dead and fell in heaps throughout the city. The only plausible theory advanced as to the source of the birds was that they had been driven inland by a recent storm along the Florida coast and had been killed by a sudden change in temperature around Baton Rouge. The editors of the *Monthly Weather Review* stated that storms and temperature changes were common, but bird falls were most assuredly not.

We move from birds to fish again when in June 1901, hundreds of small catfish, trout and perch fell during a heavy rain at Tiller's Ferry, South Carolina. After the rain showers ended, the fish were found swimming around in pools of water that had accumulated between the rows of cotton of a farm owned by Charles Raley. There is no record of what the Raleys had for dinner that night!

In November 1921, rocks began to fall from the sky over the town of Chico, California. J. W. Charge, the owner of a grain warehouse along the Southern Pacific Railroad tracks, complained to City Marshal J.A. Peck that someone was throwing rocks at his building everyday. Peck, believing it was nothing more than local youngsters playing pranks on the man, paid little attention to the report. His conclusions, after a very brief investigation, were that he had seen the stones fall but could not explain them. He suspected that "someone with a machine was to blame." The stones remained a nuisance to Charge but were largely ignored by everyone else until a few months later, on March 8, 1922. On that day, stones ranging in size from peas to baseballs came raining down on the warehouse, seemingly from nowhere. They continued to fall for days and a search by police officers of the area failed to find anyone throwing the rocks.

In the days that followed, Charge's warehouse sustained quite a bit of damage, from broken windows to split boards and collapsed roof shingles. Stones also began to rain down on a cluster of houses that were located near the railroad tracks and individuals who stood in the open, perhaps trying to determine the source of the mysterious projectiles, were often struck. The investigators and officials present often became targets too. Fire Chief C.E. Tovee and Traffic Officer J.J. Corbett were narrowly missed by a large boulder that came from nowhere and struck a wall behind the spot where they had been standing just moments before. The force of the stone's impact left a large dent in the wood.

The fall of stones continued throughout most of the rest of the month, attracting a large amount of publicity and a number of curiosity-seekers. The origin of the stones was never solved but a Professor C.K. Studley added to reports by saying that some of the rocks were so large that they "could not be thrown by ordinary means." He also noted that they did not seem to be of meteoric nature. The famous chronicler of anomalies Charles Fort asked a friend, writer Miriam Allen deFord, to go to Chico to investigate personally. Throughout March a series of articles appeared in the San Francisco Chronicle and the rocks were described as being warm and oval-shaped. Miriam Allen de Ford, wrote: "I looked up in the cloudless sky and suddenly saw a rock falling straight down, as if becoming visible when it came near enough. This rock struck the earth with a thud and bounced off on the track beside the warehouse, and I could not find it." She also stated that at one point a rock fell from the sky to "land gently at my feet."

Fish fell again on October 23, 1947, this time over the town of Marksville, Louisiana. The weather at the time was calm and it was not raining, although it was somewhat foggy. The fish came raining down without warning and included largemouth bass, sunfish, shad and minnows. Some of them were frozen and others merely cold but all were said to be "fit for human consumption." The fish came down into an area that was about 1,000 feet long and 75 or 80 feet wide and a number of them struck people who happened to be on the street at the time. The weather bureau in New Orleans reported that there were no tornadoes in the area at the time of the incident.

On the night of September 26, 1950, two Philadelphia police officers, John Collins and Joe Keenan, encountered something far beyond the range of experience expected from two veteran cops. As they were cruising the streets in their patrol car that night, they made their way down a quiet side street near Vare Avenue and 26th Street. Coming around a corner, their headlights pick up a large, shimmering object that seemed to be falling down into an open field about a half block away from them. When they stopped to investigate, their flashlights illuminated a domed mass of quivering purple jelly. It was about six feet in diameter and about a foot thick in the center. It gently sloped down toward the edges but was still an inch or two thick. The pulsating movement of the mass made them wonder if it might be alive! They quickly radioed for help and were soon joined by Sergeant Joe Cook and Patrolman James Cooper. Cook suggested that the four of them try and pick the thing up but when Officer Collins attempted to reach underneath it, the mass fell apart in his hands. Fragments of it clung to his skin but it too began to slide off of him, leaving only a sticky, odorless scum behind. Within a half-hour after Cook and Cooper arrived on the scene, the entire mass had evaporated and vanished.

On September 7, 1953, a downpour of frogs and toads of all descriptions began falling from the sky over Leicester, Massachusetts. The streets seemed to be alive with them and children gathered them into buckets using their hands, making a game of the astounding event. Officials attempted to explain the sudden appearance of thousands of the creatures by saying that they had escaped from a nearby, overflowing pond, however, this explanation did not provide a logical reason as to why so many of them were found on the roofs of houses and in the rain gutters.

Carpenters who were working on the roof of a house in Shreveport, Louisiana had to take cover on July 12, 1961 when a brief deluge of green peaches began falling from the sky. They were all about the size of golf balls and were believed to have fallen from a dark cloud that was spotted overhead. According to the local weather bureau, the conditions around the city that day were not sufficient to cause whirlwinds, tornadoes or water spouts. Even a strong updraft would not have been enough to carry peaches into the sky, leaving those who witnessed the event to scratch their heads in confusion.

In January 1969, hundreds of badly injured ducks came crashing to the earth in St. Mary's City, Maryland. Wildlife officials surmised that the ducks had received their fatal injuries, which included broken bones and mysterious hemorrhages, while they were flying. What may have caused the damage, or why so many ducks were flying in one large mass, was unknown.

And those are just a sampling of the bizarre falls from the sky that have plagued America and have been recorded in history. There are many hundreds more incidents like this that have occurred in other places around the world. But how do we explain such a thing happening?

There are naturally many theories but the standard explanation for the seemingly inexplicable falls from the sky are that the objects that come down were carried up into a whirlwind or a waterspout. This is the most logical explanation and admittedly, storms do often manage to pick objects up from one place and put them down again in others. A great variety of natural debris (plants, dust, feathers, etc.) requires little force to lift it up into the air and larger storms could certainly move rocks or perhaps even pull fish or frogs from a body of water. Much larger items have often been found moved by tornadoes, including automobiles, people and even entire structures. Few of us have any doubts (especially those living in the Great Plains or the Midwest) as to what a major storm can do. I will never forget one of my first visits to the Illinois State Museum as a child to see the display of a single piece of straw that had been driven through a solid wooden fence post!

Waterspouts have been far less observed by science but records show that they have also accomplished extraordinary things. There are records of fish being emptied from bays, ponds being sucked dry and, on at least one occasion, all water life being pulled from a lake in England and then being deposited on dry land.

That seems to show that the energy being generated by tornadoes and other storms is sufficient to lift into the sky those things that have been seen to fall from it, but does this theory really provide a solution for all of the incidents that have been recorded? How, for example, have these storms managed to be so selective about depositing the strange items? Things that fall from the sky are usually neatly segregated in that only stones, or only frogs, or only fish fall in one location. If a storm has swept up everything in its path, then how does it manage to only let fall a certain type of item?

Another interesting question would be how the fish, frogs and other assorted creatures usually manage to survive the storm and land on the ground alive? The whirlwind/tornado theory asks us to believe that the animals must survive being pulled from the water and then exist on nothing more than the moisture inside of the storm cloud for an extended period of time. This must be a long time, we have to note, because in many cases, there are no records of storms or tornadoes present in the area where the falls occur at the time they take place. Also for this theory to work, we have to

294

believe that forces powerful enough to lift the creatures from their normal habitat and into the sky are insufficient to do them any physical damage (in most reported cases) and that the sudden changes in pressure and temperature that would undoubtedly take place are just as harmless.

Needless to say, this theory makes common sense but really lacks the evidence for it to be seen as the only explanation for the phenomenon. Unfortunately, many of the other explanations that have been suggested to explain how such falls happen are nearly as hard to believe. These explanations fall into categories of extraterrestrials, the supernatural and shifts in time and space.

Those who proffer theories of aliens from outer space suggest that perhaps the otherworldly visitors have gathered up large supplies of earthly items, only to jettison them from their spacecrafts before returning to wherever they came from. The falls from the upper atmospheres might seem as if the objects were falling from nowhere. In addition, the rains of blood and meat could be waste matter from the crafts that was dumped to lighten the load for the journey.

In the supernatural theory, gods, spirits or other unnamed entities are responsible for falls from the sky, or at least some of them. Others suggest that perhaps poltergeist-like instances of psychokinesis may be responsible for falls of rocks and stones. When it comes to the falls of fish, frogs and other creatures, there have been suggestions that perhaps they are examples of some kind of supernatural benevolence. Proponents of this theory point to instances when dry ponds or new ditches have been found to contain full-grown fish after a rainstorm. This was one of the first theories to explain falls from the sky that I ever heard. As a child, a minister once told me that the oceans and lakes were stocked every time that it rained as God made the fish fall from the heavens. This fascinated me until I reached the age of perhaps 10, and after that, I looked elsewhere for the answers to a number of questions that explanation created for me!

One of the most popular theories to deal with falls from the sky is that our world consists of many times and dimensions. These parallel worlds intersect occasionally with our own and as we discussed in an earlier chapter, things sometimes vanish from our world and in turn, items mysteriously appear in our own. Many researchers of strange phenomena are inclined to this theory of teleportation—the paranormal transportation of an object from one place to another—as a sort of blanket explanation for everything from falls from the sky to mystery animals that appear in places where they don't belong. In this case though, even if we accept the idea that teleportation is possible (which is not certain, of course) it still asks the same questions as the more logical explanations for these weird events: how is that the falls manage to be so selective with the items that fall and the locations where they happen?

As the discerning reader must have already noticed, the virtue of these types of paranormal explanations is that they account for all possibilities, no matter how bizarre. The only flaw that they have, in searching for an absolute solution, is that they provide explanations using untested ideas and circumstances that go beyond the fantastic. This is not to say that there may not be some truth to the theories, but there is simply no way to know at this time. It becomes a matter of course that our explanations for why these things occur are nearly as strange and inexplicable as the unsolved mysteries themselves!

Spook Lights!

The Mystery of the Glowing Lights

Spook lights, or ghost lights as they are often called, have long been a part of anomalous history in America. Such a light is best defined as being a luminous phenomenon that, because of the way that it behaves, its location and regular manifestation, is put into a separate category from ball lightning or even ghosts themselves. However, most spook lights, especially those that appear regularly over a period of time and in one location tend to take on a supernatural air. Legends tend to grow around them concerning strange deaths and most often, a beheading for which a ghost returns looking for the severed head. The spook light is most often said to be the light of a lantern that the spirit carries to assist him in the search.

According to stories, there have long been such lights in America. A book written in 1685 by Nathaniel Crouch called *The English Empire* in America makes note of a remarkable flame "that appears before the death of an Indian or English upon their wigwams in the dead of night." Native American tales and early settler stories often told of such light appearing as a forewarning of death, perhaps hearkening back to similar tales from the Old World. Other stories told of "corpse candles" that would signify the presence of a spirit left behind by a death.

In February 1909, newspaper accounts told of strange happenings in Stockton, Pennsylvania over the nighttime appearance of an "arrow of flame" that would hover over a spot on the mountain where the body of a murdered woman had been found two years before. The locals insisted that the light was the avenging spirit of the dead woman who kept coming back to the spot on a nightly basis to insure that the history of the crime was kept alive. In that way, the legend went, she could try and make sure that her killer was someday apprehended.

Spook lights appear in hundreds of places around the country and while most of them have an eerie legend or two attached to their appearance, few explanations can be reached as to why they appear. In the instances when the lights have been thoroughly investigated, the results have been inconclusive at best and at the worst, disappointing. In some cases, the mysterious lights turn out to be nothing more than the headlights of cars on distant highways or reflections of stars and lights that refract layers of different air temperatures. But that's not always the case.

There are a number of locations where spook lights appear and manage to escape such explanations. These are locations where reports of the lights date back to well before the advent of the automobile and where claims of artificial lights in the distance just don't hold up. These are lights that serious researchers have been unable to debunk. And while it is the opinion of many with an interest in such things (myself included) that spook lights are a natural part of our world for which we do not yet have an explanation, the most compelling ones still remain unsolved.

Brown Mountain Lights

In the western hills of North Carolina stands a mountain that is not particularly striking, or even high, but it plays host to perhaps the strangest mystery in the state. The mountain is called Brown Mountain and it lies in the foothills of the Blue Ridge. For many years, it has attracted the attention of people from all over the nation and even the attention of the United States government, as two separate investigations have been conducted by the U.S. Geological survey into the strange anomalies of this mountain.

The odd events that are occurring here have been called the Brown Mountain Lights for more years than most can remember. They appear along the ridges of this mountain on a regular basis and are faithful enough that in clear weather, you can see them just about any night that you care to. Locals say the best place to view them is at Wiseman's View on Highway 105 near Morganton. Curiosity-seekers will line this stretch of road in the early evening hours and are rarely disappointed. By looking to the southeast, the watchers will suddenly see a light appear that is about the size of a basketball, or so it appears. The light will be reddish in color and it will hover in the air for a moment and then disappear. In a few minutes, it will appear again, but in another location and then all through the night, the lights will come and go, appearing and vanishing against the night sky.

As is normal with this kind of thing, almost every person

reports the lights in a different way; some see them as white and bobbing, others as pale and stationary, while others see them coming and going quite rapidly. Regardless of how they are seen, they remain a mystery. No explanation yet exists as to what the lights really are, although many have tried to solve the riddle. Some have suggested will-o'-the-wisp, that elusive gas that resides in swamps, and yet no swamps are found in this area. Others have suggested foxfire or some sort of phosphorus, radium rays, strange gases, geological anomalies with the rocks and a myriad of other explanation. Strangely though, all of them have been dismissed. Another popular solution is that the lights are simply headlight reflections from Rattlesnake Knob in the distance. However, this does not explain the fact that the lights were reported well before automobiles were common in the area. Some have even suggested that the lights could be firing of moonshine stills by liquor makers on the mountain and while this theory is certainly a romantic one, it has been quite some time since moonshine was made on the slopes of Brown Mountain.

As is the case with most ghost light report, there is a fantastic explanation and a spooky legend to explain the source of the lights. The story dates back to 1850 and a night when a woman disappeared in the area. There was a general suspicion that the woman's husband had murdered her, and everyone in the community turned out to help search for her body. One night, while the search was on, strange lights appeared over Brown Mountain. They were not like lights that anyone had ever seen before and many believed they were the spirit of the dead woman, coming back to haunt her killer. The search ended without the woman being found. Shortly after, the woman's husband disappeared without a trace and many wondered what may have become of him. A number of years later, a skeleton belonging to a woman was found on Brown Mountain and the lights that had been seen during the search started to appear again and have been seen ever since.

The first printed reference to the lights came about in 1913 with a newspaper report in the *Charlotte Daily Observer*. The article passed on the testimony of a group of fisherman and noted that the "mysterious light is seen just above the horizon almost every night." This article prompted the first U.S. Geological Survey of the mountain by D.B. Sterrett. His investigations concluded that the lights were nothing more than reflections from locomotive headlights, however a 1916 expedition reported the lights moving in an out of ravines along the southeast side of the mountain. This would have placed the lights far out of reach of mere headlights.

Continued sightings brought another U.S. Geological Survey scientist to the region in March and April 1922. George Rogers Mansfield spent seven nights observing the lights on the mountain and also compiled reports with a survey of Brown Mountain and dozens of interviews with local witnesses to the anomalies. He attributed percentages of the sightings to automobile lights, trains, stationary lights and brush fires, but still left a small percentage of the sightings as unknown and unaccounted for. His research proved that there was no single (or easy) answer to the mystery of the lights.

In the years since then, witnesses have reported lights in all shapes and sizes and in a variety of different forms. On a few occasions, witnesses also claim to have been close enough to the lights to actually hear them sizzle as they passed by. To this day, no hard explanations have appeared to really explain why the Brown Mountain Lights continue to appear or what may be the source of the enigma.

Maco Station

The mysterious lights of Brown Mountain are not the only anomalous lights in North Carolina. Perhaps just as famous, and strange, is the light that is seen at Maco Station. Over the nearby railroad crossing appears an unexplainable light and while it has many of the same characteristics as other railroad ghost lights, it has puzzled both witnesses and scientists for many years.

The story of the light dates back to 1867 and involves a railroad man named Joe Baldwin. In that year, the Atlantic Coast Line Railroad was rebuilt and now included a small station that had once been called Farmer's Turnout and was now Maco. Joe Baldwin was a conductor for the Atlantic line and his job involved riding in the last car of the train. One night, as the train was steaming along, he realized that his car seemed to be inexplicably slowing down. With one look, he realized that it had become uncoupled and there was another train following behind! He was sure they would crash into the slowly moving car!

Joe ran out onto the rear platform of the car and started wildly waving his signal lantern, trying to get the attention of the engineer of the train behind him. The engineer paid no heed to the lantern and continued on, finally crashing into the car where Joe had remained at his post. The coach was completely demolished and Joe was killed, his head severed from his body. A witness to the accident reported that Joe stayed where he was, waving the lantern, through the entire wreck. Just seconds before the engine collided with the car, Joe's lantern was hurled away as if by some unseen, but mighty, force. It hit the ground and rolled over and over again, finally coming to rest in a perfectly upright position.

Shortly after this horrible accident, the Maco light began to appear along the train tracks. It has been appearing there ever since and has become a popular curiosity to seek out on a warm summer night. Automobiles are often parked along the highway, and the curious walk the hundred or so yards down an old road to the train tracks. Rarely is anyone disappointed either, because the light is one of the most regular anomalies in the South.

It is said that the light often appears to be very small and then grows to the size of the lantern that Joe Baldwin must have been carrying. It has been reported here since 1873 and has been seen by literally thousands of people since that date. In 1886, an earthquake stopped the light for a short time and when it came back there were two lights for a short time. In 1889, the light was even seen by then president, Grover Cleveland.

No one has been able to figure out what causes the light, as just about every explanation has been discussed and tossed aside, from automobile headlights seen before cars existed to swamp gas. During one investigation, all traffic was routed away from Maco and no cars were allowed to approach the area, and yet the unearthly light still appeared. On one occasion, a machine gun attachment from Fort Bragg encamped at Maco to solve the mystery, or at least shoot it down, but they did neither.

Joe Baldwin, or whatever ghostly source for the Maco light, continues on—still swinging the signal lantern and contacting the train that journeys from this world to the next.

Gurdon Light

The most popular Halloween attraction in Clark County, Arkansas must be the "Gurdon Light," a mysterious phenomenon that has been appearing here for generations. Over the last several decades, hundreds of witnesses have observed the light. It has been seen on local television stations and has been photographed by students at nearby Henderson State University. There is no doubt that the light exists, although what it is and what legends are behind its existence remains to be seen.

Gurdon, Arkansas is located south of Little Rock and is a small, sleepy little town of only about 2,000 people. It is said that many of the local people in Gurdon have seen the light more than one hundred times in their life, and, while it is an accepted fact of this place, those same people still have no idea just how to explain why the light exists. There is a legend, which will come as no surprise to ghost light buffs, that tells of a railroad worker who was working along a stretch of tracks outside of town. He accidentally fell into the path of an oncoming train and his head was severed from his body. Of course, the ghost of this railroad worker is said to walk the tracks at night and the ghost light is from his lantern as he searches for his missing head. The only thing that makes this story a little different from other tales of the phantom brakeman is that a real-life murder did take place here and if the light is actually some sort of supernatural manifestation, this may explain why the light was seen a short time later.

According to Mark Evans, who provided information to me about the Gurdon anomaly, he has seen the light on several occasions. It is white and blue and sometimes orange in color and it has a very distinct border, almost as if it is shining through a plastic lens. It always sways back and forth and stays in motion, probably explaining why the legend of the railroad lantern was started. The light is frequently seen on the darkest nights and best when it is cloudy and overcast. The light never reflects off the tracks and because of its remote location cannot be a reflection from passing headlights or anything else that is easily explainable.

Hornet Spook Light

Located about 20 miles or so southwest of Joplin, Missouri is a roughly paved road where my favorite American spook light puts in a regular appearance. This old and otherwise forgotten track runs across the Oklahoma border but is only about four miles long. Nearby is the border village of Hornet and close to that is the site of what once was a spook light museum. The place is remote and far from civilization, so why do so many people come here?

They are searching for an unexplained enigma, a puzzle that many of them find. It has been seen along this road since 1866 and has created such a mystery that even the Army Corps of Engineers officially concluded that it was a "mysterious light of unknown origin." It has been called by many names since it started appearing here, near what is called the Devil's Promenade, but it's most commonly known as the "Hornet Spook Light." This light has appeared, looking like a ball of fire, for nearly a century and a half, varying in size from a softball to larger. It spins down the center of this gravel road at great speed, rises up high, bobs and weaves to the right and left. It appears to be a large lantern, but there is never anyone carrying it. The light has appeared inside of vehicles, seems to retreat when it is pursued, and never allows anyone to get to close to it. Does the light have some sort of intelligence? This remains just one of the many mysteries connected to this light.

No one has ever been injured by the light but many claim to have been frightened by it while walking and driving down this road at night. Sometimes it seems to come from nowhere and a few witnesses claim they have felt the heat from it as it passed close to them. Occasionally, some observer will even take a shot or two at the light, like Franklin Rossman, who lived near the Devil's Promenade for years. He twice attempted to shoot the light with a hunting rifle but the shots had no effect on it whatsoever. He told a spook light investigator that he was unable to judge the distance to the light because it had such an odd look to it. When asked what he meant by this, Rossman was unable to explain. It just looked "sort of blurry," he said.

There have been many theories that have attempted to explain why this mysterious light appears here. Originally, a number of legends sprung up around the place. One of them claimed the light was connected to the spirit of two young Quapaw Indians who died in the area many years ago. Another claimed the light was the spirit of an Osage Indian chief who had been beheaded on the Devil's Promenade and the light was said to be his torch as he searched for his missing head. Another legend tells of a miner whose children were kidnapped by Indians and he set off looking for them with only a lantern to light his way. The light is said to be that very lantern as the farmer's ghost continues looking for the children that he will never find.

Locals claim that the stories of the Hornet Light originated back in the 1800s but most printed accounts are of a much more recent vintage. As far as is known, the first account of it appeared in the *Kansas City Star* in 1936 and then in the 1947 book *Ozark*

Superstitions by Vance Randolph, the famed Missouri folklorist. Randolph was the first to put into print the oral legends of the light's origins, from beheaded Indians to lost children.

In 1958, a writer for the *Ford Times* investigated the light and described it as a diffused, orange glow that floated and weaved along the roadway. He also noted that it seemed to change size as he watched it, varying between the sizes of an apple to that of a bushel basket. While present, he also saw the light split off into three different lights and then as a single light, it settled down upon the branch of a tree and changed colors from orange to blue.

Over the years, the light has been studied, researched, chased, photographed and shot at, but, what is it? While legends give one reason for the light, its genuine origins seem to present a formidable problem. Many suggestions have been offered as to what could cause the light to appear and for many years the most popular theory was that it was merely will-o'-the-wisp, the name given to a biological phenomenon that is caused by the decay of wood and organic materials. The emission of light that comes from the decay often glows brightly and can be seen on occasion in wooded areas and damp regions. As fascinating as this is, it really doesn't explain the Hornet Light. Instances of will-o'-the-wisp simply do not give off the intensity of light that has been reported along the Devil's Promenade.

Another suggestion has been the ever-popular marsh gas. Unfortunately, while an abundance of marsh gas in a marsh or swamp would certainly be flammable, it cannot spontaneously light itself. Even if it did, wind and rain would soon extinguish any flame that appeared. Strong winds that have been reported during sightings of the Hornet Light do not seem to disturb the light and they don't keep it from moving in whatever direction it pleases.

There have also been theories that the light might be a glow coming from minerals in the area. This seems doubtful too, as the light does not always appear in the same place. One plausible suggestion theorizes that the light might be formed by electrical fields in areas where earthquakes and ground shifts take place. This is a possibility since there are fault lines in the region. Four earthquakes took place here in the early 1800s that had a devastating effect on this part of the state. It is possible that the lights starting appearing around the time of the earthquakes but were not reported until the population in the area started to grow around the time of the Civil War.

Other experts claim they have the mystery solved and that it's not unexplainable at all. They claim the light is caused by automobiles driving on the highway about five miles east of what's known as "Spook Light Road." They say the highway is on a direct line with it but at a slightly lower elevation. When it is pointed out that a high ridge separates the area from the highway, the experts explain how refraction causes light to bend and creates the eerie effect that so many people have reported as the spook light.

Believe it or not, several investigations that have been conducted at the site have shown that some of the sightings here may be attributed to this phenomenon. Dr. George W. Ward, formerly of the Bureau of Standards in Washington and later with the Midwest Research Institute, investigated the light in 1945. He said that shortly after arriving at the site, he saw a diffused glow appear over some low hills. A few moments later, a sphere of light appeared that looked to be four to six feet in diameter. Ward humorously added that the Publicity Director of the Midwest Institute remarked to the others assembled that he had seen all that he cared to and as the light approached the group, he quickly locked himself inside their automobile.

But Ward was critical about the source of the light. During his study, he decided that the light must originate to the west of the viewing site and over the range of hills in the distance. He surmised that the refraction of auto headlights from a road that was in line with the country lane could create an illusion of a traveling light. Dr. Ward checked his maps and found that such a road did exist, a section of highway that ran east and west between Commerce and Quapaw, Oklahoma. He suggested that an airplane might be used to spot cars on the highway and relay the information to observers at the Spook Light site. If the lights could be shown to correspond with the Hornet Light, the mystery would be solved.

Captain Bob E. Loftin followed these speculations with his own experiments a few years later. He discovered that colored test lights that were placed on the suspected areas of Route 66 could be seen from Spook Light Road. He further reasoned that the presence of moving cars along the highway would appear as spheres of light, closely grouped together. He also added that changing humidity and temperature would cause the lights that were created to behave strangely. This, they reasoned, would explain the number of unusual stories told about the way the light acted. And while this would admittedly explain some of the sightings of the Hornet Light, it is impossible that it could explain them all. The most important point to remember is that the light was being seen before the invention of automobiles!

These were far from the only investigations conducted at the site. Author Raymond Bayless embarked on an extensive study of the spook light in October 1963. Around dusk on the evening of October 17, he and several assistants spotted the light for the first time, as it appeared as a bright light some distance along the roadway. He reported that the light fluctuated in intensity and at times became two separate lights, hovering one above the other. The light returned again about an hour later and according to Bayless, was so bright that it caused a reflection on the dirt surface of the road. A few minutes after the light appeared, the investigation group began moving westward along the road in pursuit of it. The light receded backward, or appeared to, as they got closer to it. The group began navigating the hills and ravines of the road and the light vanished. It did not reappear until they reached a point near the old spook light museum, which was still in operation at that time.

The Spooksville Museum, operated then by Leslie W. Robertson, offered not only photographs and a collection of accounts about the light but also a viewing platform for people to observe the light with the naked eye or through telescopes and cameras. A member of Bayless' group set up a small refracting telescope on the platform and they were able to learn that what appeared to be a single light was actually composed of a number of smaller lights. Bayless stated that they moved very close together, weaving slighting, expanding and contracting back and forth. It was amber and gold in color and sometimes gained a reddish tint for a few moments at a time. Through the telescope, the edges of the light were observed to be like a flame in that they were not uniform and constantly changed.

Bayless was fascinated with the many explanations of the light and was able to rule out almost all of the ones that had been proposed, including the theory that all of the sightings could be explained away as the refraction of auto headlights. In fact, Mr. Arthur Holbrook, a resident of the area and a man who had investigated the light many times, told Bayless that he had first seen the light in 1905. At that time, Holbrook explained, there were only about a dozen automobiles in Joplin, the closest large town. There were no highways, and the few cars in existence did not travel about on remote, dirt lanes best suited for horses. He also added that autos of that time were only fitted with oil and carbide lamps, which would not have been capable of creating the long, intense beams of modern headlights. To add even more credibility to his account, Holbrook was in the automotive profession and would have been very aware of the number of autos in the region in those days and the state of the roads and highways.

But did the light actually exist before automobiles came to southwest Missouri or was this merely a part of the local legend? Many skeptics claimed that the enigma's longevity was merely a part of the light's folklore, but Bayless did not agree. After conducting a number of interviews in the area, he began to believe that it had been seen in the 1800s. He did not feel that his own sighting of the light was comparable to auto headlights, but he needed to gather as much evidence as possible to show the light pre-dated automobiles. Mr. Holbrook had experienced his first sighting of the light in 1905 and had heard of the light for several years before that. After that first sighting, he rode out in a buggy to see the light many times and told Bayless that the light was the same in the 1960s as it had been in 1905.

Bayless followed up with more interviews of local Joplin residents. He spoke with Leslie Robertson, the curator of the Spooksville Museum, who first saw the light in 1916. He was only 14 years old at the time, but continued to see the light "thousands of times." Mr. John Muening first saw the light around 1928 and had heard stories about it for a number of years before that. He told Bayless that "we have watched it all night—Highway 66 has nothing to do with the light. It couldn't have, as it didn't exist when the light was first seen, of that I am sure." Mrs. Rene Waller, also said that she had seen the Hornet Light before Route 66 was put in through Quapaw, Oklahoma. She confirmed that the original highway was a dirt road that was traveled infrequently. She had first seen the light in the late 1920s, when auto headlights would have been too seldom on the road to have created the effect of the light. Mr. and Mrs. L.C. Ferguson stated that they had been familiar with the Hornet Light even earlier. By the time they first saw it in 1910, they were told that the light had been seen along the road for many years already.

These claims of the light's longevity were further substantiated by Mr. J. Leonard, who was a member of the Miami Indian tribe at the time of his interview in the early 1960s. He told Bayless that his parents had spoke of the light many times when he was a boy. He could personally remember seeing it for as long as he had been alive (he had been born in 1896) and according to stories, the light had been in existence for several generations or at least 100 years. Another Native American from the area, Guy Jennison, recalled hearing about the light when he was a boy attending the Quapaw Mission School in 1892. By that time, it was a local topic of conversation, implying that reports of the light had been around for at least a few years. Jennison believed that, like Mr. Leonard, the light might have appeared several generations before, based on the Indian legends that had been suggested to explain its origin. Unfortunately, during the time of the Bayless investigation, there were few Native Americans left who had knowledge of when the stories originated.

Even without the earlier dates though, Bayless was able to show that the Hornet Light existed prior to the use of automobiles in the area. He did not dispute the idea that headlights could cause some sightings, but he did debunk the idea that headlights could be the only cause. Others have suggested that perhaps lights from Quapaw or from mining camps in the area could have caused a refraction of light, thus creating the Spook Light, but there is little evidence to suggest this or to suggest that these stationary lights could manage to create a light that moves about and comes and goes as the Hornet Light does.

With that in mind, Raymond Bayless' investigations of the light should be considered groundbreaking. Although he certainly did not solve the mystery of the Hornet Light, he did manage to present some compelling evidence for its early existence. The only problem to come out of his investigations was that he managed, by showing how long the light had been around and by showing that not all of the sightings could be dismissed, to make the mystery even more perplexing.

Bayless was not the first, nor would he be the last, to investigate the Hornet Spook Light. Literally thousands of curiosity-seekers visit the Devil's Promenade each year and many of those are serious researchers of the unknown. The old Spook Light Museum is gone now but long after Leslie Robertson came Garland "Spooky" Middleton, who also operated the place for a time. Along with the photographs and newspaper articles, Middleton sold soda to tourists and entertained them with his own encounters with the mysterious light, like the time he saw it in a field near the museum. He said that the light appeared one night on the road, just after sunset, and began to roll like a ball, giving off sparks as it traveled along the gravel road. It entered a field where several cattle grazed and managed to move among the animals, not disturbing them at all.

On three different occasions, starting in the late 1990s, I visited Spook Light Road, each time hoping to get a glimpse of the elusive light. My diligence was never rewarded but I didn't give up on the idea that I might be at the right place at the right time at some point. Eventually, my persistence paid off. In December 2005, I took a group of people in search of the light, and in addition to a near case of frostbite, several of us also got a look at this mysterious wonder.

The afternoon had been a cold one but it was nothing compared to how cold it got after nightfall. Even though the clear skies had made it bitterly cold, they had the benefit of treating us to a sky that was unbelievably filled with stars. With no city lights or hazy clouds to interfere with our view, we saw more stars that night than on any occasion I can ever remember. Shooting stars streaked across the sky about every few minutes or so, which made standing in the cold well worth the effort—even if we didn't see the Hornet Spook Light. Luckily though, we didn't have to make that sacrifice. The light put in its brief appearance some time around 2:30 a.m.

When the spook light finally put in its appearance, there were perhaps six of us huddled around the van, trying to stay warm. Several of the guests had fallen asleep in the van at this point, wrapped up in sleeping bags and blankets, while others had vanished to other vantage points along the roadway. We had several false alarms during the night, with several of us thinking we saw the light, but each time it turned out to be headlights approaching along this lonely road. When the light did show up, there was no mistaking it for anything else.

It was Becky Ray, a representative for the American Ghost Society in Kansas City, who spotted it first. Her quick response got the attention of the others who were standing together, and we saw the light appear at the crest of a small hill about 50 yards away.

The spook light was directly west of where we had parked the van along Spook Light Road and it did not seem to have come up the hill—it just appeared there—and it shot sideways to our right about seven or eight feet. The light was yellowish-orange in color and it left a faint trail behind it as it moved. The trail streaked out in a jagged motion, moving slightly up and down, and then blinked out into darkness. It was almost like a firework display on a summer night, shooting outward and then burning itself out as quickly as it had appeared. The sighting lasted no longer than 10 seconds but it's not something that I will soon forget.

What is the Hornet Spook Light? No one knows but I think that it's still described best in the words of the Army Corps of Engineers as a "mysterious light of unknown origin." Regardless of what it may be, one thing is certain—it's something that has to be seen if possible. There are those who believe that the Hornet Light is slowly burning itself out, that sightings of the light are going to become more and more infrequent in the years to come. I hope that this is not the case, and not only for my own selfish desire to see the light again, but also for all of those who have not had the chance to experience this wonder first hand. The Hornet Spook Light is one of America's greatest unsolved mysteries and since no one has managed to figure out the answers to this enigma just yet, we need the spook light to be around for future generations to ponder for themselves.

MOTHMAN & THE MAD GASSER

Mysterious Figures of this World or Another?

The weird events connected to the strange creature that became known as the "Mothman" began on November 12, 1966 near Clendenin, West Virginia. Five men were in the local cemetery that day, preparing a grave for a burial, when something that looked like a "brown human being" lifted off from some nearby trees and flew over their heads. The men were baffled. It did not appear to be a bird, but more like a man with wings. A few days later, more sightings would take place, electrifying the entire region.

Late in the evening of November 15, two young married couples had a very strange encounter as they drove past an abandoned TNT plant near Point Pleasant, West Virginia. The couples spotted two large eyes that were attached to something that was "shaped like a man, but bigger, maybe six or seven feet tall. And it had big wings folded against its back." When the creature moved toward the plant door, the couples panicked and sped away. Moments later, they saw the same creature on a hillside near the road. It spread its wings and rose into the air, following along with their car, which by now was traveling at over 100 miles per hour. "That bird kept right up with us," said one of the group. They told Deputy Sheriff Millard Halstead that it followed them down Highway 62 and right to the Point Pleasant city limits. And they would not be the only ones to report the creature that night. Another group of four witnesses claimed to see the bird three different times.

Another sighting had more bizarre results. At about 10:30 on that same evening, Newell Partridge, a local building contractor who lived in Salem, about 90 miles from Point Pleasant, was watching television when the screen suddenly went dark. He stated that a weird pattern filled the screen and then he heard a loud, whining sound from outside that raised in pitch and then ceased. "It sounded like a generator winding up," he later stated. Partridge's dog, Bandit, began to howl out on the front porch and Newell went out to see what was going on.

When he walked outside, he saw Bandit facing the hay barn, about 150 yards from the house. Puzzled, Partridge turned a flashlight in that direction and spotted two red circles that looked like eyes or "bicycle reflectors." The moving red orbs were certainly not animal's eyes, he believed, and the sight of them frightened him. Bandit, an experienced hunting dog and protective of his territory, shot off across the yard in pursuit of the glowing eyes. Partridge called for him to stop, but the animal paid no attention. His owner turned and went back into the house for his gun but was too frightened to go back outside again. He slept that night with his gun propped up next to the bed. The next morning, he realized that Bandit had disappeared. The dog had still not shown up two days later when Partridge read in the newspaper about the sightings in Point Pleasant that same night.

One statement that he read in the newspaper chilled him to the bone. Roger Scarberry, one member of the group who spotted the strange bird at the TNT plant, said that as they entered the city limits of Point Pleasant, they saw the body of a large dog lying on the side of the road. A few minutes later, on the way back out of town, the dog was gone. They even stopped to look for the body, knowing they had passed it just a few minutes before. Newell Partridge immediately thought of Bandit, who was never seen again.

On November 16, a press conference was held in the county courthouse and the couples from the TNT plant sighting repeated their story. Deputy Halstead, who had known the couples all of their lives, took them very seriously. "They've never been in any trouble," he told investigators and had no reason to doubt their stories. Many of the reporters who were present for the weird recounting felt the same way. The news of the strange sightings spread around the world. The press dubbed the odd flying creature "Mothman," after a character from the popular Batman television series of the day.

The remote and abandoned TNT plant became the lair of the Mothman in the months ahead, and it could not have picked a better place to hide in. The area was made up of several hundred acres of woods and large concrete domes where high explosives were stored during World War II. A network of tunnels honeycombed the area and made it possible for the creature to apparently move about without being seen. In addition to the manmade labyrinth, the area was also comprised of the McClintic Wildlife Station, a heavily forested animal preserve filled with woods, artificial ponds and steep ridges and hills. Much of the property was almost inaccessible and, without a doubt, Mothman could have hid for weeks or months and remained totally unseen. The only people who ever wandered there were hunters and fishermen and local teenagers, who used the rutted dirt roads of the preserve as lovers' lanes.

Very few homes could be found in the region, but one dwelling belonged to the Ralph Thomas family. One November 16, they spotted a "funny red light" in the sky that moved and hovered above the TNT plant. "It wasn't an airplane," Mrs. Marcella Bennett, a friend of the Thomas family, said, "but we couldn't figure out what it was." Mrs. Bennett drove to the Thomas house a few minutes later and got out of the car with her baby. Suddenly, a figure stirred near the automobile. "It seemed as though it had been lying down," she later recalled. "It rose up slowly from the ground. A big gray thing. Bigger than a man with terrible glowing eyes."

Mrs. Bennett was so horrified that she dropped her little girl! She quickly recovered, picked up her child and ran to the house. The family locked everyone inside but hysteria gripped them as the creature shuffled onto the porch and peered into the windows. The police were summoned, but the Mothman had vanished by the time the authorities had arrived.

Mrs. Bennett would not recover from the incident for months and was in fact so distraught that she sought medical attention to deal with her anxieties. She was tormented by frightening dreams and later told investigators that she believed the creature had visited her own home too. She said that she could often hear a keening sound, like a woman screaming, near her isolated home on the edge of Point Pleasant.

Many would come to believe that the sightings of Mothman, as well as UFO sightings and encounters with "Men in Black" in the area, were all related. For over a year, strange happenings continued in the area. Researchers, investigators and monster hunters descended on the area but none so famous as author John Keel, who has written extensively about Mothman and other unexplained anomalies. He has written for many years about UFOs, but dismisses the standard extraterrestrial theories of the mainstream UFO movement. For this reason, he has been a controversial figure for decades. According to Keel, man has had a long history of interaction with the supernatural. He believes that the intervention of mysterious strangers in the lives of historic personages like Thomas Jefferson and Malcolm X provides evidence of the continuing presence of the "gods of old." The manifestation of these elder gods comes in the form of UFOs and aliens, monsters, demons, angels and even ghosts. He has remained a colorful character to many, and yet remains respected in the field for his research and fascinating writings.

Keel became the major chronicler of the Mothman case and wrote that at least 100 people personally witnessed the creature between November 1966 and November 1967. According to their reports, the creature stood between five and seven feet tall, was wider than a man and shuffled on human-like legs. Its eyes were set near the top of the shoulders and had bat-like wings that glided, rather than flapped, when it flew. Strangely though, it was able to ascend straight up "like a helicopter." Witnesses also described its murky skin as being either gray or brown and it emitted a humming sound when it flew. The Mothman was apparently incapable of speech and gave off a screeching sound. Mrs. Bennett stated that it sounded like a "woman screaming."

John Keel arrived in Point Pleasant in December 1966 and immediately began collecting reports of Mothman sightings and even UFO reports from before the creature was seen. He also compiled evidence that suggested a problem with televisions and phones that began in the fall of 1966. Lights had been seen in the skies, particularly around the TNT plant, and cars that passed along the nearby road sometimes stalled without explanation. He and his fellow researchers also uncovered a number of short-lived poltergeist cases in the Ohio Valley area. Locked doors opened and closed by themselves, strange thumps were heard inside and outside of homes and often, inexplicable voices were heard. The James Lilley family, who lived just south of the TNT plant, was so bothered by the bizarre events that they sold their home and moved to another neighborhood. Keel was convinced that the intense period of activity was all connected.

And stranger things still took place. A reporter named Mary Hyre, who was the Point Pleasant correspondent for the Athens, Ohio newspaper the *Messenger*, also wrote extensively about the local sightings. In fact, after one very active weekend, she was deluged with over 500 phone calls from people who saw strange lights in the skies. One night in January 1967, she was working late in her office in the county courthouse and a man walked in the door. He was very short and had strange eyes that were covered with thick glasses. He also had long, black hair that was cut squarely "like a bowl haircut." Hyre said that he spoke in a low, halting voice and he asked for directions to Welsh, West Virginia. She thought that he had some sort of speech impediment and for some reason, he terrified her. "He kept getting closer and closer to me," she said, " and his funny eyes were staring at me almost hypnotically."

Alarmed, she summoned the newspaper's circulation manager to her office and together, they spoke to the strange little man. She said that at one point in the discussion, she answered the telephone when it rang and she noticed the little man pick up a pen from her desk. He looked at it in amazement, "as if he had never seen a pen before." Then, he grabbed the pen, laughed loudly and ran out of the building. Several weeks later, Hyre was crossing the street near her office and saw the same man on the street. He appeared to be startled when he realized that she was watching him, and he turned away quickly and ran for a large black car that suddenly came around the corner. The little man climbed in and it quickly drove away.

By this time, most of the sightings had come to an end, and Mothman had faded away into the strange twilight zone from which he had come, but the story of Point Pleasant had not yet ended. At around 5:00 in the evening on December 15, 1967, the

700-foot bridge linking Point Pleasant to Ohio suddenly collapsed while filled with rush hour traffic. Dozens of vehicles plunged into the dark waters of the Ohio River killing 46 people. On that same tragic night, the James Lilley family (who still lived near the TNT plant at that time) counted more than twelve eerie lights that flashed above their home and vanished into the forest.

The collapse of the Silver Bridge made headlines all over the country, and the local citizens were stunned with horror and disbelief at the tragedy. As reporters and television crews from everywhere descended on the town, Hyre went days without sleep Then, during Christmas week, a short, dark-skinned man entered her office. He was dressed in a black suit with a black tie, and looked vaguely Asian. He had high cheekbones, narrow eyes and an unidentified accent. The man was not interested in the bridge disaster, she said, but wanted to know about local UFO sightings. Hyre was too busy to talk so she handed him a file of related press clipping instead, but he was uninterested. He insisted on speaking with her until, she finally dismissed him from her office.

That same night, an identically described man visited the homes of several witnesses in the area who had reported seeing the lights in the sky. He made all of them very uneasy, and while he claimed to be a reporter from Cambridge, Ohio, he inadvertently admitted that he did not know where Columbus, Ohio was even though the two towns are just a few miles apart.

So was this the Mothman? And what was behind the strange events in Point Pleasant?

Whatever the creature may have been, it seems clear that the Mothman was no hoax. There were simply too many credible witnesses who saw "something." At the time, it was suggested that the creature might have been a sandhill crane, although not native to the area, could have migrated south from Canada. That was one explanation, anyway, but it was rejected by Mothman witnesses, who stated that what they saw looked nothing like a crane.

But there could have been a logical explanation for some of the sightings. Even John Keel (who believed the creature was genuine) suspected that a few of the cases involved people who were spooked by recent reports and saw owls flying along deserted roads at night. Even so, the Mothman remains hard to easily dismiss. The case is filled with an impressive number of multiple-witness sightings by individuals that were deemed reliable, even by law enforcement officials.

But if the Mothman was real—and was some unidentified creature that cannot be explained—what was behind the UFO sightings, the poltergeist reports, the strange lights, the sounds, the men in black and, most horrifying, the collapse of the Silver Bridge? John Keel believes that Point Pleasant was a "window" area, a place that was marked by long periods of strange sightings, monster reports and the coming and going of unusual persons. He thinks that it may be wrong to blame the collapse of the bridge on the local UFO sightings, but the intense activity in the area at the time does suggest some sort of connection.

Others have pointed to another supernatural link to the strange happenings, blaming the events on the legendary Cornstalk Curse that was placed on Point Pleasant in the 1770s. Could such a curse explain the bizarre happenings of the 1960s?

The Cornstalk Curse

Almost two centuries before the shadow of the Mothman reared its head in Point Pleasant, West Virginia, the land around the Ohio River ran red with blood. As the inhabitants of the American colonies began to push their way to the west, and later fought for their independence from Britain, they entered into deadly combat with the Native American inhabitants of the land. Perhaps their greatest foe in these early Indian wars was Chief Cornstalk, who later became a friend to the Americans. But treachery, deception and murder would bring an end to the chief's life and a curse that he placed on Point Pleasant would linger for 200 years, bringing tragedy, death and disaster.

There is no denying that the southeastern corner of Ohio and the surrounding area of West Virginia is considered by many to be one of the most haunted areas of the country. West Virginia has long been thought of as one of the strangest parts of the country in regards to ghosts, legends and strange happenings. The Native Americans regarded this part of the country, which was originally a part of the state of Virginia, as a haunted spot, plagued with ghost lights, phantoms and strange creatures. The town of Parkersburg, just north on the river from Point Pleasant, has more than its share of ghosts, and nearby is Athens County, Ohio, the most haunted city in the state.

But how did this region gain such a reputation? Why are many people not surprised to find stories of the Mothman, phantom inhabitants and mysterious creatures roaming this part of the country? There have been a number of theories to explain the large number of haunted happenings here, including that this area may be some sort of windo" between dimensions. This would, according to the theories, allow paranormal phenomenon to come and go and vanish at will, just as the Mothman did after thirteen months of appearing around Point Pleasant.

Those researchers with a historical bent have offered their own solutions. They have traced the supernatural roots of the region back to a bloody event from the days of the American Revolution, and a great curse.

As the American frontiersmen began to move west in the 1770s, seven nations of Indians (the Shawnee, Delaware, Wyandot, Mingo, Miami, Ottawa and Illinois) formed a powerful confederacy to keep the white men from infringing on their territory. The Shawnee were the most powerful of the tribes and were led by a feared and respected chieftain called *Keigh-tugh-gua*, which translates to mean Cornstalk. In 1774, when the white settlers were moving down into the Kanawha and Ohio River valleys, the Indian Confederacy prepared to protect their lands by any means necessary. The nations began to mass in a rough line across the point from the Ohio River to the Kanawha River, numbering about 1,200 warriors. They began to make preparations to attack the white settlers near an area called Point Pleasant on the Virginia side of the Ohio River. As word reached the colonial military leaders of the impending attack, troops were sent in and faced off against the Indians. While the numbers of fighters were fairly even on both sides, the Native Americans were no match for the muskets of the white soldiers. The battle ended with about 140 colonials killed and more than twice that number of Indians. The tribes retreated westward into the wilds of what is now Ohio and in order to keep them from returning, a fort was constructed at the junction of the Kanawha and Ohio Rivers.

As time passed, the Shawnee leader, Cornstalk, made peace with the white men. He would carry word to his new friends when the British began coaxing the Indians into attacking the rebellious colonies in 1777. Soon, the tribes again began massing along the Ohio River, intent on attacking the fort. Cornstalk and Red Hawk, a Delaware chief, had no taste for war with the Americans and they went to the fort on November 7 to try and negotiate a peace before fighting began. Cornstalk told Captain Arbuckle, who commanded the garrison, that he was opposed to war with the colonists, but his tribe was the only one holding back from fighting on the side of the British. He was afraid that the Indian Confederacy would force him to join the war.

When he admitted to Arbuckle that he would allow his men to fight if the other tribes did, Cornstalk, Red Hawk and another Indian were taken as hostages. The Americans believed that they could use him to keep the other tribes from attacking. They forced the Native Americans into a standoff, for none of them wanted to risk the life of their leader. Cornstalk's name not only stuck fear into hearts of the white settlers up and down the frontier, but also garnered respect from the other Indian tribes. He was a gifted leader with great oratory skills, fighting ability and military genius. In fact, it was said that when the Americans adopted Cornstalk's fighting tactics, they were able to defeat the British in a number of battles where they had been outnumbered and outgunned.

Although taken as hostage, Cornstalk and the other Indians were treated well and were given comfortable quarters, leading many to wonder if the chief's hostage status may have been voluntary in the beginning. Cornstalk even assisted his captors in plotting maps of the Ohio River Valley during his imprisonment. On November 9, Cornstalk's son, Ellinipisco, came to the fort to see his father and was also detained.

The following day, gunfire was heard from outside of the walls of the fort, coming from the direction of the Kanawha River. When men went out to investigate, they discovered that Indians had ambushed two soldiers who had left the stockade to hunt deer. One of them had escaped but the other man had been killed. When his bloody corpse was returned to the fort, the soldiers in the garrison were enraged. Acting against orders, they broke into the quarters were Cornstalk and the other Indians were being held. Even though the men had nothing to do with the crime, they decided to execute the prisoners as revenge. As the soldiers burst through the doorway, Cornstalk rose to meet them. It was said that he stood facing the soldiers with such bravery that they paused momentarily in their attack. It wasn't enough though and the soldiers opened fire with their muskets. Red Hawk tried to escape up the chimney but was pulled back down and slaughtered. Ellinipisco was shot where he had been sitting, and the other unknown Indian was strangled to death. As for Cornstalk, he was shot eight times before he fell to the floor.

And as he lay there dying in the smoke-filled room, he was said to have pronounced his now legendary curse. The stories say that he looked upon his assassins and spoke to them: "I was the border man's friend. Many times I have saved him and his people from harm. I never warred with you, but only to protect our wigwams and lands. I refused to join your paleface enemies with the red coats. I came to the fort as your friend and you murdered me. You have murdered by my side, my young son. For this, may the curse of the Great Spirit rest upon this land. May it be blighted by nature. May it even be blighted in its hopes. May the strength of its peoples be paralyzed by the stain of our blood."

Cornstalk spoke these words, says the legend, and then he died. The bodies of the other Indians were then taken and dumped into the Kanawha River, but Cornstalk's corpse was buried near the fort on Point Pleasant, overlooking the junction of the Kanawha and Ohio Rivers. Here he remained many years, but he would not rest in peace.

In 1794, the town of Point Pleasant was established near the site of the old fort. The Indian's grave lay undisturbed for several years, but in 1840 his bones were removed to the grounds of the Mason County Court House where, in 1899, a monument was erected in Cornstalk's memory. In the late 1950s, a new court house was built in Point Pleasant and the chief's remains (which now consisted of three teeth and about fifteen pieces of bone) were placed in an aluminum box and reinterred in a corner of the town's Tu Endie-Wei Park, next to the grave of a Virginia frontiersman that Cornstalk once fought and later befriended. A twelve-foot monument was erected in his honor.

And this is not the only monument dedicated to the period in Point Pleasant. Another stands 86-feet tall and was dedicated in August 1909, one month behind schedule. Originally, the dedication ceremony had been set for July 22 but on the night before the event, the clear overhead sky erupted with lightning and struck the upper part of a crane that was supposed to put the monument into place. The machine was badly damaged and it took nearly a month to repair it. The monument was finally dedicated and stood for years, until July 4, 1921. On that day, another bolt of lightning struck the monument, damaging the capstone and some granite blocks. They were replaced and the monument still stands today. But what is this bedeviled obelisk that seems to attract inexplicable lightning on otherwise clear evenings? It is a monument to the men who died in the 1774 Battle of Point Pleasant, when Cornstalk and his allies were defeated.

Could the freak lightning strikes have been acts of vengeance tied to Cornstalk's fabled curse? Many believed so and, for years residents of the triangular area made up of western West Virginia, southwest Pennsylvania and southeastern Ohio spoke of strange happenings, river tragedies and fires as part of the curse. Of course, many laughed and said that the curse was nothing more than overactive imaginations, ignoring the death toll and eerie coincidences that seemed to plague the region for 200 years after the death of Chief Cornstalk. Many tragedies and disasters were-blamed on the curse including the following.

1907: The worst coal mine disaster in American history took place in Monongah, West Virginia on December 6, when 310 miners were killed.

1944: In June of this year, 150 people were killed when a tornado ripped through the tri-state triangular area.

1967: The devastating Silver Bridge disaster sent 46 people hurtling to their death in the Ohio River on December 15.

1968: A Piedmont Airlines plane crashed in August near the Kanawha Airport, killing 35 people on board.

1970: On November 14, a Southern Airways DC-10 crashed into a mountain near Huntington, West Virginia, killing 75 people on board.

1972: A flash flood from Buffalo Creek, a tributary of the Kanawha River, roared through an 18-mile canyon and wiped out towns in its path and killed 120 people who were unlucky enough to be in the way.

1976: In March of that year, the town of Point Pleasant was rocked in the middle of the night be an explosion at the Mason County Jail. Housed in the jail was a woman named Harriet Sisk, who had been arrested for the murder of her infant daughter. On March 2, her husband came to the jail with a suitcase full of explosives to kill himself and his wife and to destroy the building. Both of the Sisk's were killed, along with three law enforcement officers.

1978: In January, a freight train derailed at Point Pleasant and dumped thousands of gallons of toxic chemicals. The chemicals contaminated the town's water supply and the wells had to be abandoned.

1978: In April of that same year, the town of St. Mary's (north of Point Pleasant) was struck with tragedy when 51 men who were working on the Willow Island power plant were killed when their construction scaffolding collapsed.

And there have been many other strange occurrences, fires and floods. Most would say however that floods are a natural part of living on the river, although Point Pleasant was almost obliterated in 1913 and 1937. It might be hard to tie such natural occurrences into a curse, but what about the barge explosion that killed six men from town just before Christmas 1953? Or the fire that destroyed an entire downtown city block in the late 1880s? Some have even gone as far as to blame the curse for the death of Point Pleasant's local economy, an event linked to the passing of river travel and commerce. Largely, the curse has been forgotten over time and today, Point Pleasant is better known for its connection to otherworldly visitors like the Mothman than for Indian curses and bloody frontier battles.

But how real was the curse? Was it simply a string of bloody and tragic coincidences, culled from two centuries of sadness in the region? Could it be used to explain why the area seems to attract strange happenings and eerie tales? Or is the area somehow blighted, separate from any curse, and attractive to the strangeness that seems to lurk in the shadowy corners of America? And if such things can happen in West Virginia, then why not elsewhere in the country? Could the idea that this region was some sort of "window area" explain other phantom attackers, mysterious creatures, mad gassers and more that have been reported all over America? Perhaps so, for the Mothman was certainly not the first mystery figure to wreak havoc in the annals of the paranormal in America!

The Botetourt County Gasser

In 1933, Botetourt County, Virginia was a quiet area of the state and had never really experienced much out of the ordinary. That all began to change on December 22 when the home of Mrs. and Mrs. Cal Huffman, near Haymakertown, was attacked by a mysterious figure that was unlike anything seen, or even heard of, in the region before.

At around 10:00 that evening, Mrs. Huffman stated that she grew nauseated after smelling a strange gas that had been apparently sprayed into her house. She decided to go to bed, but her husband remained awake to see if the lurker who had sprayed the gas might return. A half-hour later, another wave of gas filled the room and Huffman immediately went to the home of his landlord, K.W. Henderson. The Huffman house was located on the Henderson property and was only a short distance away. Here, Huffman telephoned the police. An Officer Lemon was dispatched to the scene and stayed until midnight. Immediately after he left, another gas attack was launched on the property, filling both floors of the house. All eight members of the Huffman family, along with Ashby Henderson, were affected by the gas. Ashby and Cal Huffman had been keeping watch for the return of the prowler and thought that they saw a man running away after the attack.

According to reports, the gas caused the victims to become very nauseated, gave them a headache and caused the mouth and throat muscles to restrict. Alice, the Huffman's 19-year-old daughter, was most affected by the gas and had to be revived with artificial respiration. She was said to have experienced convulsions for some time afterward. Her physician, Dr. S.F. Driver, later reported that while part of her condition was caused by extreme nervousness over the attack, he had no doubt that the gas attack was responsible for the fact that her condition continued.

However, no one could determine what kind of gas was used (Dr. W.N. Breckinridge, who assisted with the police investigation, ruled out ether, chloroform and tear gas) or who could have sprayed it into the house. The only clue that Officer Lemon found at the scene was the print of a woman's shoe beneath the window the attacker was thought to have sprayed his gas through.

The next attack took place in the Botetourt County town of Cloverdale. Clarence Hall, his wife and two children came home from a church service at around 9:00 on Christmas Eve. Five minutes after they entered the house, they smelled a strange odor. Hall went into one of the back rooms of the house to investigate and came back moments later, staggering and swaying. His wife, who also felt nauseated and weak, had to drag him outside. The effects of the gas did not linger with Mr. Hall but Mrs. Hall experienced eye irritation for the next two days. Dr. Breckinridge again helped the police and he noted that the gas "tasted sweet" and that he detected a trace of formaldehyde in it. He still had no idea what the gas was though and investigators again found only one clue at the scene. Apparently, a nail had been pulled from one of the windows. Was this to make it possible to spray the gas inside?

Another attack occurred on December 27 when A.L. Kelly, a welder and his mother were sprayed in their home in Troutville. Oddly, the police learned that a man and a woman in a 1933 Chevrolet had been seen driving back and forth in front of Kelly's house around the time of the attack. A neighbor managed to get a partial plate number on the car, but the police were unable to locate it.

No attacks took place over the next two weeks, but on January 10 the Gasser struck again at the home of Homer Hylton, near Haymakertown. Hylton and his wife were upstairs asleep and their daughter, Mrs. Moore, whose husband was out of town on business, was sleeping downstairs. Around 10:00, she got up to attend to her baby and later recalled that she heard mumbling voices outside and someone fiddling with the window. Moments later, she said the room filled with gas, and as she grabbed her child, she experienced a "marked feeling of numbness." The window where the noises came from had been slightly broken for some time and this may have allowed the Gasser access to the house. Author Michael T. Shoemaker, in an excellent article on the subject for *Fate* magazine in 1985, suggests that we could theorize that Mrs. Moore was simply spooked by the wind blowing through the crack in the glass, if not for the voices that she heard. Again, some might say this was only her imagination, but for the fact that a neighbor, G.E. Poage, also heard voices around the same time.

Also on January 10, a Troutville man named G.D. Kinzie was attacked, but the case was not reported until later. Apparently, Dr. Driver investigated this case and stated that the gas used in the attack was chlorine. Chlorine was then mentioned in several subsequent accounts until a Roanoke chemistry professor later ruled it out as a possible cause.

After a few quiet nights, the Gasser returned on January 16, this time attacking the home of F.B. Duval near Bonsack. Duval left the house to summon the police and as he reached a nearby intersection, saw a man run up to a parked car and speed away. He and Officer Lemon spent several hours driving around searching for the car, but they found nothing. The next day, Lemon again found the prints of a woman's shoes, this time where the car had been parked.

On January 19, the Gasser struck again. This time, gas was sprayed into the window of a Mrs. Campbell, a former judge's wife, near Cloverdale. She was sitting near the window in question and moments after seeing the shade move, became sick.

A few nights later, the gas attacks reached their peak with five attacks taking place over a period of three nights. The first attack took place on January 21 when Howard Crawford and his wife returned to their home between Cloverdale and Troutville. Mr. Crawford went into the house first to light a lamp but quickly came stumbling back out. He was overwhelmed by the gas, which Dr. Driver again said was chlorine. Police officers were again able to find only a single clue at the house—the crank of an old automobile. The metal crank seemed to have absolutely nothing to do with the attack, but it was simply too strange of an item to be left behind. On the other hand, it was also too common of an item in those days to be traced.

On January 22, three separate attacks occurred in Carvin's Cove. In just one hour's time, the Gasser covered a distance of about two miles, attacking in order, the homes of Ed Reedy, George C. Riley and Raymond Etter. In each of the houses, the victims all claimed to have numbness and nausea. Riley called his brother, a Roanoke police officer, and a blockade of the nearby roads was quickly put into place. Although the Gasser managed to elude the authorities, one of Mr. Etter's sons claimed to see a figure disappearing from the direction of the house. He gave chase and even fired a few shots at the man from a distance of 30 yards, but the unknown figure got away.

On January 23, Mrs. R.H. Hartsell and her family spent the night with some neighbors and when they returned to their Pleasantdale Church home at 4:30 a.m., they discovered that the house had been filled with gas. For some bizarre reason, someone had also piled wood and brush up against their front door. The only possible motive that I can see for this would have been to keep the family from easily escaping once the house was filled with gas. This means that the elusive Gasser must have believed the family was home at the time of the attack.

This new series of gassings had the entire community in an uproar. Families who lived in more isolated areas began spending the night with friends and neighbors, hoping to find security in numbers. Local men began patrolling the roadways at night, armed with shotguns and rifles. The local newspaper, the *Roanoke Times*, was sure the gassers would be caught and pleaded with the farmers not to shoot anyone.

The authorities were now growing more concerned. Prior to this, they believed the gassings had been nothing more than pranks played by some mischievous boys. Now the county sheriff's office was forced to admit that if this had been the case, the boys would have been caught long before. They began to investigate the idea that a mentally deranged person might be the culprit, perhaps even an unhinged gas victim from World War I.

On January 25, the Gasser may have attempted to strike again, but this time was foiled. Around 9:00 at night, a dog at the home of Chester Snyder began barking. Alerted, Snyder jumped out of bed and grabbed his shotgun. Darting outside, he ran across the yard and fired a shot at a man that he saw creeping along a ditch about 20 feet from the house. But the shot went wide, and Snyder only had one shell in his gun. He ran back inside for more ammunition but by the time he returned, the man was gone.

He called the police and a deputy sheriff named Zimmerman investigated the scene. He managed to find footprints that led from the road to the ditch and signs that the prowler had hidden behind a tree on the property for some time before the dog sounded the alarm. More tracks led from the tree to the house and then stopped, marking the point where the man had retreated. Visitors who had left the Snyder home shortly before the incident recalled seeing a man about a half-mile away on the road. There was, of course, no real evidence to say that the prowler was actually the Gasser, but based on recent events any sort of incident like this was immediately suspect.

On January 28, the Gasser managed to pull off another attack on the home of Ed Stanley of Cloverdale. Frank Guy, a hired hand on the farm, ran outside immediately after the gas filled the house and stated that he saw four men running away in the direction of the Blue Ridge Mountains. He ran back inside to get his gun and when he returned to the yard, he couldn't see the fleeing figures, but could hear them in the woods. He fired several shots in the direction of the voices but felt that it was unlikely that he hit anything. The Gasser returned two nights later and again attacked the Stanley House. This time, however, Stanley heard a sound outside of the window before the attack took place. What happened after that remains a mystery, as no further details were reported in the contemporary accounts.

The last of the likely authentic gas attacks took place in Nace, two miles from Troutville, on February 3. The house that was attacked belonged to A.P. Scaggs, and he and his wife, along with five other adults, were all affected by the gas. The group was so badly hurt by the gas that Sheriff Williamson would tell the skeptics who later emerged over the gassing cases that "No amount of imagination in the world would make people as ill as the Skagges are." Once again, the gas has some pretty strange effects including one child who screamed hysterically that he was trapped in the house and a dog who rolled over and over in the snow as though a skunk had sprayed him. The Skaggs incident was as dramatic as the first attack on the Huffman family leading author Michael T. Shoemaker to note that perhaps the Gasser wanted to mark his entrance and exit with striking attacks.

It was at this point that the story began to deteriorate. During the following week, there were twenty attacks reported in nearby Roanoke County and a number of other reports in Lexington, about 30 miles away. And while a few of the later attacks may have been genuine, they lacked the detail of the original incidents and most were likely hysterical reactions to ordinary odors or the result of hoaxes perpetrated by pranksters. In one of these hoaxes, a teenager threw a bottle of insecticide into a woman's window; a similar incident on February 9 gave the police and the newspapers the opportunity to declare that the Gasser mystery was over.

The last insecticide case did have some interesting aspects to it . On February 9, when J.G. Shafer of Lithia believed his house was gassed, he went outside and scooped up some snow that contained a sweet-smelling substance. It was analyzed and determined to contain sulfur, arsenic and mineral oil, which was commonly used in insecticide sprays. This caused the police to dismiss the attack as a hoax, but was it really? Strangely, investigators found footprints leading from the front porch of the house to the barn, but no trail that led away from this building. It was as if whoever had been on the porch had walked into the barn and simply vanished. Also, as with some of the other earlier cases, a woman's tracks led from the yard to the road.

The later cases that came along led the general public to swallow the unconvincing theory that faulty chimney flues and wild imaginations had caused the entire affair. However, the gas victims and investigating police officers, including Lemon, never accepted this explanation. The ongoing cases of panic did not help to convince the nonbelievers to reconsider. Looking back now, the later cases helped to show that the original occurences were not hysteria. The later cases did not follow the pattern of the original attacks, occurred outside the already established area, took place at no particular times, and did not cause any lasting physical effects. It should also be noted that the original attacks, while taking place in Botetourt County, were spread out enough throughout the area that neighbors could not infect one another with hysteria.

So if mass hysteria was not the answer in the Mad Gasser of Botetourt County case, then could a natural explanation have been to blame? Explanations like pollution and faulty chimney flues don't hold water when the reader examines the factors in the case, including the selection of victims, times of the evening, intense police investigations and of course, the fleeing figure (or figures) that were seen running away from the residences in question. The hoaxer, or the lone lunatic, theories are not much better either. Even though a mysterious figure was often seen, there were never any useful clues left behind and the identity of the Gasser was never discovered.

It was almost as if the strange figure left Virginia and vanished without a trace, never to return again. And while perhaps the Gasser did not return to Botetourt County, could he have possibly surfaced in Illinois 11 years later?

The Mad Gasser of Mattoon

Mattoon, which is located in the southeastern part of Central Illinois, is a fairly typical Midwestern town. The strange events that took place here in 1944 were anything but typical. These events would place the small city under the scrutiny of the entire nation and would one day become a textbook case of what authorities and psychologists called mass hysteria. But was it really? Could the legendary "Mad Gasser of Mattoon" be simply starting over again in a new location?

The whirlwind of events would begin in the early morning hours of August 31. A Mattoon man was startled out of a deep sleep and complained to his wife that he felt sick. He questioned her about leaving the gas on in the kitchen because his symptoms seemed very similar to gas exposure. The woman tried to get out of bed and check the pilot light on the stove, but found to her surprise that she could not move. Just minutes later, according to published reports, a woman in a neighboring home also tried to get out of bed and discovered that she too was paralyzed.

The next evening, a woman named Mrs. Bert Kearney was awakened by a peculiar smell in her bedroom. The odor was sweet and overpowering and as it grew stronger, she felt paralysis creeping into her legs and lower body. She began screaming, and, drawing the attention of her neighbors, was able to alert the police. The following day, she would complain of having burned lips and a parched mouth and throat from exposure to the gas. A hasty search of the yard by police officers and her shaken neighbors revealed nothing. But that would not be the last strange event to occur at this particular house.

Later that night, when Mr. Kearney returned home from work, it was just after midnight. He spotted a man lurking near the house who would later fit the descriptions of the Mad Gasser. The stranger, according to Kearney, was tall and dressed in dark clothing and a tight-fitting black cap. He was standing near a window when Kearney spotted him and the odd man ran away. Kearney pursued but was unable to catch up with him.

The events in Mattoon soon became public knowledge and panic gripped the town. The story was badly handled by the authorities and the local newspaper reported the Kearney case, and subsequent others, in a wildly sensational manner. The newspaper is believed by many to be the culprit behind the "Gasser hysteria." Years later, the newspaper would be blamed for everything that happened in the case and for manufacturing the scare. The frightened citizens, according to these skeptics, took leave of their senses and began to imagine that a mad gasser was wreaking havoc in the town. This particular approach has been considered by many to be the simple explanation for the affair, but it certainly does not eliminate all of the evidence for something very bizarre to have happened in Mattoon.

By the morning, of September 5, the Mattoon police department had received reports of four more gas attacks. All of the victims complained of a sickeningly sweet odor that caused them to become sick and slightly paralyzed for up to thirty minutes at a time. That night would be the occasion when the first real clues in the Mad Gasser case would be discovered. They were found at the home of Carl and Beulah Cordes, but what these clues meant has yet to be discovered. The Cordes were returning home late that evening when they found a white cloth lying on their porch. Mrs. Cordes picked it up and noticed a strange smell coming from it. She held it up close to her nose and was overwhelmed with nausea. In minutes, she seemed to have a severe allergic reaction to it as her lips and face swelled and her mouth started to bleed. The symptoms would disappear in about two hours. The police investigated and took the cloth into evidence. They also found a skeleton key and an empty tube of lipstick on the porch. They decided the prowler was probably trying to break into the house but had failed.

The police believed that the cloth was connected to the other gas attacks. It should be noted, however, that the odor on the cloth caused different symptoms in Mrs. Cordes than in the other victims. She did feel sick to her stomach but there were no sensations of paralysis. The case itself is also unique because if this was the Gasser, it is the only time when he actually tried to gain access to the home of his victims. Could his intentions in this case have been different?

The Gasser attacked again that same night, but he was back to his old tricks and sprayed his gas into an open window. There would only be one other report that even hinted that the attacker tried to break into the house. The woman in this instance claimed that a person in dark clothing tried to force open her front door. Was it really the Mad Gasser?

The attacks continued, and Mattoon residents began reporting fleeting glimpses of the Gasser, always describing him as a tall, thin man in dark clothes and wearing a tight black cap. More attacks were reported and the harried police force tried to respond to the mysterious crimes that left no clues behind. Eventually, the authorities even summoned two FBI agents from Springfield to look into the case, but their presence did nothing to discourage the strange reports. Panic was widespread and rumors began to circulate that the attacker was an escapee from an insane asylum or was an odd inventor who was testing a new apparatus. Interestingly, I was sent a letter in 2002 from a woman whose father grew up in Mattoon during the Mad Gasser period. He told her that there had been two sisters living in town at the time who had a brother who was allegedly insane. A number of people in town believed that he was the Gasser, so his sisters locked him in the basement until they could find a mental institution to put him in. After they locked him away, her father told her, the gas attacks stopped.

Armed citizens took to the streets, organizing watches and patrols to thwart any further attacks, but several took place anyway. The gas attacks were becoming more frequent and the attacker was leaving behind evidence like footprints and sliced window screens. This evidence would become particularly interesting after the revelations of the authorities in the days to come.

A group of citizens did manage to arrest one suspect but after he passed a polygraph test, he was released. Local businessmen announced that they would be holding a mass protest rally on Saturday, September 10 to put more pressure on the already pressured Mattoon police force. Now, the Gasser was becoming more than a threat to public safety, he was becoming a political liability and a blot on the public image of the city.

The Gasser, apparently not impressed with armed vigilantes and newspaper diatribes, resumed his attacks. The first residence to be attacked was that of Mrs. Violet Driskell and her daughter, Ramona. They awoke late in the evening to hear someone removing the storm sash on their bedroom window. They hurried out of bed and tried to run outside for help, but the fumes overcame Ramona and she threw up. Her mother stated that she saw a man running away from the house.

A short time later that night, the Gasser sprayed gas into the partially opened window of a room where Mrs. Russell Bailey, Katherine Tuzzo, Mrs. Genevieve Haskell and her young son were sleeping. At another home, Miss Frances Smith, the principal of the Columbian Grade School, and her sister Maxine were also overwhelmed with gas and fell ill. They began choking as they were awakened and felt partial paralysis in their legs and arms. They also said that as the sweet odor began to fill the room (as a thin, blue vapor), they heard a buzzing noise from outside and believed that it was the Gasser's "spraying apparatus" in operation.

By September 10, Mad Gasser paranoia had peaked. FBI agents were trying to track down the type of gas being used in the attacks, and the police force was trying to not only find the Gasser, but also to keep the armed citizens off the streets. None of the law enforcement officials were having much luck with any of these tasks. By Saturday night, several dozen well-armed farmers from the surrounding area had joined the patrols in Mattoon. In spite of this, six attacks took place anyway, including the three just mentioned. Another couple, Mr. and Mrs. Stewart B. Scott, returned to their farm on the edge of Mattoon late in the evening to find the house filled with sweet smelling gas.

This period seemed to mark a turning point in the case. Now it was the idea of the gas attacks moving from the city of Mattoon to the surrounding country that pushed the scales of official acceptance in the wrong direction. In the words of Thomas V. Wright, the City Commissioner of Public Health: "There is no doubt that a gas maniac exists and has made a number of attacks. But many of the reported attacks are nothing more than hysteria. Fear of the gas man is entirely out of proportion to the menace of the relatively harmless gas he is spraying. The whole town is sick with hysteria and last night it spread out into the country."

At this point, newspaper accounts of the affair began to take on a more skeptical tone and despite claims by victims and material evidence left behind, the police began to dismiss new reports of attacks and suggested that local residents were merely imagining things. The episode had gone so far that it was really the only thing left for them to do. The Gasser, if he existed at all, could not be caught, identified, or tracked down. They started to believe that if they ignored the problem, it would just go away. After all, if the man were real, how could he have possibly escaped detection for so long? Psychology experts opined that the women of Mattoon had dreamed up the Gasser as a desperate cry for attention, as many of their husbands were overseas fighting in the war. This theory ignored the fact that many victims and witnesses were men and that this so-called fantasy was leaving behind evidence of his existence.

On the night of September 11, the police received a number of phone calls but after half-hearted attempts to investigate, dismissed all of them as false alarms. Just days before, a crime specialist with the State Department of Public Safety named Richard T. Piper told reporters that "This is one of the strangest cases I have ever encountered in my years of police work" but now new calls were only worthy of perfunctory examination. This is in spite of the fact that a doctor who appeared on the scene shortly after one of the evening's attacks stated that there had been a "peculiar odor" in the room. The officials were just no longer interested.

The Mattoon police chief issued what he felt was the final statement on the gas attacks on September 12. He stated that large quantities of carbon tetrachloride gas were used at the local Atlas Diesel Engine Co. and that this gas must be causing the reported cases. It could be carried throughout the town by wind and could have left the stains that were found on the rag at one of the homes. As for the Mad Gasser himself, well, he was simply a figment of their imaginations. The whole case, he said, "was a mistake from beginning to end."

Not surprisingly, a spokesman for the plant was quick to deny the allegations that his company had caused the concern in town, maintaining that the only use for that gas in the plant was in their fire extinguishers and any similar gases used there caused no ill effects in the air. Besides that, why hadn't this gas ever caused problems in the city before? And how exactly was this gas cutting the window screens on Mattoon homes before causing nausea and paralysis?

The official explanation also failed to cover just how so many identical descriptions of the Gasser had been reported to the police. It also neglected to explain how different witnesses managed to report seeing a man of the Gasser's description fleeing the scene of an attack, even when the witness were unaware that an attack had taken place.

The last Gasser Attack took place on September 13 and while it was the last appearance of the attacker in Mattoon, it was also possibly the strangest. It occurred at the home of Mrs. Bertha Bench and her son, Orville. They described the attacker as being a woman dressed in man's clothing who sprayed gas into a bedroom window. The next morning, footprints that appeared to have been made by a woman's high-heeled shoes were found in the dirt below the window. And while this report does not match any of the earlier attacks in Mattoon, readers will undoubtedly recognize the claims of a woman's shoe prints from several attacks in Botetourt

County in 1933. After this night, the Mad Gasser of Mattoon was never seen or heard from again.

The real stories of what happened in Mattoon and Botetourt County are still unknown and it is unlikely that we will ever know what was really behind these strange events. It is certain that something did take place in both locations, however strange, and theories abound as to what it may have been. Was the Mad Gasser real? And if he was, who was he? Could he have been the same figure in both cases? It's hard to ignore the similarities between the two cases, from his method of operation to the unusual form of attacks. In Botetourt, the Gasser was not always reported as being alone as he was in Mattoon, but then again, what about the identical reports of prints left by a woman's shoe?

Stories have suggested that Mattoon's Gasser was anything from a mad scientist to an ape-man (although who knows where that came from?) and researchers today have their own theories, some of which are just as wild. Could he have been some sort of extraterrestrial visitor using some sort of paralyzing agent to further a hidden agenda? Or could the Gasser have been an agent of our own government, who came to an obscure Midwestern town to test some military gas that could be used in the war effort? It might be telling that once national attention came to Mattoon, the authorities began a policy of complete denial and the attacks suddenly ceased.

Whoever, or whatever, he was, the Mad Gasser has vanished into time and, real or imagined, is only a memory in the world of the unknown. Perhaps he was never here at all—perhaps he was, as Donald M. Johnson wrote in the 1954 issue of the *Journal of Abnormal and Social Psychology*, simply a "shadowy manifestation of some unimaginable unknown."

But was he really? How do we explain the sightings of the Mad Gasser that were made by people who did not even know the creature was alleged to exist? Or identical sightings from independent witnesses who could not have possibly known that others had just spotted the same figure. Was the Gasser, as some have suggested, a visitor from a dimension outside of our own, thus explaining his ability to appear or disappear at will? Was he, like the Mothman and the Botetourt Gasser, a creature so outside the realm of our imaginations that we will never be able to comprehend his motives or understand the reason why he came to Mattoon?

Which brings us back to a question that I posed earlier: could the appearances of a creature like the Mad Gasser or the Mothman be connected to the idea of a window area that allows people and things to pass between this world and another? Could such a window explain not only the appearance of mystery figures that seem to come from nowhere but the disappearances of people from this world as well? Perhaps it can, but to consider this, we have to consider an even more chilling question—where will the next window area be?

What Lies Beneath?

The Secrets Under the Earth

For centuries, there have been stories and legends surrounding the mysteries of what lies beneath the earth. Of course, not all of these stories involve lost cities or mysterious civilizations. A few of these strange tales involve sites that could be called a curiosity, and they range from being simply odd to downright spooky.

For example, in places like Tacoma, Washington, southern Illinois, and Hannibal, Missouri, there have been stories told of what might best be called sinkholes. They are depressions in the ground, or pits, that simply cannot be filled. There are stories of such holes that people use to throw in extra dirt from gardens and yards and have been doing so for generations. The situation seems harmless, but only until you begin to question the reality of such sinkholes. Where is the dirt actually going? Why do the pits only sink so far, even though it is filled over and over again? Why doesn't the sinkhole continue sinking until there is a deep shaft into the earth?

In some cases, these sinkholes become the source of a local legend or a curse. In many cases, the story goes that a man was hanged on the spot and his executioners were forced to dig a hole when the weight of his body stretched the limb of the hanging tree too close to the earth. The story normally continues with the addition that the hole has not filled since, no matter how much dirt has been tossed into it. Pretty strange stuff—but not as strange as others.

In Tacoma, Washington, a man named Johnson discovered a hole in his yard that was about four feet in diameter, with the top three feet bricked in. He didn't notice the hole until he moved into the house and his dog found the opening. He apparently dropped a rope into the hole about fifty feet but failed to reach the bottom. Assuming that it was an abandoned well, he loaded it with old tires and the hole actually seemed to be getting close to being filled. Johnson asked around the neighborhood about the hole and was told that the previous owners of the house had dumped a load of marble into it and a short time later "an explosion blew everything out." The former residents moved away soon after. By the summer of 1974, the tire level in the hole began dropping, as if the hole was digesting them, and soon the top of the pile disappeared from sight. Neither Johnson, nor anyone else was inclined to get into the hole to see where the tires had gone.

In southern Illinois, not far from the small town of Cave-in-Rock, there have long been stories told of sinks that will appear in the woods. These holes literally open overnight in the middle of farm fields and become ponds and small lakes, filling with water in a matter of hours. Local fishermen find that the holes are somehow stocked with fish from the moment they appear, as if the water was being channeled in from somewhere else. No local lakes or creeks have been documented to drop when the sinks open. When the sinks do appear, they may last for days, weeks or even months before suddenly being drained of their water. One man that I spoke with told me that his father was fishing one day and heard a loud gurgling sound from one of the sinks. The water began to swirl and then drain out of the hole as mysteriously as it had come. He recalled that he had filled his pickup truck with fish that afternoon!

One summer in the 1970s, a group of men from the National Forest Service (the area is located within the Shawnee National Forest in southern Illinois) poured gallons and gallons of a harmless dye into one of the sinks. It had been filled for some time and it was assumed that it would soon empty again. When it did, a line of men in boats were stationed along the nearby Ohio River, believing that the dye from the sink would soon become visible as the river was the only body of water capable of holding the water drained from the sink. They waited for several days after the sink emptied but no dye was ever seen.

Locals have come to accept the sinks as an oddity of nature but still wonder where the water comes from and where it goes. They also ponder the fish that appear overnight in a new sink. They are not blind fish that appear to have come from some underground cavern, but rather fresh carp, bluegill and catfish that are commonly found in freshwater lakes and ponds. During the time when the sinks are empty, farmers till the ground and plant crops on the site, never knowing if the field might be lost when another sink decides to open!

For years, I also heard about a hole near Hannibal, Missouri that was locally rumored to be bottomless. According to the stories, a number of cattle and animals had been lost in the hole and had never been found. It was located in the woods outside of town and became a place to be shunned and avoided by nearby residents. And while I have never been able to find any records that proves this hole actually exists, the story persists. The fellow who owned the land on which the hole was located decided one day to check the hole out for himself, and he tied a rope around a nearby fence post and slid down into the blackness. The story relates that some friends discovered him shortly after his adventure in the pit and his hair had turned completely white and he was wildly insane.

Whatever he had encountered down in the cave had broken his sanity. This is strange, but it gets even stranger.

In the northern part of Arkansas is Boone County and within the county is a small village called Self. It's a remote place and is not very accessible anymore, but it is home to a story that is both elusive and fascinating. Similar to the story from Missouri, it deals with a strange and largely unexplored cavern called the Devil's Hole Cave. One day, an indeterminate number of years ago, the owner of the land where the cave is located decided to explore the cavern. He climbed down a rope about 200 feet to a ledge where the shaft narrows to a point that can only be crawled through. He suddenly heard a vicious hissing from the darkness, perhaps like a large lizard would do, and he made a hasty retreat. Some time later, he and some men from town dropped a flatiron tied to a rope to the same place in the cave. They heard a hissing sound and the rope was pulled hard. When they pulled it back up, they found the flatiron had been badly bent and scored with scratches and teeth marks. They next tried a stone and the rope was pulled taut again. They pulled it back up and the stone was gone. Not surprisingly, no one wanted to dare and climb down to see what was in the cave.

Occasionally, new local stories about the cave are heard, but the "gowrow," as the natives call it, seems to prefer staying down in the darkness. The tale dates to around 1900, and many believe the creature may be some sort of giant lizard, but nobody knows for sure what it is or even if it is still alive. Arkansas spelunkers have informed me that they have visited this cave on several occasions, and while much of it remains unexplored, they have yet to encounter the gowrow.

The Lost Civilization of Death Valley

America is riddled with caves and strange tunnels about which there are stories of lost routes to secret cities and underground civilizations. Even the most ancient records of past societies tell of

343

reasonable people who have wandered into holes and tunnels, where they find artifacts and paintings pointing to some subterranean world. The Spanish conquistadors even noted that the Indians often seemed to vanish into underground caverns through the Southwest that were too complex and vast to explore.

The idea that the earth possesses a hollow core and that these same civilizations exist in such a place is an even older notion. Many religions believe that the physical location of "hell" might be at the center of the earth and perhaps this has been the source of the stories that still exist today. In the early 1800s, an eccentric named John Cleves Symmes tried to prove that the earth was hollow, theorizing that the earth is made of up concentric spheres with 4,000-mile wide holes at the north and south poles. Despite the ridicule he faced, Symmes wrote and lectured on the subject and tried hard to organize an expedition through one of the poles to the interior of the planet. Here, he was convinced, his expedition would meet the Inner-Earth people and could open new sources of trade and commerce. Symmes is largely forgotten today, but readers may remember him as the inspiration for Edgar Allan Poe's science fiction story, "The Narrative of Arthur Gordon Pym."

While dismissed by most, Symmes was the first to suggest the idea that there could be people living below the earth. His son, Americus, followed in his footsteps and kept in touch with the Hollow Earth disciples that his father had created. He published a collection of his father's lectures in 1878, and this book joined others on the subject like *The Hollow Globe* (1871) by M.L. Sherman, which purported to be a series of communications with the dead at the center of the earth. Famous mystic Helene Petrova Blavatsky, the founder of the occult school of Theosophy, wrote of the Hollow Earth in two of her books, *Isis Unveiled* (1877) and *The Secret Doctrine* (1888).

For most of us though, the idea of the Hollow Earth is most memorably presented in the works of science fiction and fantasy authors like Jules Verne and Edgar Rice Burroughs. It seems to be the stuff of imagination but writers of those days, and many today, took the ideas very seriously. Civilizations that are located beneath the earth are an important part of many movements and of some aspects of ufology these days as well.

The idea that we could somehow gain access to these forbidden worlds has intrigued man long before any of these books were written. One such civilization could be accessed through the treacherous Death Valley desert, the lowest and hottest place in America. According to Native American legends, there existed an entrance to a city called *Shin-au-av*. Located near an area called Wingate Pass, it was said to be inhabited by fair-skinned people who spoke an unknown language and who lived in hidden caverns that were illuminated by green light.

A Native American guide named Tom Wilson said that his grandfather had stumbled into the caverns some time around 1920 and had become totally lost. He ended up stumbling into an underground city, where he found white people who wore shiny leather clothing. They spoke a language that he had never heard before, but they showed him a way to get out of the tunnels and back to the surface. The guide told the tale after meeting a prospector named White who claimed to have fallen through the floor of an abandoned mine where he found various chambers containing bars of gold and mummies dressed in leather. The prospector said that he went back to the cave several times with his wife and a partner named Fred Thomason to see the mummies (and likely to haul away some of the gold), but when he tried to lead an archaeological team to the site, he was unable to find it.

The cavern was again lost for many years—or was it? Many people in the area speculated as to the source of wealth enjoyed by an eccentric old prospector named Walter Scott. He built a castle in the valley and a racetrack that still exists today. Those who knew him stated that when his funds were running low, "Death Valley Scotty," as he was known, would disappear for a few days and return with some suspiciously refined-looking gold that he claimed he prospected. Many believe that the old man, who spent millions on his castle, got his gold from the stacks of bars that were hidden in the caves beneath Wingate Pass.

The cavern remained lost until 1931 when an amateur archaeologist and physician named Dr. F. Bruce Russell literally stumbled onto it again. He soon made an announcement that he had discovered a variety of strange artifacts and eight-foot-tall mummified bodies, along with 32 similar caves within seven miles of the original site. He spent the next 20 years exploring the caverns and trying to generate interest in them and funding for a major dig. After putting the money together, he issued invitations throughout the academic community to accompany him to the caves and to bring back artifacts that could be studied scientifically. All of those he invited refused to come. They would only go to the site after first seeing the artifacts. Discouraged, but not hopeless, Dr. Russell returned to Death Valley to bring back proof of his discovery. He was never seen again.

The mysterious caverns were forgotten until 1947 when a new announcement came from a man named Howard E. Hill, an amateur archaeologist who claimed to have rediscovered Dr. Russell's lost caverns. He stated that the caves contained mummies of men and animals and implements of a culture that was thousands of years old but "in some respects more advanced than our own." In a newspaper report, Hill admitted that Dr. Russell had discovered the caves and that he "tried for years to interest people in them, but nobody believed him." According to the report, Hill and his team found one cave that seemed to contain a ritual hall with designs and markings similar to Freemason design. A long tunnel from this temple took the group into another room, where they found the preserved remains of dinosaurs, saber-toothed tigers, elephants and other extinct beasts. The animals had been placed in pairs as if on display. He believed that perhaps some sort of catastrophe in the past had driven the civilization into the caves ,and they had left all of the implements of their culture behind, including household utensils and stoves "which apparently cooked by radio waves."

The story made the newspapers and then mysteriously vanished. If it was true, what ever became of the artifacts and mummies? The stories were apparently too unbelievable, and the Los Angeles County Museum, which at first expressed interest in the find, soon broke off contact with the group when the story grew too incredible. Once again, the caverns were lost.

Interest in them was revived in the 1960s, thanks to the attention of cult leader and alleged killer Charles Manson. He came to believe that a water-filled cavern entrance in Wingate Pass was a passageway to the underground civilization from the earlier tales about the area. He was arrested here in 1969 before he could lead his followers into the portal to the other side.

While such interest in the site is questionable (at best), there have been many others who have come to believe there may be more to the area than meets the eye. Since Manson's brush with Wingate Pass, at least two people have died trying to swim through the hundreds of feet of water that blocks the entrance to the cavern. One has to wonder what they hope to find inside. Relics of some forgotten, ancient culture, or the entrance to another world?

Mount Shasta and the Lemurians

Stories of an underground civilization under Mount Shasta in California date back hundreds of years. They are a part of Native American legend and existed long before the white settlers came to the region. The Modoc, Shastika and Wintun people living near the mountain considered Shasta the home of the gods and a pillar that reached up to the heavens, rooted in the underworld. In those days, Mount Shasta was still an active volcano and appears to have last erupted between 1810 and 1825, just before the first explorers came in 1827.

Shasta was the focus of other tribal beliefs as well. In the 1870s, during the last of California's Indian wars, the Modocs were

347

inspired to battle by their shamans, who prophesied that their ancestors would be resurrected and would come to their aid, rising up out of the earth and allowing the land to swallow the white soldiers. At the same time, one of the Shastika elders announced that a crow had brought him news that the spirits of slain Shastika men were waiting above the peak of Mount Shasta, ready to come down and join the battle.

Many of the Native Americans also told of mysterious beings living inside of the mountain. There was a race of giants, and according to Hopi legend, the mountain was one of the thirteen homes of the Lizard People. Small, invisible people also lived on the mountain and they could sometimes be seen for a moment before vanishing. Most often their eerie laughter, like that of a small child, could be heard echoing among the rocks and trees.

Stories like these, passing from the Indians to the settlers who came to the area, helped continue the mountain's strange and wondrous reputation. The first piece of literature that could be connected to the mountain, and the book that allowed the reputation to grow, was a curious occult novel called *A Dweller on Two Planets; or, the Dividing of the Way* by "Phylos the Thibetan." The author of the book, Frederick S. Oliver, claimed that it had been channeled to him and that it was the true story of an ancient master who dwelt inside of Mount Shasta. According to reviews, it's a pretty lousy book, but it did establish all the main elements of the Mount Shasta story for generations to come, telling of an old underground city beneath the sleeping volcano.

When *A Dweller on Two Planets* was published around 1900, it became quite popular with the alternative-reality community. The book made a very strong impression on H. Spencer Lewis, the advertising man who founded the Ancient Mystical Order Rosae Crucis, better known as the Rosicrucians. He later wrote a book called *Lemuria: the Lost Continent of the Pacific* in 1931. According to Lewis, the Lemurians were much like the people of the fabled city of Atlantis and had created a progressive culture and a vast continent that took up most of the area now covered by the Pacific Ocean. Eventually, the continent was covered by water and the most advanced members of Lemurian society escaped to the highest peak of Lemuria, which was, of course, Mount Shasta. On the mountain, they have secretly remained to this day.

Of course, with all of the people who were visiting Mount Shasta by the 1930s, it seems likely that people would have had a hard time missing the Lemurians. As described by Lewis, they averaged more than seven feet in height with long arms, large heads, long foreheads and short legs. They wore their hair quite long and often arranged in "very fancy forms across their shoulders or down their back." The most interesting feature on them however would have had to have been the third eye that was said to have been placed in the center of their forehead. This would have definitely gotten some attention by hikers or hunters near the mountain!

And while it seems that the world Lewis created must have sprung from the older legends of the mountain, there were those who seemed to embrace the idea of the Lemurians. One of them was a journalist named Edward Lanser, who wrote a sensationalistic article about a society of people who wore white robes and who lived on the mountain in 1932. They allegedly possessed a huge supply of pure gold and claimed to be descendants of the Lemurians. According to the article, only one man had ever penetrated the wall of secrecy around the Lemurian colony, an "eminent scientist, Professor Edgar Lucien Larkin, for many years the director of the Mt. Lowe Observatory in southern California." Lanser wrote that Larkin used a powerful telescope to spy on the Lemurian village and saw huge temples that marked the entrance to the underground world. Of course, it should be noted that Lanser seems to have written a large part of the article in a tongue in cheek manner. By the time he wrote the piece, most of Shasta had been explored and no temples had been discovered. He also noted that the "really incredible" thing about the Lemurians was their ability to resist neon signs and hot dogs; and anyone who researched the article would find that

Professor Edgar Lucien Larkin was no eminent scientist. He was a rather eccentric occultist who had died in 1924, eight years before Lanser's article was published. His Mt. Lowe Observator" was not a scientific establishment either, but rather a tourist attraction railway north of Los Angeles. The only telescope here showed tourists the lights of the city, not the distant slopes of Shasta.

In spite of this, Lanser's story was seized upon by the fringe groups and the lost continent enthusiasts as further proof of Lemuria. The tales of Shasta continued to grow and while the idea of lost Lemurians seemed pretty silly, were all of the stories pure bunk?

In 1904, an explorer for a the British Lord Cowdray Mining Company named J.C. Brown reported that he discovered a caved-in hollow on the side of Mount Shasta. He had been hired to prospect for gold in the region and on his second trip, he found the manmade tunnel. When he wandered inside, he discovered a large cavern that had been carved from the rock. The walls were lined with hammered copper and strange shields of gold. Hidden in various niches were odd artifacts and a series of hieroglyphic writings which led Brown into another room filled with very large skeletons. According to the prospector, they may have belonged to some ancient race.

Brown later quit his job and settled in Stockton, California. He waited more than 30 years before announcing his discovery in the mountain so that his former employers could not lay claim to it. In 1934, he finally told his tale and lined up a number of people to help him excavate the cave. On June 19, 1934, Brown and his team set out on their journey into the mountains. The night before Brown was to have shown the party the entrance to the cavern, they camped out near a small stream. At some point during the night, Brown mysteriously disappeared. The Stockton police investigated the case but they had no clues and could find no trace of the prospector. He had simply vanished. It was suggested that perhaps Brown had assembled the team as part of a scam, leading them into the mountains and then disappearing, but team members insisted that no money had ever changed hands. With everything else ruled out, it was assumed that

Brown had been abducted, but by who or for what reason, was unknown. He was never seen or heard from again.

Based on this report, one has to wonder just what Brown may have found on Mount Shasta. Could his story have been true? Did he actually find an entrance to a lost cache of ancient artifacts? And if he did, was there some truth to the old stories and Indian legends about a tribe of people living inside of the earth?

According to reports, stories were common in California many years ago of strange-looking people who would emerge from the forests around Mount Shasta on occasion. They would usually run back into the woods and hide if seen by anyone, but at times, they would come into town and trade for modern goods using gold nuggets or dust for payment. They never accepted change for the items they purchased and rumors about these unusual people suggested that gold was of no real value to them and that they had no use for modern money. Descriptions were always the same: the people had fair features, were tall and graceful and wore clothing that was not recognized by the American Indians or later inhabitants of the region. Could these mysterious figures have been responsible for the lore that was created about the mountain?

There were a number of people who claimed to have been in contact with these mystery inhabitants, but in 1930 perhaps the greatest of the alleged contact with the mystery creatures was said to have taken place. While many believe that the stories told by Guy W. Ballard of his encounters in the region are the stuff of fantasy, I will withhold my own opinions and allow the reader to judge for himself.

According to Ballard, he was working near Mount Shasta for a mining company in the summer of 1930. He was aware of the mountain's reputation, so he decided to climb the peak and pray to God to show him the right path to take with his life. When he stopped at a spring for lunch, he felt an "electric charge" pass through his body. He looked up to see a young man standing nearby. He asked Ballard for the cup that he was drinking out of and then filled it with an odd, creamy liquid. He handed it back to Ballard and asked him to drink it. Ballard did so and was over-whelmed by an electric feeling in his mind and body. The young man told him that he was an ancient master, Saint Germain, and that he had given Ballard the gift of life.

This encounter would be the first of many that Ballard was to have with Saint Germain (the Comte de Saint-Germain was a noto-rious eighteenth-century occultist who, it was rumored, had discov-ered the secret of eternal life. He has allegedly appeared in various guises for centuries). Ballard was then taken into the mountain and shown a huge subterranean world and given all sorts of gifts of wis-dom and the ability to understand the laws of the universe.

Soon after, Ballard wrote a book on his encounter and his mys-tical experiences called *Unveiled Mysteries*. He and his wife Edna began attracting followers to the teachings in the book and were enormously successful from 1934 until Ballard's death in 1939. Bearing the title of the "Ascended Messengers" of the Masters, the Ballards and their son, Donald, traveled around the United States preaching about the "coming Crystal Age" to Americans. In a short time, the cult, now called the "I AM" Activity, surrounded itself with a controversial message and might even be seen as the spiri-tual parent of the modern Scientology movement. The Ballards used a multi-sensory approach to indoctrinating their followers and were obsessed with the values of colors, particularly pink, blue and violet. They dressed in pastel clothing and stressed love and virtue for all.

The I AM Activity collected hundreds of thousands of dollars in "love gifts" during meetings, and by 1939, the Ballards claimed a worldwide membership of 400,000 with an impressive head-quarters in Chicago. Ballard's death in 1939 almost shattered the movement though. In 1938, he had declared that he would not die before his Ascension to becoming one of the Masters. Unable to accept Edna Ballard's assurances that her husband did take his place at Mount Shasta with the other Masters, many followers abandoned the fold. In 1940, Edna and Donald Ballard, along with several I AM leaders, were indicted for obtaining money under false pretenses. The messy trial caused the membership to dwindle even more. Eventually, the group was acquitted, and the movement continued on for a time.

In the 1940s, Edna established the I AM Youth Foundation near Mount Shasta City on a piece of land that her husband had bought for the purpose. The local residents were not happy with the influx of cult members but the two groups co-existed quietly, despite the No Trespassing signs erected by the I AM folks and the rumors concerning secret rituals and mysterious invocations that were shocking for its day.

Edna Ballard passed away in 1971, and while the I AM movement still exists today, it is hardly the presence that it once was in America. The strange beginning of the group at Mount Shasta are nearly forgotten now, but once again, it shows how the original legends of the place gave birth to high strangeness in later times.

The legends of Mount Shasta continue to exist. In a 1993 publication, Commander X (who is allegedly a retired military officer with access to government secrets about UFOs) wrote that Mount Shasta "has a highly charged aura which prevents the forces of darkness from penetrating nearby. Teams of space brothers, Lemurians and elementals, working jointly, meditate daily underground here to heal the planet and to keep this scared spot from either physical or mental attack."

Another ufologist claimed to meet "a young, very pretty blond girl with almond-shaped eyes and small perfect teeth" who said she was born in a city called Telos, which is located inside an artificial, domed-shaped cavern about one mile beneath Mount Shasta. The woman, who identified herself only as "Bonnie," described how the inhabitants of Telos travelled by tube shuttle to visit other subterranean cities. According to her claims (or the ufologist's, if you prefer), they are Lemurians and members of a cosmic federation that links them to extraterrestrial intelligence.

And just to show that all of the strangeness at Mount Shasta has come full circle, the reader is asked to recall the fact that the Native Americans considered the mountain to be one of the 13 homes of the Lizard People in their mythology. In 1972, a man from San Jose who was hiking along the southern slopes of the mountain reported an encounter with what was described as a "reptilian humanoid." I guess that it just goes to show that all things old are new again.

The Amazing Stories of Raymond Palmer

Perhaps the greatest story of the Hollow Earth came about thanks to the Golden Age of Pulp Magazines in America. The pulps were cheap, newsprint paper magazines and were immensely popular in the time between the two World Wars. The magazines were made up of all types of genres and the science fiction pulps—*Amazing Stories*, *Science Wonder Stories*, *Astounding Stories*, and many others—sold hundreds of thousands of copies each month. They held great appeal, especially to legions of young men, with their lurid covers, exciting tales and escapist fiction about the worlds of tomorrow.

Before the era of the pulps, nearly all of the early depictions of the Hollow Earth consisted of the inner world's inhabitants being members of an advanced, benevolent race that human beings would want to meet and befriend. That soon began to change, and in a matter of time, the wise and superior beings were making certain, for humanity's good of course, that the intrepid explorers who stumbled into lost caverns never returned to the surface alive. The transformation of the Hollow Earth into a place of menace was largely the work of one man, Raymond Palmer, who became the editor of *Amazing Stories* in 1938.

Palmer was born in Milwaukee in 1910 and over a 40 year career would edit a wide range of science fiction and alternative reality magazines, including *Amazing Stories, Fate, Other World, Flying Saucers* and many more. He was responsible for introducing the idea to the public that UFOs were piloted by extraterrestrial visitors and promoted many of the early flying saucer stories and tales of the government's cover-up of the elusive craft.

Long before this though, his life would be considered a tragedy by most. Palmer was always an avid reader, and his love for books, magazines and newspapers would serve him well in life after a butcher's truck ran over him at the age of seven cracking one of the vertebrae in his spine. Over the next two years, the pressure on his spine increased until he could neither stand nor walk. The doctors performed a spinal graft on him, and it appeared to be successful until one day it loosened and he collapsed with his spine bent so badly that any attempt to straighten it would have killed him. He was given only 24 hours to live, but Palmer survived, although he was permanently disabled. He grew up as a hunchback and was never free from pain. As an adult, he stood four feet, eight inches tall but he never let that stop him from becoming "larger than life."

Palmer was hospitalized many times during his teens and early 20s, and while bedridden, he developed a passionate appetite for science fiction, especially the novels of Jules Verne, H.G. Wells and the burgeoning pulps. In 1926, a story that he penned was accepted at *Science Wonder Stories* and Palmer was determined to become a writer. He submitted a second story 100 times and it was rejected on 99 occasions, but he did not let this slow him down. Over the next 11 years, he wrote hundreds of stories of mystery, murder and science fiction for the pulps. He wrote mostly at night, and worked as a bookkeeper during the day. He also wrote numerous letters to his favorite magazine, *Amazing Stories*, and in 1938, Ziff-Davis, the magazine's publisher, offered him the editor's position.

Palmer achieved almost instant success at the magazine by publishing straightforward and hard-hitting science fiction. He also kept the writers hard at work, and while he was seen as a tyrant around the office, he made many friends with his good-natured wit and staff poker games. He negotiated a contract that paid him a percentage of the profits (unheard of at the time) and managed to increase sales of the magazine to the point that he managed to take home more money than the publisher's vice-president.

Then in September 1943, Palmer received a letter that had been written to *Amazing Stories* that would change his career and the magazine forever. Sent from a reader named Richard Sharpe Shaver, the letter detailed an "ancient alphabet," but Palmer's managing editor tossed it into the trash as the work of a crackpot. After rescuing the letter, Palmer tried experimenting with the alphabet that Shaver called "definite proof of the Atlantean legend," and while he didn't feel that it was proof of anything, it did turn out to be an interesting code alphabet. Palmer decided to print the alphabet in the next issue of the magazine.

By itself, the letter as it was published would have seemed like the product of an unbalanced mind, but Palmer decided to include an invitation for the readers to try the alphabet for themselves. And while he certainly must have meant the whole thing as an experiment to attract reader response, the number of letters that he received back was astounding. People from all over the country wrote in to say that they had tried the alphabet and it had worked!

Palmer was now sure that he was on to something, and so he wrote to Shaver to ask for more information. He received back a 10,000-word letter that was entitled "A Warning to Future Man." Shaver stated that he did not know how long he had to live and before he died, he wanted to warn humanity of the terrible dangers it faced. He was anxious to see the letter published in *Amazing Stories* and hoped that Palmer would do so as soon as possible. Palmer took one look at the jumbled and badly written manuscript and knew that he had a gold mine in his hands. Using the letter as a basis, he sat down and wrote a 31,000-word story that was called "I Remember Lemuria!" The story was published in the March 1945 issue of the magazine, and all of the copies quickly sold out. Palmer introduced it as a true story, told from Shaver's own experiences, and he gave the author's credit to Shaver alone.

"I Remember Lemuria!" is a bizarre story, as were all of the stories written by Shaver and rewritten by Palmer. Shaver wrote of his encounters with evil creatures known as "deros," which was apparently short for "detrimental robots." They were not the robots of usual science fiction but rather the name given to races produced by genetic engineering performed by the giant residents of Lemuria, the "Titans." These creatures, some of whom could be as tall as 300 feet, lived on the earth's surface until about 12,000 years ago, when they were forced to flee the earth for distant planets. Most of the deros fled into huge underground caverns to avoid radiation from the sun. Those who remained on the earth's surface later mutated into the forerunners of the human race. The deros were twisted and sadistic half-wits who had access to advanced Titan technology, making them especially dangerous. They used the technology to mostly heighten their sexual pleasure during the orgies to which they were addicted. They also used machines to torture kidnapped surface dwellers and "teros" (good subterraneans who, although outnumbered, were fighting the evil deros). They also used the machinery to cause accidents, madness and other disasters in the surface world. This was what Shaver was trying to warn the world about, as he claimed to witness the terrible deeds of the deros first hand.

Soon after the story went to print, a flood of letters began pouring into the magazine's offices and readers wanted to know more about Shaver and Lemuria. Many of those who wrote also professed to have encountered the deros and had barely lived to tell the tale. Chester S. Geier, one of the magazine's regular contributors, started the Shaver Mystery Club as a way of handling the incoming mail and "investigating" the stories of those who had also been abducted by the deros.

Palmer and Shaver caused quite a stir and between 1945 and 1948. *Amazing Stories* and it companion pulp, *Fantastic Adventures*, began filling up with terrifying stories of Shaver's adventures in the underworld. In his disconnected writings, (which were published in a book called *The Hidden World* by Palmer in the 1960s) Shaver placed the blame for nearly every bad event in history on the deros. He insisted that they used a death ray to sever blood vessels in the brain of Franklin Delano Roosevelt, killing him near the end of World War II, and that the Nazis were mere puppets of the deros, who designed the death camps and organized the Third Reich. Even Jesus Christ was crucified on orders from the inner earth.

Shaver was always a bit of a mystery himself. The details of his life are hazy and often seemed to change. He was born in 1908 (or 1910) in rural Pennsylvania, and his father operated restaurants throughout the state. Shaver's mother wrote poetry and stories for women's magazines and true confession pulps while his older brother, who died when Shaver was a boy, wrote fiction for *Boy's Life* and other periodicals. Shaver showed little interest in writing and was always considered a restless and unstable young man. He never kept a job for long and only worked when he felt like it. After he got out of high school, he hauled trees for a landscaper for a while and then worked as a meat cutter in a slaughterhouse, a crane operator and a welder. He was also married three times, although his first two marriages lasted for less than one year each. His third wife, Dorothy, married him in 1947 and they remained together until his death.

While never much of a writer, Shaver was an avid reader and loved science fiction. He bought his first copy of *Amazing Stories* in 1926 and was a fan of the pulps until they eventually faded from view. He was also fascinated by the paranormal collections of Charles Fort and all manner of occult writings, from the Rosicrucians to Madame Blavatsky. Influences from all of these sources can be seen throughout the Shaver stories of the under-world.

But if the stories were true, as Shaver claimed, how could a welder from rural Pennsylvania have encountered the deros in the first place? He told several versions (not surprisingly) of how this came about but the most popular version had Shaver working as a welder at a Ford Motor Plant in Highland Park, Michigan in 1932.

As he was working on the assembly line, his welding gun turned into a transmitter (bear with me as I am not sure I get this either), and he began picking up voices and signals from the underworld. He heard a woman's screams, the cracks of whips and bizarre voices and shouts. He soon quit his job and bummed around until he reached Montreal. He stowed away on a ship that he thought was bound for England and ended up in Newfoundland instead. He was arrested and sent to jail and then deported to Boston, where he broke his leg and spent the winter in a charity hospital. Another version of his life states that he was not arrested at all and instead spent eight years in a mental hospital.

Whatever occurred, it was during one of the prison or hospital stays when Shaver discovered the truth about the deros. He was visited in his room by a blind teros girl named Nydia who told him the story of the Titans and the secrets of the underground world. After she had visited him several times, Nydia helped Shaver to escape and then led him to a concealed cave entrance, located not far from the hospital (or prison, or whatever). Shaver then joined a group of teros and lived with them for several years. He learned that the voices that he heard coming from his welding gun were those of the deros and their prisoners. Shaver witnessed horrible torture sessions and some pretty graphic sexual scenes, both of which managed to make it into his writings. The perverted deros seemed to be aroused by torture and dismemberment and Shaver himself seemed especially fond of writing about the mostly naked young women and buxom Titan women that could be found in the early stories.

The phenomenal success of "I Remember Lemuria!" caused Palmer to begin including Shaver material in almost every issue of *Amazing Stories*. The magazine's circulation increased more than 50,000 issues a month and what had once been perhaps 50 reader letters a month, now expanded to more than 2,500. Readers wrote Palmer to tell him that they had heard voices, had strange dreams of the underworld, and had been prisoners of the deros but had escaped. Palmer was delighted with the flood of new mail (however strange) and increased the size of the letter column. He even added a new department to the magazine to handle the best developments in what he called "The Shaver Mystery."

From 1945 to 1948, the magazines were filled with Shaver and fan clubs started all over the country. But not all of the *Amazing Stories* readers were happy with the situation. Many science fictions fans began to write letters to protest the magazine's fixation on stories for crackpots. One group even wrote that the stories endangered the sanity of the reader and brought a resolution before the Vice Board to get the magazine banned. Another group petitioned the Philadelphia post office to get the magazine banned from the mail.

Palmer loved the attention the protests brought the magazine and used the threats and hostile letters as an excuse to question those who would suppress the truth. The Shaver Mystery peaked in June 1947 with an entire issue of the magazine devoted to it. It described the mystery as the "most sensational true story ever told." But the Shaver stories would not last much longer within the page of *Amazing Stories*. Late in 1948, the series was stopped. The magazine ran a few more Shaver stories that had already been purchased over infrequent intervals into the 1950s, but the letters, columns and editorials had ended. Palmer gave several different explanations as to why the series had been stopped: the publisher had received too many complaints from older readers of the magazine; Palmer himself decided that true stories did not belong in a fiction magazine; and even the deros had tampered with the presses.

Palmer went on to co-found *Fate* magazine with Curtis Fuller in 1948 and then left Ziff-Davis and moved to Amherst, Wisconsin. Here, he began producing his own magazines including *Flying Saucers* and *Mystic* (later called *Search*). Until his death in August 1977, Palmer unearthed, sensationalized and defended one mystery after another without ever actually admitting that he believed them to be true. He was a clever writer and his true feelings about the Shaver

Mystery and journeys to the inner earth remain a mystery.

While Palmer was a showman, Shaver was even more of a puzzle. He died of lung cancer in November 1975 with most of the world unconvinced about the validity of the Shaver Mystery. In many histories of science fiction and the pulps, it is referred to as the "Shaver Hoax"—but was it really a hoax? From Ray Palmer's point of view, it likely was, but he had a great feel for what people liked to read and he loved to stir up controversy. Despite his many protests that he was dedicated to uncovering the truth behind the mystery, he actually managed to scatter and confuse any so-called evidence that could back up Shaver's claims. By encouraging the readers to write in with their own experiences in the underworld, he prolonged the story, entertained the masses and gave people the chance to participate in the adventure. However, Shaver really seemed to believe in it. His disjointed letters to Palmer laid out a story that he truly claimed to believe. Was he a madman or a prophet—or was he really connecting with the technological fears that were shared by a huge number of Americans in those days?

There are those who have questioned Shaver's sanity and those (albeit dwindling) followers who maintain that no one could have concocted a story as fantastic as his and a story that he believed so whole-heartedly. Shaver continually asserted the reality of the underworld but when asked where the entrances were, he contended that the deros camouflaged the tunnel mouths with their insidious machines. He could provide no proof of his beliefs and yet this never seemed to bother him. The story was true, he insisted, but was he really fooling himself into believing in the creations of his own fevered mind?

Perhaps he was, or perhaps there are not only things that are stranger in heaven and earth than are dreamt of in our own philosophies—but under the earth as well!

Bibliography &
Recommended Reading

Allen, Robert Joseph, *The Story of the Superstition Mountain & the Lost Dutchman Mine* (1971)

Aron, Paul, *Unsolved Mysteries of American History* (1997)

Barker, Gray, *The Silver Bridge* (1970)

Barnard, Barney, *Superstition Mountain & Its Famed Lost Dutchman Mine* (1964)

Bayless, Raymond, "Report on the Ozark Spook Light," *Fate Magazine* (Sep./Oct. 1964)

Bell, Horace, *On the Old West Coast* (1930)

Bielski, Ursula, *Chicago Haunts* (1998)

Bleiler, E.F., ed., *Ghost & Horror Stories of Ambrose Bierce* (1964)

Brandon, Ruth, *Life & Many Deaths of Harry Houdini* (1993)

Cannell, J.C., *Secrets of Houdini* (1989)

Canning, John, *Great Unsolved Mysteries* (1984)

Casebook of Jack the Ripper Website (www.casebook.com)

Cashman, John, *Gentleman from Chicago* (1973)

Chicago Daily Sun-Times (1957 editions)

Childress, David Hatcher, *Lost Cities of North & Central America* (1992)

Citro, Joseph A., *Passing Strange* (1996)

Clark, Jerome, *Unexplained!* (1999)

Coleman, Loren, *Curious Encounters* (1985)

Coleman, Loren, *Mothman & Other Curious Encounters* (2002)

Coleman, Loren, *Mysterious America* (1983/2000)

Corliss, William R., *Handbook of Unusual Natural Phenomena* (1977/1983)

Davies, Rodney, *Supernatural Vanishings* (1996)

Dunninger, Joseph, "Dunninger Discusses the Houdini-Ford Controversy," *Fate* (Nov. 1971)

Evans, Stewart & Keith Skinner, *The Ultimate Jack the Ripper Companion* (2000)

Fate Magazine, Various Issues (see detailed listings)

Feder, Kenneth L., *Frauds, Myths and Mysteries* (1999)

Ford, Arthur, "How I Broke the Houdini Code," *Fate* (July 1959)

Fortean Times Magazine, Various Issues

Floyd, Randall, *Ghost Lights* (1995)

Floyd, Randall, *Great American Mysteries* (1990)

Fort, Charles, *Complete Books of Charles Fort* (1941)

Gaddis, Vincent H., "Mystery of Houdini's Death," *Fate* (August 1963)

Gentry, Kurt, *The Killer Mountains* (1968)

Ghost Tracker's Newsletter (July 1983 edition)

Ghosts of the Prairie Website (www.prairieghosts.com)

Gibson, Edmund P., "Is This Houdini's Telepathic Code?", *Fate* (April 1961)

Gilmore, John, *Severed* (1994)

Godwin, John, *This Baffling World 2*, (1968)

Gresham, William Lindsay, *Houdini: The Man Who Walked Through Walls* (1959)

Guiley, Rosemary Ellen, *Atlas of the Mysterious in North America* (1995)

Guiley, Rosemary Ellen, *Encyclopedia of Ghosts & Spirits* (2000)

Hauck, Dennis William, *Haunted Places: The National Directory* (1996)

Houdini & Dunninger, *Magic & Mystery* (1967)

Houdini, Harry, *A Magician Among the Spirits* (1924)

Hunt, Gerry, *Bizarre America* (1988)

Jameson, W.C., *Unsolved Mysteries of the Old West* (1999)

Jarvis, Sharon, *Dark Zones* (1992)

Jarvis, Sharon, *Dead Zones* (1992)

Joltes, Richard E., *The Burrows Cave Controversy* (2001)

Kafton-Minkel, Walter, *Subterranean World* (1989)

Keel, John, *Complete Guide to Mysterious Beings* (1970/1994)

Keel, John, *Disneyland of the Gods* (1988)

Keel, John, *The Mothman Prophecies* (1975)

Keel, John, *Our Haunted Planet* (1971)

Knight, Damon, *Charles Fort: Prophet of the Unexplained* (1970)

Kolb, Ellsworth, *Through the Grand Canyon from Wyoming to Mexico* (1914)

Kurland, Michael, *Complete Idiot's Guide to Unsolved Mysteries* (2000)

Lindberg, Richard, *Return to the Scene of the Crime* (1999)

Lopes, Lianne Bruynell, *Who Really Discovered America First?* (2000)

Martinez, Lionel, *Great Unsolved Mysteries of North America* (1988)

Miller, R. DeWitt, *Impossible, Yet it Happened!* (1947)

Monaco, Richard, *Bizarre America 2* (1992)

Nash, Jay Robert, *Among the Missing* (1978)

Nash, Jay Robert, *Murder, America* (1980)

Ness, Eliot with Oscar Fraley, *The Untouchables* (1957)

Newton, Michael, *Encyclopedia of Serial Killers* (2000)

Norman, Michael & Beth Scott, *Historic Haunted America* (1995)

Olcott, Henry S., *People from Other Worlds* (1875)

Peithman, Stephen, ed., *Annotated Tales of Edgar Allan Poe* (1981)

Picknett, Lynn, *Flights of Fancy?* (1987)

Platnick, Kenneth, *Great Mysteries of History* (1971)

Randolph, Vance, *Ozark Magic & Folklore* (1947)

Readers Digest, *Great Mysteries of the Past* (1991)

Readers Digest, *Mysteries of the Unexplained* (1982)

Readers Digest, *Strange Stories, Amazing Facts* (1976)

Rumbelow, Donald, *The Complete Jack the Ripper* (1975)

Shaffer, Tamara, *The Crime that Time Forgot*

Shoemaker, Michael T., "The Mad Gasser of Botetourt," *Fate* (June 1985)

Shuker, Karl P.N., *The Unexplained* (1996)

Sifakis, Carl, *Encyclopedia of American Crime* (1982)

Sifakis, Carl, *The Mafia Encyclopedia* (1987)

Silverman, Kenneth, *Edgar A. Poe* (1991)

Silverman, Kenneth, *Houdini!* (1996)

Steiger, Brad, *Strange Disappearances* (1972)

Strange Magazine, Various Issues

Sugden, Phillip, *The Complete History of Jack the Ripper* (1994)

Taylor, Troy, *Beyond the Grave* (2001)

Taylor, Troy, *The Ghost Hunter's Guidebook* (1999/2001)

Taylor, Troy, *Haunted Illinois* (2001)

Taylor, Troy, *Haunted St. Louis* (2002)

Taylor, Troy, *No Rest for the Wicked* (2001)

Trento, Salvatore M., *Field Guide to Mysterious Places of Eastern North America* (1997)

Trento, Salvatore M., *Field Guide to Mysterious Places of the West* (1994)

Walsh, John Evangelist, *Midnight Dreary* (2000)

Wanner, Jayne, *A Consideration: Was America Discovered in 1170?* (1995)

Wilkins, Harold T., *Strange Mysteries of Time & Space* (1959)

Wilson, Colin, *Unsolved Mysteries Past & Present* (1992)

Wilson, Colin & Damon Wilson, *Mammoth Encyclopedia of the Unsolved* (2000)

Winer, Richard & Nancy Osborn, *Haunted Houses* (1979)

Yenne, Bill, *Lost Treasure* (1999)